Power and Victimization

The Rhetoric of Sociopolitical Power and Representations of Victimhood in Contemporary Literature

Proceedings of a Symposium
Held by the Department of American Culture and Literature
Haliç University, Istanbul, 13-15 April 2005

Editors
Oya Berk
Sırma Soran Gumpert

Oya Berk and Sırma Soran Gumpert (eds.)

POWER AND VICTIMIZATION

The Rhetoric of Sociopolitical Power and Representations of Victimhood in Contemporary Literature

Proceedings of a Symposium
Held by the Department of American Culture and Literature
Haliç University, Istanbul, 13-15 April 2005

ibidem-Verlag
Stuttgart

Bibliografische Information Der Deutschen Bibliothek

Die Deutsche Bibliothek verzeichnet diese Publikation in der Deutschen Nationalbibliografie; detaillierte bibliografische Daten sind im Internet über <http://dnb.ddb.de> abrufbar.

∞

Gedruckt auf alterungsbeständigem, säurefreien Papier
Printed on acid-free paper

ISBN: 3-89821-533-4

Printed in Germany

CONTENTS

Foreword

The Department of American Culture and Literature at Haliç University, Istanbul, conducted a symposium on 'The Rhetoric of Sociopolitical Power and Representations of Victimhood in Contemporary Literature' from 13–15 April 2005. This symposium, hosting 24 participants from various countries, was the third in a series providing a platform for literary scholars to discuss literary works from contemporary literatures in light of the leading questions and issues in contemporary literary criticism. The papers presented at the symposium touched upon a wide range of topics, including the entanglements between politics and literature, the relationship between oppressors and oppressed, problems of minority groups, colonization, racial and gender discrimination, war, and terrorism. While the emphasis was on Anglophone literatures and works from Britain, the United States, Canada, the West Indies, and South Africa, treatments of French, German, Egyptian, Turkish, Argentine, and Japanese writing were also included. Such a wide spectrum made it possible for participants to approach the subject from multiple perspectives and led to fruitful discussions on how today's literature concerns itself with the role of the subject as both victimized and victimizer.

We would like to take this opportunity to give our warm thanks to our keynote speakers, Professor Dr. Sibel Irzık (Sabancı University, Istanbul) and Associate Professor Dr. Dane Johnson (San Francisco State University) for their enlightening presentations. We are deeply thankful to the Academic Committee, the Organizing Committee and the participants for their valuable work: without their contributions this conference could not have been realized. We extend our warmest thanks to Koray Melikoğlu, co-editor of the 'Studies in English Literatures' series, for his invaluable help in making these published proceedings a reality. We also want to express our sincere gratitude to faculty members Professor Yusuf Eradam and Banu Özel from the Department of American Culture and Literature at Haliç University, and Dr. Ayşe Ece from the Department of English Language Teaching at Marmara University for their commitment and support in the organization of the symposium and the preparation of this book.

We are indebted to Dr. Atok Olgun for his kind technical support in preparing the call for papers, the invitation, and the printed proceedings of the symposium.

Our special thanks go to the Vice Rector and the Dean of the Faculty of Arts and Sciences at Haliç University, Professor Atilla Özalpan, for his generous help and encouraging support. We are also grateful to our Rector, Professor Ahmet Çakır, and the Chairman of the Board of Trustees of Haliç University, Professor Gündüz Gedikoğlu, for their help and encouragement.

Last, but certainly not least, we would like to thank Öz-el Ticaret for their financial support.

The Editors
Dr. Oya Berk – Haliç University
Dr. Sırma Soran Gumpert – Haliç University

Contributors

Alban, Gillian, Dr.
Instructor – Boğaziçi University, Istanbul.

Berk, Oya, Dr.
Assistant Professor – Haliç University, Istanbul.

Bulutsuz, Sema, Dr.
Research Assistant – Istanbul University.

Dedebaş, Eda.
Research Assistant – Boğaziçi University, Istanbul.

Ece, Ayşe Dr.
Lecturer – Marmara University, Istanbul.

Gumpert, Matthew, Dr.
Associate Professor – Kadir Has University, Istanbul.

Göze, Gülfer.
Research Assistant – Boğaziçi University, Istanbul.

Gülçur, Lâmia, Dr.
Assistant Professor – Boğaziçi University, Istanbul.

Gürle, Meltem, MA.
Instructor – Boğaziçi University, Istanbul.

Hope, Trevor, Dr.
Assistant Professor – Ankara University.

Johnson, Dane, Dr.
Associate Professor – San Francisco State University.

Kayışçı, Burcu.
Research Assistant – Yeditepe University, Istanbul.

Kıran Raw, Meltem, Dr.
Assistant Professor – Başkent University, Ankara.

Melikoğlu, Esra, Dr.
Professor – Istanbul University.

Öğüt, Özlem, Dr.
Assistant Professor – Boğaziçi University, Istanbul.

Özdağ, Ufuk, Dr.
Assistant Professor – Hacettepe University, Istanbul.

Özel, Banu, MA.
Instructor – Haliç University, Istanbul.

Seçkin, Murat, Dr.
Associate Professor – Istanbul University.

Soran Gumpert, Sırma, Dr.
Assistant Professor – Haliç University, Istanbul.

Tomkinson, Fiona, MA.
Instructor – Yeditepe University, Istanbul.

Turan, Ayşegül.
Research Assistant – Boğaziçi University, Istanbul.

Academic Committee

Prof. Dr. Yusuf Eradam
Haliç University, Istanbul

Prof. Dr. Esra Melikoğlu
Istanbul University

Assoc. Prof. Dr. Dane Johnson
San Francisco State University

Assist. Prof. Dr. Çiler Özbayrak
Haliç University, İstanbul

Assist. Prof. Dr. Özlem Öğüt
Boğaziçi University, Istanbul

Organization Committee

Assist. Prof. Dr. Çiler Özbayrak
Assist. Prof. Dr. Oya Berk
Assist. Prof. Dr. Sırma Soran
Banu Özel, MA
Haliç University, Istanbul

I

POWER AND VICTIMIZATION IN ANGLOPHONE LITERATURES

The Narrator's Tale:
Life Stories in Philip Roth's *The Human Stain*

Meltem Kıran Raw
Başkent University

Abstract: When Nathan Zuckerman, the narrator of Philip Roth's *The Human Stain*, begins to write a book about his late friend Coleman Silk, he initially displays a sympathetic outlook: he portrays Coleman as a victim of political correctness and anti-Semitism. Nathan's sympathetic view changes drastically, however, in his account of Coleman's passing (Coleman came from an African American family but passed as a white and a Jew as a young man, keeping his assumed identity until his death). Ironically enough, Nathan becomes very much a "passing figure" like his friend, at least in his writing. If Coleman negotiated the borders between racial identities in his life, Nathan comes to negotiate the borders between life story and fiction in his book. Through an analysis of how Nathan turns his narrative into a cross between life story and fiction, this paper will ask why Nathan ultimately victimizes Coleman by presenting him as a reckless man in denial of his racial identity, although Nathan himself has performed a similar act of passing in writing his book. The paper concludes that, in condemning Coleman, Nathan himself unwittingly falls victim to essentialist notions of race.

The narrator of Philip Roth's *The Human Stain* is Nathan Zuckerman, a writer of fiction who meets the main character Coleman Silk in 1996, two years before Coleman's death. A successful classics professor forced into retirement when accused of making a racist remark, Coleman asks Nathan to write a book about his and his late wife's victimization by what he sees as the petty political correctness of academia: he attributes his wife's sudden death to her anguish caused by the scandal that ended his academic career. Initially, Nathan is not interested in undertaking such a project: as he puts it, Coleman's "ordeal wasn't a subject I wished to address in my fiction" (13). After Coleman's death, Nathan obviously changes his mind and starts writing the book. When it is finished, however, Nathan's book is a far cry from what Coleman originally intended him to do. Going far beyond the academic scandal that terminated Coleman's career and caused his wife's death, it now includes a great "secret" (45) Nathan learns after his friend's death: although he came from a "model Negro family" (86), the light-complexioned Coleman started to pass as a white and a Jew in the late 1940s, at the expense of cutting his ties with his paternal family and concealing his past from his Jewish wife and his four children.

In the opening chapter, Nathan makes no explicit reference to Coleman's passing: the main reason for his decision to finally write the book seems to be related to the fond memory of his friendship with Coleman. Having suffered from prostate cancer, Nathan is grateful to Coleman for enabling him to resume his "entanglement with life" (44). Nathan suggests two specific reasons for his decision to write the book about Coleman. The first, which he refers to as Coleman's "disaster," has to do with Coleman's death; the second, which he describes as Coleman's "disguise" and "secret," with his passing (45).

On the face of it, the circumstances leading to Coleman's death seem to be as significant a motive for Nathan to write the book as Coleman's passing. To summarize briefly, two years after his wife's death, Coleman, now 71, starts a passionate affair with a much younger woman called Faunia Farley. When, only a few months later, both Coleman and Faunia die in a car accident, Nathan becomes convinced that the culprit is Faunia's ex-husband Les Farley. A Vietnam veteran still suffering from PTSD, Les has followed them with his truck and caused their car to swerve off the road. In Nathan's view, Les has been driven towards this crime not only by his jealousy of Faunia but also by his anti-Semitist feelings against Coleman. In the last chapter, Nathan tells of his desperate efforts to prove Les's crime: he informs the police of how Les kept stalking Coleman and Faunia; he tries to get hold of Faunia's diaries, which he thinks might contain details to incriminate her ex-husband; he even braves confronting Les himself, in the hope of wrenching something in the way of a coded confession out of him. When all his efforts fail, the last resort, Nathan suggests, was writing the book, which in fact subtly raises himself to the status of a martyr. Once the book is published, Nathan believes, Les will be after him. As he puts it, "I knew that if and when I finished the book, I was going to have to go somewhere else to live" (360). What, if anything else, could best testify to Nathan's altruism than this book which, in exposing the man who caused Coleman's death, also places Nathan's own life at risk?

Nathan is equally adamant to defend his friend against those academics who forced Coleman to retire. He particularly targets Delphine Roux, the head of Coleman's department: not only did she bring on the charges of racism against Coleman, but also hounded him over his affair with Faunia, blaming him of "sexually exploiting an abused, illiterate woman" (39). Nathan opens his narrative by juxtaposing Coleman's sufferings at the hands of Delphine Roux with President Clinton's impeachment trial over his affair with Monica Lewinsky: the summer of 1998, when Coleman and Faunia started their affair, also happened to be the time when the Clinton scandal "revived America's oldest communal passion, historically perhaps its most treacherous and subversive pleasure: the ecstasy of sanctimony" (2). If the hysterical Delphine Roux represents the American "ecstasy of sanctimony," or political correctness at its worst, then Coleman becomes its victim: for Nathan, Coleman's plight epitomizes nothing less than the moral maladies of America in the 1990s.

Nathan's determination to expose Coleman's victimization by an enthusiast of political correctness (Delphine Roux) and an anti-Semitist madman (Les Farley) seems to be a natural outcome of his friendship with Coleman. His treatment of Coleman's passing, however, takes an entirely different course. Although at the beginning Nathan refers to Coleman's passing with such words as his friend's 'disguise' or 'secret,' his tone gradually becomes much more judgmental. In the last chapter, for example, Coleman has turned into the perpetrator of a "crime" of epic proportions in Nathan's eyes: his passing is "like the savagery in *The Iliad*, Coleman's favorite book about the ravening spirit of man. Each murder there has its own quality, each a more brutal slaughter than the last" (335). What is it, then, that disturbs Nathan so much about Coleman's passing?

Negotiating, confusing, and ultimately mocking the black/white binary that still dominates the American views of race, the act of black-white passing elicits different responses from those identified as black and those classified as white. African American discussions on the issue generally revolve around two conflicting interpretations. On the one hand, passing can be seen as a denial of one's racial identity, a betrayal of one's historical community. On the other hand, it can be regarded as a subversive act, whereby racially defined individuals challenge arbitrary racial classifications that deny them the opportunity to participate in American life as citizens on a par with the white majority. Published in 1929, Nella Larsen's novel *Passing* summarizes the ambivalent feelings evoked by the phenomenon of passing, when one African American character makes the following comment: "It's funny about 'passing.' We disapprove of it and at the same time condone it. It excites our contempt and yet we rather admire it. We shy away from it with an odd kind of revulsion, but we protect it" (56). For the white community, the implications of passing are much simpler: it is a fraudulent act. With reference to the 1924 Virginia Act to Preserve Racial Integrity, Werner Sollors explains that passing was seen as a "threat" by the white community (254). Elaine K. Ginsberg succinctly points out the disparity between African American and white views of passing: "Although for the legally or culturally black individual race passing is an attempt to move from the cultural margin to the center, from the perspective of a dominant race, passing is deception, an attempt to claim status and privilege falsely" (8).

In this context, Nathan indeed seems to assume the outlook of the white community, as he refers to Coleman's passing as a "disguise" (45). However, his condemnation of Coleman operates on a much more sophisticated plane. In depicting Coleman as a traitor to his paternal family, Nathan shows Coleman's passing not as a transgression against the white community, but as an unspeakable crime against the African American community. While recounting a quarrel between Coleman and his father, for example, Nathan indeed transforms Coleman to a *de facto* killer. At high school, Coleman secretly takes up boxing, learning many of the tricks of the trade from a white man called Macmachrone. Discovering his son's secret, Coleman's father tries to make him give up boxing in a provocative way:

> "You know, if I were your father, Coleman, you know what I'd tell you now?"
> "You are my father," Coleman said.

> "Oh, am I?" his father said.
>
> "Well, sure..."
>
> Well – I'm not sure at all. I was thinking that maybe Macmachrone, at the Newark Boys' Club, was your father."
>
> "Come on, Dad. Mac's my trainer."
>
> "I see. So who then is your father, if I may ask?"
>
> "You know. You are. You are, Dad."
>
> "I am? Yes?"
>
> "No!" Coleman shouted. "No, you're not." (92)

Although the passage puts part of the blame for Coleman's rebellion on to his authoritative father, the implications of the dialogue are clear: by disowning his father, Coleman is also denying his own racial background, as the substitute father in this scene, Macmachrone, is white. Even though Coleman eventually reconciles with his father and does not actually start to pass until after his father's death, he has already crossed the color line in his mind. In the critic Jeffrey Mehlman's words, Coleman thus becomes "an American Oedipus, his flight from his race a virtual parricide" (124).

In driving Coleman's "crime" home, Nathan adds matricide to parricide. As Coleman begins to pass only after his father's death, it is his mother who survives to bear the full impact of her son's actions. In line with his decision not to tell about his past to his bride-to-be, Coleman finally severs all his ties with his family, despite his mother's heart-breaking protests. "There was no explanation that could begin to address the outrage of what he was doing to her," Nathan says (138). Now, Coleman has also committed matricide, as the following comment by Nathan makes clear: "This man and his mother. This woman and her beloved son. If, in the service of honing himself, he is out to do the hardest thing imaginable, this is it, short of stabbing her" (139).

Nathan thus portrays Coleman's passing as a crime against his family, and, by extension, against the African American community. In this way, Nathan proves that he is not motivated by a racist agenda: although a white man himself, he can judge Coleman from an African American perspective, from the one that sees passing as betrayal. Significantly, Nathan overlooks the other African American perspective which characterizes passing as an act that challenges arbitrary racial classifications. In fact, Nathan has internalized the black/white binary to such an extent that he cannot see his own inconsistencies in identifying Coleman racially. Before he learns about Coleman's passing, Nathan does not suspect of his friend's identity as a white and a Jew. After he learns about it, though, he immediately categorizes Coleman as black. Although he also learns that Coleman has white as well as black ancestors, it never occurs to him to think of his friend as white or racially mixed. Nathan thus falls victim to the dictates of the specifically American "one-drop rule," according to which having but one ancestor of African origin automatically renders an individual black, and not white or racially mixed. Gayle Wald states that the one-drop rule "has disproportionately shaped the U.S. social and cultural imagination of race throughout the twentieth century and promises to affect racial discourse [. . .] into the twenty-first" (13). Through Nathan's unquestioning acceptance of the impermeability of racial borders, *The Human Stain* demonstrates the persistence of this rule.

Nathan's failure to conceptualize passing as a challenge to the racialist structure of American society becomes conspicuously ironic when he himself becomes a 'passing figure' like Coleman, at least in writing his book. A writer of fiction himself, Nathan is keenly aware that the book negotiates life story and fiction. Accordingly, he painstakingly identifies his sources of information. He takes special care, for example, to explain how he learned about a series of events that took place a few months before Coleman's death. Coleman "himself never told me about the visit to the college or the phone call from the student union to his son Jeff," Nathan says, and continues:

> I learned of his having been on the campus that day because he'd been observed there [. . .] by his former colleague Herb Keble [. . .]. I knew about the phone call because Jeff Silk, whom I spoke with after the funeral, mentioned something about it [. . .]. It was directly from Nelson Primus [Coleman's lawyer] that I learned of the visit Coleman had made to the attorney's office earlier on the same day [. . .]. (202)

Nathan is particularly keen to authenticate his account of Coleman's passing as well. Having devoted a long part of Chapter II to Coleman's past, he returns to it in the final chapter, and explains that it was Coleman's sister Ernestine who told him of her brother's passing.

Nathan's anxiousness to state his sources of information becomes all the more evident when he admits to his failure to do so on several occasions. In the last chapter, for instance, he gives a somewhat long-winded explanation of how, after Faunia's death, he was unable to secure her diaries from her father. Similarly, he cannot substantiate his conviction that Coleman had told Faunia of his passing:

> Faunia alone knew how Coleman Silk had come about being himself. How do I know she knew? I don't. I couldn't know that either. I can't know. Now that they're dead, nobody can know. For better or worse, I can only do what everyone does who thinks that they know. I imagine. I am forced to imagine. It happens to be what I do for a living. It is my job. It's now all I do. (213)

However uncomfortable to invent parts of his book, then, Nathan will – and does – cross the border between fiction and life story, enhancing his account of the lives of the major personages with details from his own imagination. To give a few examples, although he does not personally know Delphine Roux, the academic who brought the charges of racism against Coleman, he turns her into a neurotic woman whose vindictiveness over Coleman's affair with Faunia is motivated by her secret sexual attraction to him. In addition, he invents a scene in which Faunia's ex-husband Les plans the car accident that will kill both Faunia and Coleman. Moreover, as the critic Elaine B. Safer notes, both "the romantic action in Coleman's bedroom" with Faunia and "Faunia's depressed thoughts in the wildlife habitat" are of Nathan's making (224).

All in all, then, Nathan's attempt to cross the line between fiction and life story enables him to create a compelling book, if nothing else. And yet, when it comes to crossing the color line personally, he ultimately fails. This despite the fact that Coleman's sister Ernestine offers him the chance to become a member of Coleman's African American family. Getting acquainted with Nathan after Coleman's death, Ernestine takes him into her confidence and tells him of Coleman's passing. Shocked by this revelation, Nathan admits to his confusion: "Look, learning this from you today, there is nothing about Coleman that I don't have to rethink," he tells Ernestine. "Well, then, you're now an honorary member of the Silk family," she says, and continues: "Aside from Walter [Coleman's brother], in matters pertaining to Coleman none of us has known what to think" (326). Welcoming Nathan into Coleman's family and, by extension, into the African American community, Ernestine thus offers him the opportunity to cross the color line.

In a gesture to confirm Nathan's symbolic admission into Coleman's family, Ernestine also invites him to a family dinner. Initially, Nathan is exhilarated as much as he is bemused by the prospect of assuming a new identity: "I wonder what I had in mind by accepting the invitation," he writes, "Strange to think that Coleman's sister and I had been taken so by each other's company [. . .]" (343). However, Nathan shies away from making the final imaginative leap, which shows that he is helplessly conditioned by the rigid racial boundaries still sanctioned and maintained by American society. On his way to dinner at Coleman's "boyhood house" in the final scene of the book, he refers to himself as "the white guest at Sunday dinner" (360).

To conclude, Nathan establishes a sympathetic, even emphatic, bond with Coleman in his account of his friend's victimization by social ills such as anti-Semitism and the vagaries of political correctness. And yet, he fails to understand how arbitrary racial classifications, crystallized in the one-drop rule, have played an equally significant part in determining the course of Coleman's life. Nathan's unquestioning acceptance of the impermeability of racial borders thus victimizes Coleman, whom Nathan turns into an arch criminal with regard to his passing. Sadly, Nathan fails to understand how he too has been victimized by his essentialist outlook: he is unaware that his attempt to effect a "proper presentation" (45) of his friend's passing has liberated him as a writer, enabling him to negotiate the borders between life story and fiction. Even more sadly, his essentialist outlook prevents him from acquiring a new family, a new community, when he fails to respond to Ernestine's welcoming gesture. At the beginning of the book, Nathan described himself as a man living a "secluded" life (45). At the end, he goes back to square one: his inability to cross the color line, even on a symbolic level, traps him once again into that secluded life.

Works Cited

Ginsberg, Elaine K. "Introduction: The Politics of Passing." *Passing and the Fictions of Identity*. Ed. Elaine K. Ginsberg. Durham and London: Duke UP, 1996. 1-18.

Larsen, Nella. *Passing*. 1929. Ed. Thadious M. Davis. New York: Penguin, 2003.

Mehlman, Jeffrey. "Against France: An American Novelistic Fantasy." *Diogenes* 203 (2004): 121-132.

Roth, Philip. *The Human Stain*. 2000. New York: Vintage, 2001.

Safer, Elaine B. "Tragedy and Farce in Roth's *The Human Stain*." *Critique* 43 (2002): 211-227.

Sollors, Werner. *Neither Black nor White yet Both: Thematic Explorations in Interracial Literature*. New York, Oxford: Oxford UP, 1997.

Wald, Gayle. *Crossing the Line: Racial Passing in Twentieth-Century U.S. Literature and Culture*. Durham and London: Duke UP, 2000.

The Rise of Anti-Novel: Victims of Allegory in *Left Behind*

Matthew Gumpert
Kadir Has University

Abstract: This essay focuses on *Left Behind*, a fundamentalist and evangelical Christian sci-fi series whose success in recent years can only be described as one of Biblical proportions. The popularity of this apocalyptic narrative, I argue here, is symptomatic of a new America (or, rather, an old America whose contours have only become more distinctly defined), an anti-hermeneutical America: an America, that is, hostile to interpretation itself.

Left Behind looks, at a first glance, like a triumph of the semiotic: everything depends on the reading of signifiers and prophecies, signs that point to the (admittedly, Christian) truth. A closer look shows us to what extent this process of decipherment is a sham. The truth to which those signs point is absolute and self-evident (which means signs are now redundant); the prophecies have, in fact, come true (and thus are no longer prophecies). Hermeneutics has become obsolete.

Perhaps our only recourse, faced with such an anti-hermeneutical narrative, is to read it carefully, despite its rejection of the very act of reading itself. *Left Behind* is, after all, a novel, even if it is an *anti-novel*, a text opposed to textuality itself.

Hermeneutics is dead! Long live hermeneutics!

Reading the signs: Janet Jackson's breast as the *apocalypse*

Halfway through his Super Bowl half-time dance spectacle, Justin Timberlake appeared to become entangled in Janet Jackson's outfit, which suddenly "tore" away – too easily for some – to *reveal* a naked breast. And so began a semiotic scandal of national proportions. It was imperative, from the moment that breast made its *appearance* upon the American scene, to *interpret* it. Was this an accident? Or a carefully choreographed stunt? Janet Jackson's breast was a *sign*, it was clear, of something. Here, it seemed, was the naked truth: but what truth? Here, was a glimpse, perhaps, of what America has increasingly become: a truly *apocalyptic* culture. A culture in love, that is, with cataclysm; not just as something imminent, but etymologically, hermeneutically speaking, as that which has already been *revealed.*[1]

At the very moment it is waging war against theocracy in other parts of the world, America, many have suggested, has become a theocracy in its own right.[2] At first glance this new theocracy looks like a semiotic phenomenon. America, it would seem, is a place dedicated to the pursuit, now, not of happiness, but of *meaning*. It has become a nation, it would appear, of soothsayers and semioticians, for whom everything is a sign pointing somewhere else. Today Americans spend much of their time reading semiological thrillers, like Dan Brown's *The DaVinci Code* (2003), and watching lurid forensic fantasies, like *Crime Scene Investigation*. Their politicians have become prophets, *reading* events *allegorically*, as a transcendent struggle between good and evil.

This is all exactly wrong. It is not the *sign* Americans are worshipping, but the *conversion of the sign into meaning itself.* It is not that they believe in *allegory*, they believe *allegory is at an end*. In this apocalyptic world, a world at allegory's end, signs have given way to *things*. Seen thus, Bush's manichaean predications may not be fanciful *figures* of speech, but assertions to be taken *literally*. That is to say, our world, perhaps, really *is* spinning around an *axis of evil*. Truth here is essentially *tautological*. It is a profoundly anti-hermeneutic stance.[3]

America's fascination with mysteries and conspiracies is a *sign* of this anti-hermeneuticism. From the American perspective everything *is* a mystery; but one that has, in fact, already been solved. There really *is* a conspiracy, always, everywhere, leading to some terrible truth. All the signs *have been read*.

---

1 From the Greek verb, *apokalupto*: *to disclose, to uncover, to reveal* (Liddell 1985).

2 Frank Rich writes recently in the *New York Times*, "our culture has been screaming its theocratic inclinations for months now."

3 And, indeed, Bush is a (self-proclaimed) anti-reader, telling *Time* magazine, "I'm not a textbook player, I'm a gut player" (Gibbs 33); and, "I'm not the historian, I'm the guy making history" (38).

Left Behind: novel or anti-novel?

We have been talking about what America is reading. Apparently, 1 in every 8 Americans are reading the Christian apocalyptic thriller *Left Behind: A Novel of the Earth's Last Days* (1995),[4] by Tim LaHaye and Jerry Jenkins.[5] The *Left Behind* series tells the story of the war against the Antichrist that begins when Jesus *raptures* his true believers (that is, takes them back to heaven), and which ends with the victory of Christ at the battle of Armageddon.[6]

The *Left Behind* series has been tied to America's resurgent fundamentalism. But few have really bothered to *read* these books (at least few ostensibly trained in the art of reading books). Which is understandable, given the fact that they are appallingly bad, even by the standards of popular fiction (although there is, I will argue later, a certain logic to this badness). But I think there is something to be learned from the exercise. For the *Left Behind* series, I want to argue, is a carefully executed anti-hermeneutic enterprise, an assault on textuality itself.

---

4 A few more statistics: out of the series' 12 volumes, five have debuted at number one on the *New York Times* Bestseller List; the 12th and final volume sold two million copies before even hitting the shelves; and over 62 million copies have been sold so far in total. *Newsweek* describes the success of the series in these terms: "arguably [. . .] the most successful literary partner- ship of all time [. . .] their Biblical-techno-thrillers about the end of the world are currently outselling Stephen King, John Grisham, and every other pop novelist in America" (Gates).

5 Tim LaHaye, along with Jerry Fallwell and Pat Robertson, was one of the primary architects of the religious right in the 1980's. *Left Behind* can be seen as part of a larger evangelical, apocalyptic, and fundamentalist trend in publishing. See, for example, Pat Robertson's *The End of the Age* (1996), Paul Meier's *The 3rd Millenium* (1993), and, more recently, Bruce Wilkinson's Jabez series (see *The Prayer of Jabez*, 2000)

6 On the rapture, see Thessalonians. The theology, if it can be called that, to which *Left Behind* subscribes, is thus *premillenial* and *pretribulationist*. *Newsweek* offers a few handy definitions for the layman: *premillenialism*: "The belief that Christ will rise before the Millenium [i.e., Christ's thousand-year-rule on earth] to lead his armies at Armageddon"; *pretribulationalism*: "The premillenialist doctrine, popularized by 19th-century British evangelist John Darby, that Jesus would rapture the faithful before the Tribulation." This theological, it can be seen, is a fairly recent trend in Christian thinking; it can hardly be said to represent mainstream doctrine.

A strange task to undertake in a *novel*, one might think, with all its *polysemic* possibilities. Indeed, *Left Behind* does not fail to capitalize upon the genre's strengths, profiting (in more ways than one) from the very signs it appears to be eviscerating, promulgating a predictable political and cultural ideology through innuendo and implication. The business of hermeneutics goes on then, as it must; but in *Left Behind*, we will see, *business* is precisely what hermeneutics has become: a way of distributing information (the commodity, in this case, of truth itself).

Voyage of the Hermeneuts?

And yet, those who emerge victorious in *Left Behind* are the ones able to interpret the signs: the fate of one's very soul depends on it.[7] The first novel in the series, the eponymous *Left Behind*, looks very much, on a first glance, like a fable on the urgency of *exegesis*. In the novel's opening chapter, Captain Rayford Steele discovers that a considerable number of his passengers, bound for London on a 747, have inexplicably disappeared. We soon become aware this is a global phenomenon. Among the passengers still on board is journalist Buck Williams, who receives a note from his editor, urging him to "[b]egin thinking about the causes. Military? Cosmic? Scientific? Spiritual?" (39). In the words of Rayford's daughter, Chloe, "[t]here's every kind of theory you want on every TV show in the country" (138).

Meanwhile, a series of mysterious gatherings seem to be linked: a conference on the possibility of a "new world order government" (40); a religious conclave debating the viability of a "one-world religious order" (40); an international monetarist summit seeking to launch a unified global currency. At the same time, a charming, populist Romanian official rises from obscurity to become Secretary General of the U.N. (Yes, it's the Antichrist!).

---

7 *Exegesis* itself has become something heroic in this novel. Indeed, the very way these books were written appear to privilege exegesis. According to the article in *Newsweek*, LaHaye would regularly send Jenkins prophecies and commentaries based on the Bible, which Jenkins would then proceed to turn into fiction (Gates).

Left Behind, then, would appear to be a novel about enigmas and explanations. The spiritual explanation – that these disappearances are indeed the rapture prophesied in the Bible – appears to be one explanation among many, struggling to gain acceptance. Rayford is searching for answers, too: his wife Irene has disappeared along with the others. It is true that from the beginning Rayford suspects it has something to do with Jesus; his wife, a devout Christian, had urged him long ago to mend his ways.

Thus Rayford begins by "searching for a Bible" (87), that supreme hermeneutical object. It is not, Rayford discovers, an easy book to understand: "maybe he'd start at the end. If *genesis* meant 'beginning,' maybe *revelation* had something to do with the end, even though it didn't mean that" (88). Answers, however, prove elusive. Rayford encounters numerous hermeneutical roadblocks:

> The very last verse of the Bible meant nothing to him [. . .] Jesus said he was coming quickly. Had he come? [. . .] what did "quickly" mean? [. . .] Rayford could make no sense of the text [. . .] he read, "Let the one who is thirsty come; let the one who wishes take the water of life without cost" [. . .] That, Rayford assumed, referred to the reader. It struck him that he was thirsty, soul thirsty. But what was the water of life? [. . .] Rayford idly leafed through the Bible to other passages, none of which made sense to him." (88-89)

But thanks to Pastor Bruce Barnes and a series of sermons based on Biblical prophecy, Rayford, Chloe, and Buck are led swiftly to the truth.

Anti-Hermeneutics

This hermeneutic saga is a charade. Consider Rayford Steele's struggle to make sense of the Bible. What we are really watching, in fact, is Steele's efforts to *avoid* struggle: "He started by searching for a Bible, not the family Bible that had collected dust on his shelf for years, but Irene's. Hers would have notes in it, maybe something that would point him in the right direction" (87-88). Rayford is not wrestling with the text here, he's looking for the shortest route past it: "Would there be some guide?" he wonders, "[a]n index?" (88).

In Roland Barthes' *S/Z* (1970), the *hermeneutic code* refers to the various strategies the novel relies upon to defer or disguise, or lure us away from, the truth; something which, among other things, is a way of keeping us reading. In *Left Behind*, however, the *hermeneutic code* is itself a *lure*. For the truth has been revealed from the beginning. There is no enigma here, and thus no possibility of revelation.[8] Even before he picks up his wife's Bible, Rayford knows what he's looking for. As the last sentence of the first chapter informs us: "The terrifying truth was he knew all too well. Irene had been right. He, and most of his passengers, had been left behind" (14).

There is a show of hermeneutics here; but only a show. Answers are self-evident. Pastor Barnes tells a still-skeptical Chloe, "we know exactly what happened" (138); "Or you think you do," Chloe replies. But Chloe is wrong; and we know she is wrong. Indeed, the many theories that appear to compete for acceptance are not allowed, even briefly, to appear credible or convincing; they are ridiculous, self-serving, patently false.

Nor is there room in this novel for mysteries or conspiracy theories. As events unfold, we know exactly where things are headed: the creation of a global tyranny under the control of Antichrist Nicolae Carpathia. At a meeting of political leaders, as Buck watches Nicolae assassinate the last of his opponents, "[t]here wasn't a doubt in his mind" – nor in ours – "that the Antichrist of the Bible was in this room."[9]

---

8 This despite the fact that the last novel in the series is called *The Glorious Appearing* (2004), and narrates the manifestation, or revelation, of Jesus himself upon earth. But Jesus has, in fact, already revealed himself to those who can see.

9 Nicolae diabolically expunges this event from the memories of those who witnessed it. Only Buck, armed with his faith, remains aware of what has happened. Along with the reader, of course.

The fifth, and transparent, horse of the apocalypse

To the extent that *Left Behind* is organized as a series of *homilies*, it would seem to be part of a venerable Judeo-Christian interpretive tradition. From Jewish Sabbath gatherings in the Hellenistic period, the assembly of the faithful had assumed the form of a *homily*, a reading of scripture followed by exegesis.[10] Since Origen, Christian exegesis had been formalized as an allegorical method. For Origen, *figures* (*typoi*) are not obstacles to understanding, but valuable points of resistance, leading to a more refined understanding of the truth – a truth one has to struggle for.[11]

Let's look more closely at one of these homilies in *Left Behind*. Pastor Barnes begins by instructing his parishioners to turn to the book of Revelations. "I've been reading the Bible," the pastor tells his congregation, and "books on the subject, and here's what I found [. . .] if I'm reading it right, the Antichrist will soon come to power" (224-225). And that is about as close as we get to a hermeneutical method in *Left Behind*. (A great many questions go unanswered here and, indeed, are not even acknowledged: *How* is Pastor Barnes "reading the Bible"? *Which* "books" has he consulted? *How* does he know he is, in fact, "reading it right"?)

At the center of this homily is what appears to be a *tour de force* of exegetical prowess:

> Bruce explained that the first four seals in the scroll were described as men on four horses: a white horse, a red horse, a

10 By the Second Sophistic period, around A.D. 200, homilies had become sophisticated, even sophistic, and powerfully influenced by the Greek rhetorical tradition. And, indeed, the relation between *hermeneutics* and *homiletics* corresponds precisely to that between *rhetoric* and *dialectic* (see Kennedy 155-157).

11 On Origen, see Kennedy 157-159. The figure who most powerfully formalizes the allegorical approach is Augustine, whose hermeneutics becomes the dominant interpretive model for the West. It is central, for example, to Dante's discussion of *polysemy* in the *Divine Comedy* in his "Letter to Can Grande Scala" (1319). It is in the course of that discussion that Dante famously distinguishes between *literal* and *allegorical* levels of meaning (1962, 199-206).

> black horse, and a pale horse. "The white horse apparently is the Antichrist, who ushers in one to three months of diplomacy while getting organized and promising peace. The red horse signifies war [. . .] the Bible predicts inflation and famine – the black horse [. . .] the fourth horseman on the pale horse – the symbol of death." (226-27)

It certainly looks like a textbook lesson in hermeneutics, all this sifting and assaying of signs. Sometimes a horse is just a horse; but not here. Here, a horse stands for something else, doesn't it? Isn't the pale horse, for example, a *typos*, an image whose plasticity functions as a point of resistance, a screen we must traverse in order to reach the promised land of meaning?

No; for meaning here is not achieved by way of resistance, or reading of any kind. Truth here is transparent, and tautological.[12] "I only believe what the Bible says" (4), Irene insists. This is pure *literalism*, a way of reading in which signifiers offer no resistance, but dissolve instantly into signifieds; in which, indeed, the very distinction between signifier and signified is annulled. For Bruce, that is to say, the pale horse, like his white, red, and black counterparts, is a transparent horse. (Such a horse is not a horse; but neither is it a sign of something else.)[13]

The end of style: the Pauline novel

With the allegorical approach *style* became essential to hermeneutics and homiletics. (*What* was being said, that is, was understood to be a function of *how* it was being said.) But in *Left Behind*, *style* is a concept that has ceased to function. This is true of the novel's execution in its own right – and one explanation for why it is so atrociously written. "I wish I was smart enough to write a book that's hard to read," says Jenkins (Gates).

---

12 If one were a Derridean, one might say: fully *logocentric*.

13 What we are witness to here, in fact, is the rejection of hermeneutics in general. Gone is the gap between *style* and *content*, or *delight* and *utility*, which has long been central to the Western approach to textuality, at least since Horace.

This kind of *anti-text* would appear to be the logical extension of Paul's anti-dialectical and anti-rhetorical approach to scripture. For Paul, Christian truth is a matter of *grace*, bestowed by god, rather than something achieved by human effort. Truth for Paul is authoritative, self-evident, and tautological. In Jenkins contempt for "a book that's hard to read" we hear the contemporary echo of the "Jews" who "demand signs" and the "Greeks" who "seek wisdom" mocked by Paul in 1 Corinthians 2.1-5. As for the homiletic side of the business, that is to say, in terms of spreading the Word, Christian truth is for Paul a matter of *proclamation*, or *kerygma*, not *persuasion*, or *pistis* (Kennedy 150). Pastor Barnes, in just this fashion, is *proclaiming*, not *explaining*, the truth.

One might describe the long Christian allegorical tradition as an effort to reconcile Greco-Roman rhetorical and philosophical hermeneutics with Christian truth as absolute.[14] In book 11 of the *Confessions*, Augustine attempts, just as Rayford does, a reading of Genesis:

> Moses wrote these words [. . .] if he were here, I would lay hold of him [. . .] beg and beseech him to explain these words to me [. . .] If he spoke in Hebrew, his words would strike my ear in vain and none of their meaning would reach my mind. If he spoke in Latin, I should know what he said. But how should I know whether what he said was true? If I knew this too, it could not be from him that I got such knowledge. But deep inside me, in my most intimate thought, Truth, which is neither Hebrew nor Greek nor Latin nor any foreign speech, would speak to me [. . .] (*Confessions* 101)

Augustine's understanding seems to be just as tautological as Rayford's. But the way there is full of incomprehension and uncertainty. Truth as something

14 After all, despite Paul's rejection of truth as a rhetorical matter, the standard word for *faith* from the earliest texts of Christianity is, in fact, *pistis*, or *persuasion* (Kennedy 146). There has thus always been a central place given to Greek rhetoric in the Christian approach to the text.

authoritative and absolute – something granted ultimately by God – is only achieved at the expense of struggle: mediation, misunderstanding, processes essentially *textual* in nature.

There is no sign of that struggle in *Left Behind*, a truly Pauline novel. Rayford, "furiously taking notes" (227) as Pastor Barnes' proclaims his dire prophecies, is the perfect Pauline student. "How could he have missed this? God had tried to warn his people by putting his Word in written form centuries before [. . .] Now he couldn't get enough of this *information*" (227; italics mine). One would think a "written form" authored by God himself would deserve a little more respect. For Rayford, it has become pure and simply a form of *information.*

The heresy of paraphrase:[15] from signs to things

This shift from the *semiotic* to the *informational* is clearly illustrated by a second homiletic moment in *Left Behind*: the Reverend Vernon Billings' prophetic "reading" of the (Pauline) epistle 1 Corinthians 15: 51-57. It is during the course of this very homily that Rayford Steele is "born again." We know we are in the realm of *information*, not *semeiosis*, because Rayford is listening to this sermon on his VCR:[16]

> Let me show you from the Bible exactly what has happened [. . .] ask yourself, how did he know? Here's how, from 1 Corinthians 15: 15-57 [. . .] Rayford was confused. He could follow some of that, but the rest was gibberish to him. He let the tape roll. Pastor Billings continued: "Let me paraphrase

15 I refer here to New Critic Cleanth Brooks' seminal essay "The Heresy of Paraphrase" (192-214).

16 Billings has, in fact, been raptured, and his sermon recorded on a tape. I return later to the role of technological mediation in the *Left Behind* series. Suffice it to say for now that if the signifier itself has been annulled, and style or textuality been rendered transparent, then the sign becomes something to be disseminated, replicated, or transmitted, whether by mobile telephone, internet, or television.

> some of that so you'll understand it clearly. When Paul says we shall not all sleep, he means that we shall not all die [. . .] (152-53)

How to reconcile the *paraphrasing* of Holy Scripture with the *literalism* to which *Left Behind* appears to subscribe?[17] But there is nothing literal about Reverend Billings' reading of Paul's phrase "we shall not all sleep." And when Pastor Barnes interprets the "pale horse" of Revelations as "death," he turns it into a metaphor. Elsewhere, LaHaye is forced to admit he is not, well, *literally*, a literalist: "The Bible says Jesus is going to slay his enemies with a sword that comes out of his mouth," says LaHaye; "We don't believe there's an actual sword in his mouth. The sword is his word" (Gates). We should hardly be surprised, then, by the Reverend Billings' paraphrase of the Bible. So harmless, so helpful, and yet so virulently hermeneutic, the paraphrase is the perfect anti-textual weapon. And if the paraphrase is a weapon, then we, the reader, at whom it is ultimately aimed, are its real victims.

Literalism: from the realm of signs to the realm of things

There is another sense, however, in which LaHaye and Jenkins *are* indeed *literalists*: for them, as for George Bush, *figures* are *prophecies* which have now, in effect, *come true*. "Let me show you from the Bible exactly what has happened," we have seen the Reverend Billings telling Rayford; he continues: "You won't need this proof by now, because you will have experienced the most shocking event of history" (152).[18] Literalism is possible in *Left Behind* because *history has arrived*.

---

17 In the interview with *Newsweek*, LaHaye proclaims: "Those millions that I'm trying to reach take the Bible literally. It's the theologians that get all fouled up on some of those smug ideas that you've got to find some theological reason behind it. It bugs me that intellectuals look down their noses at we ordinary people" (Gates). "We ordinary people" know what the Bible means, of course. It means what we know it means.

18 Later Billings defines "Bible prophecy" as "history written out in advance" (156).

In *On Christian Doctrine*, Augustine portrays the universe in which we exist as a realm made of *signs* and *things*. All signs are also things; all things, or almost all things, are signs. The distinction, however, remains a crucial one. To put it simply, a sign is a thing which refers to another thing. Signs are things that are *used* (*uti*), that is to say, or exchanged for other things. Things, on the other hand, *qua* things, are *enjoyed* (*frui*) in and of themselves. I have said that almost all things are also signs. There is, however, one thing in our universe to which everything else refers, but which does not itself refer to anything else: that thing is God.[19] For Augustine, then, the universe itself is an allegory; a textual screen that both shuts us off from God and, if we work hard enough, if we read carefully enough, points to him.

That struggle, we have seen, is over in *Left Behind*. For in the last days of our world, allegory has reached its appointed end. In this world, there are no figures.[20] All the prophecies have come true; signs have now become the things which, once upon a time, they pointed to. "I believe," says Reverend Billings, of the raptured, "that all such people were literally taken from the earth, leaving everything material behind" (153). Perhaps that is what it means to be left behind, in the realm of things.[21] Perhaps what has been taken from us is the sign itself.

---

19 Augustine's semiotic God in this sense occupies the position of the Derridean *transcendental signified*. On Augustinian semiotics in *On Christian Doctrine*, see Kennedy 170-182.

20 Because figures, as in the rhetoric of George Bush, have now literally come true. Thus the following, apparently innocent exchange between Rayford and Chloe: "'Didn't your mother tell you she believed that Jesus could come back some day and take his people directly to heaven before they died?' 'Sure, but she was always more religious than the rest of us. I thought she was just getting a little carried away.' 'Good choice of words.' 'Hm?' 'She got carried away, Chloe'" (118).

21 It is worthwhile considering, for a moment, a classic medieval example of allegory; for example, Petrarch's "Letter to Dionisio da Borgo San Sepolcro," from *Rerum familiarium libri* [*Letters on familiar matters*] 4.1 (*Correspondence*). In this letter Petrarch offers us an allegorical reading of his ascent of Mount Ventoux with his brother. As with allegory in general, we begin in the realm of the concrete, the realm of things, and then move to the plane of the conceptual. This is not an easy process. On the contrary, it is marked by struggle. That struggle suggests the labor of interpretation itself, here reflected (indeed, allegorically), by the physical pain of the ascent. That struggle is made

From text to information

We return to Rayford Steele, kneeling before his television set, poised to give himself to Christ. It is portrayed as an act of courage; one unaccompanied, however, by any corresponding sign of intellectual struggle. At the moment of his conversion, Rayford "paused the tape [. . .] and saw the concern on the pastor's face, the compassion in his eyes" (156). It is ironic that this moment of perfect communion is one with a technologically mediated image:

> Rayford slid to his knees on the carpet. He had never knelt in worship before, but he sensed the seriousness and the reverence of the moment. He pushed the play button and tossed the remote control aside. He set his hands palm down before him and rested his forehead on them, his face on the floor. The pastor said, "Pray after me," and Rayford did. (157)

No matter that Rayford's conversion here is purely imitative, his very gestures miming the exhortations of his pastor. Here, Rayford's understanding of the truth seems to cancel out the distances and delays of mediation, and is achieved instantaneously. The proof is that Rayford tosses the *remote control* aside and pushes the *play button.* No matter that the entire hermeneutical-semiotic enterprise has always functioned by *remote control,* has always been a struggle to overcome mediation or textuality. Not here; now, truth is as simple as the pressing of a button that says: *play.*

---

difficult by mediations, hesitations, uncertainties, and deferrals. The truth that Petrarch ascends to here – that gaining perspective upon a landscape is less difficult than gaining perspective upon one's self – is itself based on the allegorical labor performed by others before him; that is, other texts (specifically, here, Augustine's conversion in the garden as recorded in the *Confessions* – itself an emulation of a still prior moment of conversion provoked by the reading of a text). But in *Left Behind,* not only is allegory instantaneous and effortless, achieved without labor, without reading or writing, but its essential course has been reversed. Here we move from the realm of abstractions to the plane of things, objects, and events. A rather depressing scenario: for this is a world in which there are no mysteries, and no miracles, and no metaphors.

If *Left Behind* is in love with technological gadgetry, it is not just an effort to add the e-generation to its unwitting victims. Because truth is no longer something semiotic, but a material substance, fully present, it can be disseminated without distortion or deferral. Hence the preponderant role played by information technology in the novel – newspapers, televisions, mobile telephones and the internet – as well as transportation – souped-up Range Rovers and super-747's. Rayford's conversion, we have seen, is, in fact, a tele-conversion; Buck propagates the resistance through his newspaper; and Pastor Barnes' sermons are downloaded, after his death, from his computer.[22]

The return of the novel

This is exactly the way the *Left Behind* novels have, in fact, been marketed: as information to be accessed and disseminated, that is, bought and sold. In fact, promoting the novel depends on erasing the very distinction between the novel and its promotion; for the novel itself, we have seen, has become nothing but a truth to be promoted, by whatever means necessary. The goal here is to expunge writing itself: to offer pure *logos*, delivered without distortion or delay. With "Left Behind Mobile Prophecies," for example, as an advertisement posted on *The Official Left Behind Series Site* promises, "the [t]ruth is in your hands".

There is thus a sense in which the *Left Behind* series is a carefully orchestrated textual suicide. One might well wonder why, when truth can be so easily accessed, one need buy the novel at all. And, indeed, much of the promotional campaign surrounding *Left Behind* offers what are, in effect, substitutes for the novel itself, packaged in increasingly concentrated and textually eviscerated forms. In fact these opportunities to buy instant truth are not meant to substitute for the reading of the novel, but to supplement it. It is hard to imagine anyone would require help in making sense of what these books are trying to say, and yet that is the strategy employed to sell these products: as explanatory guides to

22 All of which, one would add, corresponds very closely to the state of Christian techno-

the novel itself. It is a strategy, ironically enough, that turns *Left Behind* back into a novel; one which, like any text, requires interpretation.

The *Left Behind* series and its vast promotional apparatus thus becomes an industry dedicated to the production of meta-narratives. Members of the "Left Behind Club [. . .] get breaking news and complete analysis each week" by way of a "newsletter" entitled, "Interpreting the Signs". A video entitled "Have You Been Left Behind?," and "[b]ased on the video that [. . .] Pastor Vernon Billings created," purports to "explain [. . .] what happened and what the viewer can do now" (*The Official Left Behind Series Site*). Of course, there should be no need for explanation: truth, in the Pauline sense to which the novel subscribes, is supposed to be self-evident. Meanwhile, it is instructive to see Jenkins and La-Haye resorting here to the classic dissimulations of fiction itself. We know that this video is not, in fact, based on Pastor Billing's video, which (like Pastor Billings himself) never existed.[23]

It would appear then, that the *Left Behind* series remains inscribed, for better or worse, within the realm of the novel, a hermeneutical landscape made up of underground passages and quick-sands of polysemy. When, in the very first paragraph of *Left Behind*, we meet Rayford Steele "[w]ith his fully loaded 747 on autopilot above the Atlantic en route to a 6 A.M. landing at Heathrow" (1), we don't have to be literary critics – or airplane pilots – to know exactly the kind of vehicle this novel is: the phallic express, with all of its familiar ideological baggage. Truths here, again, are tautological: men are men, women are women, lesbians are unattractive, and angry.

Of course this particular novel has a good deal more baggage than most. The entire ethico-political agenda of the religious right is fully operative here: international organizations are understood to be satanic instruments; and among those raptured back to heaven are unborn fetuses taken straight from the womb. Meaning in *Left Behind* may indeed be said to be on *auto-pilot* (or *remote-*

---

worship in America today.

23 We know the reverse is closer to the truth: it is the supplementary video, apparently inspired by Pastor Billings, which has, in fact, inspired *it*. Which turns all twelve volumes of the *Left Behind* series into the exegesis of a truth, not truth itself.

control): its course has been set in advance, its target unmistakable. Which is to say, truths are not just *tautological*, but *teleological*.

Every novel, it is true, may be said to be born out of a teleological paradox: for every novel is designed to reach its end. The novel, we might say, is always an act of suicide. But when *teleology* becomes *eschatology*, when the end is *The End*, then the question of how, and when, we get there, takes on a great deal more urgency.[24]

Works Cited

Alighieri, Dante. "Letter to Can Grande Scala." *Literary Criticism: Plato to Dryden*. Ed. Allan H. Gilbert. Detroit: Wayne State UP, 1962. 199-206.

Augustine, Saint, Bishop of Hippo. *Confessions*. Trans. R. S. Pine-Coffin. NY: Penguin, 1961. Trans. of *Confessiones*.

---. *On Christian Doctrine*. Trans. D. W. Robertson. New York: Macmillan, 1987. Trans. of *De doctrina Christiana*.

Barthes, Roland. *S/Z*. Paris: Éditions du Seuil, 1970.

Brooks, Cleanth. *The Well Wrought Urn: Studies in the Structure of Poetry*. New York: Harcourt, Brace, & World, 1947.

Brown, Dan. *The Da Vinci Code*. New York: Doubleday, 2003.

Gates, David. "Religion: The Pop Prophets." *Newsweek* 24 May 2005. MSNBC News: Newsweek Society. 17 July 2005 <http://www.msnbc.msn.com/id/4988269/site/newsweek/>.

Gibbs, Nancy and John F. Dickerson, "Inside the Mind of George W. Bush." *Time* 6 September 2004.

Jenkins, Jerry B. and Tim LaHaye. *The Glorious Appearing*. Wheaton, Ill.: Tyndale House, 2004.

---. *Left Behind: A Novel of the Earth's Last Days*. Wheaton, Ill.: Tyndale House, 1995.

---

24 Frank Rich writes, 27 March 2005, in the *New York Times*: "The Armageddon-fueled world view of the 'Left Behind' books extends its spell by the day, soon to surface in a new NBC prime-time mini-series, 'Revelations,' being sold with the slogan, 'The End is Near.'"

Kennedy, G. A. *Classical Rhetoric and its Christian and Secular Tradition from Ancient to Modern Times.* 2nd ed. Chapel Hill: U of North Carolina P, 1999.

The Official Left Behind Series Site. 2001-2005. Tyndale House. 3 April 2005 <http://www.leftbehind.com>.

Liddell, H. G., ed. *Greek-English Lexicon.* 1889. Oxford: Oxford UP, 1985.

Meier, Paul D. *The Third Millenium.* Nashville: WestBow Press, 1993.

Petrarca, Francesco. *Correspondence: English Selections.* 1975. Trans. Aldo S. Bernardo. Albany: State U of New York P, 1985. Trans. of *Rerum familiarium libri.*

Rich, Frank. "The God Racket, from DeMille to DeLay." *New York Times* 27 March 2004.

Robertson, Pat. *The End of the Age.* Dallas: Word, 1996.

Wilkinson, Bruce H. *The Prayer of Jabez.* Sisters, Oregon: Multnomah, 2000.

Tracing the Carnival Spirit in *A Confederacy of Dunces*: Modern Re-workings of the Grotesque in Defying Authority

Meltem Gürle
Bogaziçi University

Abstract: This article traces the re-workings of the grotesque in John Kennedy Toole's *A Confederacy of Dunces*, and demonstrates from a Bakhtinian perspective how laughter functions as a major way of defying authority. Laughter provides the victims of power with a strong tool for resistance, which negates the solemn nature of authority by placing a mirror before its eyes, making it see itself in the light of the absurd, and thereby reducing it to merely a parody of itself. Ignatius Reilly, the main character of *A Confederacy of Dunces*, performs the function of what Bakhtin would call a carnivalesque uncrowning and debasing of the official culture. Ignatius debases all the pretentious middle class values, as Don Quixote degrades the medieval ideals of chivalry and ceremonial. Arguing that a reconfigured carnival spirit finds its way into Toole's novel, this article explores the ways in which the author offers a modern version of the popular festive elements, especially the clown or the 'Fool,' who signifies the symbolic destruction of authority and a resistance to the mechanisms of power.

Modernity conceives itself as a dynamic process, which is based on not only a concept of a linear, irreversible time that is flowing onwards, but also an understanding of human awareness that is capable of shaping that time, i.e., creating history. According to Calinescu, the bourgeois idea of modernity is characterized by this doctrine of progress which rests on the cult of reason, the ideal of freedom defined within the framework of an abstract humanism, and an orientation towards pragmatism, i.e., "the cult of action and success" (Calinescu 45).

Having its points of departure in rationality, the humanist ideal of modernity is grounded in the belief that humanity is essentially benevolent, and, therefore, on its way of gradual progress toward an emancipated state. It is in this homogenizing attitude where we find indications of the totalizing effect of modernity's project. The problem with the modernist project is that emancipating rationality itself becomes a totality with the goal of normalizing differences, a unifying whole with the promise of absolute knowledge.

In its search for the absolute as the sum-total of human experience, modernity ended up totalizing different forms of existence, silencing and victimizing anything that does not fit into the prescribed ways of life. 'The Other,' being robbed of its voice, is silenced and reduced to the "economy of the same" (Derrida 120).

Having witnessed the horrors of the totalitarian regimes and the two world wars, the Russian ideologue and literary critic Bakhtin, like his contemporaries, was fully aware of the fact that the modernist project of progress had failed. In *Rabelais and His World* – his doctoral dissertation, which he wrote in the 1930s but could not publish until 1965 because of the political climate in Russia under the Stalinist regime – Bakhtin states that under the influences of rationalism and modernity from the 17th century onwards the European history witnesses the fragmentation of the militantly anti-authoritarian attitude to life which is characteristic of the carnivalesque Middle Ages. According to Bakhtin, the medieval aesthetic that celebrates the anarchic and grotesque elements of popular culture was swallowed up by modernity. The voice of the radically other, which Bakhtin characterizes as carnival laughter, has been tamed or transformed. Like the utopias of Enlightenment, the modern laughter is monological (*Problems* 82). Being just a safety-valve for social tensions, it fails to bear the mock-serious ambivalent tone of the carnival laughter – or the grotesque laughter – which is set against the official and totalizing seriousness of authority. Medieval laughter, Bakhtin claims, being the expression of a "free and critical *historical* consciousness" has been silenced (*Rabelais* 73).

Although Bakhtin specifically refers to the varied popular festive life of the Middle Ages when he talks of the *carnivalesque* in *Rabelais and His World*, he also admits the possibility of observing traces of carnival spirit in modern literature. The carnival spirit survives in carnivalized writing, which, in its own practice, makes use of the characteristic inversions, parodies, crownings and uncrownings of carnival. When it enters writing, carnival spirit offers a crownings of carnival. When it enters writing, carnival spirit offers a liberation from "all that is humdrum and universally accepted" (34).

Considering his contempt for the totalizing attitude of modernity and his emphasis on freedom, it is possible to read Bakhtin's work as a hidden polemic against the Stalinist regime's cultural politics. Similarly, John Kennedy Toole's only novel, *A Confederacy of Dunces*, in which the echoes of carnival laughter are still heard, can be read as a manifesto against the so-called "cult of success" that lies at the heart of the "American Dream."

Ignatius Reilly, the eccentric character of Toole's novel, in his own way voices Bakhtin's attitude towards modernity, when he talks about the ideal education that the youth should be provided with:

> [. . .] you must begin a reading program immediately so that you may understand the crises of our age," Ignatius said solemnly. "Begin with the late Romans, including Boethius, of course. Then you should dip rather extensively into early Medieval. You may skip the Renaissance and the Enlightenment. That is mostly dangerous propaganda. Now that I think of it, you had better skip the Romantics and the Victorians, too. For the contemporary period, you should study some selected comic books [. . .]" (266)

Ignatius maintains an open contempt for the ways of the modern world. He has a very refined world-view – or *Weltanschauung* as he calls it – celebrating the medieval ideals of Boethius and Aquinas, while having the bad fortune of being born into the working-class of 1960s New Orleans. He regards the Renaissance and the Enlightenment as downfalls in mankind's history, a degeneration resulting in the current junk of plastic, pop, and commercial cinema, which fill him with a constant rage that he often experiences in the form of intestinal problems.

Early in the novel we see Ignatius lying in bed being bloated as he contemplates the disastrous course of events that began with the Reformation.

> Doris Day and Greyhound Scenicruisers, created an even more rapid expansion of his central region [. . .] Recently, his pyloric valve snapped shut indiscriminately and filled his stomach with trapped gas, gas which had character and being and resented its confinement. He wondered whether his pyloric valve might be trying, Cassandralike, to tell him something. (41-42)

Ignatius is a man of learning. He is an intellectual and an ideologue, who believes his power lies in his ability to see the true nature of things. Owing much to Gargantua in his gluttony, Oblomov in his idleness, and Don Quixote in his thunderous contempt and one-man war against modernity, he is a grotesque figure. His eccentricity knows simply no limits and he is usually treated as a madman though most of the time Toole assures the reader that there is reason in Ignatius' madness. As Danow argues, the theme of madness is "inherent to all forms of grotesque" (169) usually appearing in the form of "festive madness" challenging authority.[1]

In *Rabelais and his World*, Bakhtin argues that the bourgeois conception of the grotesque gave rise to the splitting of the mental/bodily, spiritual/material principles of being, which was once united in the ambivalent images of medieval figures. The sharp splitting of the upper and lower strata, Bakhtin suggests, finds its initial and best expression in Cervantes' Don Quixote and Sancho Panza, where the two principles are not intermingled but represented in two isolated individuals.

> Sancho's materialism, his potbelly, his appetite, his abundant defecation are on the absolute lower level of grotesque real-

---

1 Danow makes a reference to Bakhtin at this point stating that the Russian critic registers a duality concerning madness: "In folk grotesque, madness is a gay parody of official reason, the narrow seriousness of official 'truth'. It is a 'festive' madness. In Romantic grotesque, on the other hand, madness acquires a somber tragic aspect of individual isolation" (Bakhtin, *Rabelais* 22). In the case of Ignatius, we see these two aspects being employed interchangeably. Ignatius celebrates his own festive madness though it is also possible to view him as a misfit, an isolated individual trapped in modern society.

> ism of the gay bodily grave (belly, bowels, earth) which has been dug for Don Quixote's abstract deadened idealism. (22)

In Ignatius, however, we see the regeneration of the medieval synthesis of the spiritual and the material. Ignatius is both Don Quixote and Sancho Panza representing both the upper and the lower levels of the body. The bodily principle is not sacrificed for the sake of the mental; on the contrary, the process is always blended with a 'gay relativity,' through which the purely spiritual is transformed into the level of the material, and vice versa.

Ignatius' bloating body is the outcome of a typical carnivalistic gesture of turning things 'upside down,' a continuous reversal of the spiritual and the material (the upper and the lower) levels, which is an essential quality of grotesque realism. Ignatius' contempt for modernity is not an abstract idea. It is transferred to the lower stratum of the body, and thereby is given a presence, a fullness. References to his valve, bowels, belly, appetite are all grotesque in their nature bearing "a deeply positive character" (Bakhtin, *Rabelais* 62).

As a grotesque figure, Ignatius is the reincarnation of the market place fool being truly ambivalent in his nature, i.e., containing both folly and wisdom in his attitude, and praise and abuse in his language. The medieval fool/jester and the modern grotesque clown are part of a continuing evolution, and are best explained when viewed as belonging to the literary tradition of Menippean satire,[2] as described by Bakhtin. The fool is not a comic actor playing his part on the stage; he is rather the incarnation of carnival spirit that transfers anything that is regarded as absolute, stable or mythical into the gay level of popular festive degradation.

---

2 For Bakhtin, carnivalization has a long and rich historical foundation in the genre of the ancient Menippean satire. Bakhtin says that "menippea" or "the carnivalesque" enters into all kinds of relationships, transforms itself, and combines with other genres. He believes the "menippea lives in such dialogized and carnivalized medieval genres as 'arguments, debates', morality and miracle plays and later in the mystery and *sotie*" (*Problems* 182). He says "the Menippean satire has the capacity of insinuating itself into larger genres" (161) and that it "absorbed the diatribe, the soliloquy and the symposium" (160).

> [. . .] they [the fools and clowns] were not actors playing their parts on a stage, as did the comic actors of a later period, impersonating Harlequin, Hanswurst, etc., but remained fools and clowns always and wherever they made their appearance. As such they represented a certain form of life, which was real and ideal at the same time. They stood on the borderline between life and art, in a peculiar mid zone as it were, they were neither eccentrics nor dolts, neither were they comic actors. (Bakhtin, *Rabelais* 8)

Owing much to the carnivalistic gesture of his medieval counterparts – like those of the Feast of Fools[3] – Ignatius Reilly turns every quality upside down and brings out the worst in every single character he meets in the novel. He is one of the all time great jesters taking the carnival spirit with himself wherever he goes. Like the Rabelaisian Gargantua, his grotesque quality challenges all forms of authority – even that of the reader. With his sticky fingers and gorgeous appetite, his unending obsessions and weird sexual fantasies he is a loathsome individual. Yet, we can not help being intrigued by the power of his personality, because it offers a joyful alternative to the tedious monotony of 'dunces' in the novel. Ignatius is a true monster, an anti-hero, who surprises and entertains us equally. Unlike the other characters he possesses the power of laughter and refuses to be treated like a victim. On the contrary, being full of judgment and contempt towards the society he lives in, he behaves like an executioner most of the time. From the first time we see him in the novel until the very end, we are being constantly reminded that Ignatius does not like what he sees:

> In the shadow under the green visor of the cap Ignatius J. Reilly's supercilious blue and yellow eyes looked down

3 According to Bakhtin, the carnival can be traced to the Feast of Fools, a medieval festival originally of the sub-deacons of the cathedral, held about the time of the Feast of the Circumcision (1 January), in which the humbler cathedral officials burlesqued the sacred ceremonies.

> upon the other people waiting under the clock at the D. H. Holmes department store, studying the crowd of people for signs of bad taste in dress. Several of the outfits, Ignatius noticed, were new enough and expensive enough to be properly considered offenses against taste and decency. Possession of anything new or expensive only reflected a person's lack of theology and geometry; it could even cast doubts upon one's soul. (13)

The many dunces around Ignatius are a series of characters somehow linked to Ignatius and to each other, who occasionally come together in the novel forming crowded – and often scandalous – scenes. All these characters, except for Ignatius, believe in the 'cult of action and success,' and are possessed by the desire to become a part of the constantly moving and 'improving' American society. All they want to do is to move into a higher social class, to have a better life, to possess more, or to make themselves more visible. Ignatius' babbling alcoholic mother Irene is ready to send her son to an asylum so that she can marry Claude, an old McCarthy supporter who suspects that even the police force is made up of communists. Patrolman Mancuso, the hapless police officer who comes from a family of Italian immigrants, spends half of his time in the novel under disguise in a bus station rest room hoping to arrest someone so that he can get promoted. Lana Lee, who runs a bar and leads a pornography ring; Darlene, an exotic dancer in Lana's bar with aspirations of becoming a great actress; Burma Jones, a talkative black custodian who sweeps the floors in the same bar while dreaming of a middle class life; Gus Levy and his neurotic wife, who keep having domestic quarrels about the future of a pants factory they own; Dorian Greene, who introduces Ignatius to the sexual underworld of New Orleans; and the liberal Myrna Minkoff, a supposed girlfriend from college, who keeps sending bombastic letters from New York urging Ignatius to get out of his filthy room and find himself a good cause, be it sex or politics, or better sexual politics. All these characters have one thing in common: they want to move, move forward . . . while Ignatius doesn't. Yet, he is forced to work, and this is how the novel – and the carnival – begins.

There are numerous instances in the novel that might be considered as typical examples of the primary carnivalistic act of crowning and uncrowning, where praise and abuse go hand in hand, and ambivalence dominates. Throughout the novel we see Ignatius backing curiously progressive causes despite his extreme rejection of modernity. First he goes for collective struggle at Levy Pants showing efforts to establish the Divine Rights Party under which he hopes to unite all the workers, then he discovers the virtues of free enterprise and becomes hot-dog vendor – and a devoted capitalist trying to the expand the business – and finally we see him attempting to stage a mass infiltration of the world's armed forces with homosexuals to bring down global government, based on that group's perceived love of uniforms.

His adventures at Levy Pants are particularly interesting and deserve to be mentioned here. Being forced to work by his nagging mother, Ignatius finds a job at this company which produces old-fashioned trousers. The first thing he does is decorating the office to celebrate puritan work ethics while receiving very little resistance from his co-workers Miss Trixie, an ancient, senile, incompetent employee of Levy's whose sole aim is to get retired, and Gonzalez, the chief who is pleased to see Ignatius is so dedicated and interested in business:

> Looking happily about Mr. Gonzalez noticed the results of Mr. Reilly's handiwork in the office. Tacked to Miss Trixie's desk was a large sign that said MISS TRIXIE with an old-fashioned nosegay drawn in crayon in one corner. Tacked to his desk was another sign that said SR. GONZALEZ and was decorated with the cross of King Alfonso. A multi-sectioned cross was nailed to a post in the office, the LIBBY'S TOMATO JUICE and KRAFT JELLY on two sections awaiting what Mr. Reilly had said would be brown paint with some black streaks to suggest the grain of the wood. (120)

When Ignatius finally finishes painting the cross, he applies on it the motto GOD AND COMMERCE in gold leaf letters. The scene ends with Miss Trixie leaning beneath it and praying on her way back from the ladies' room (125).

The debasing quality of the carnivalistic act is obvious in the way that Ignatius decorates the cross made up of cartoon boxes that used to contain food. Toole deliberately uses images that refer to food and excrement[4] all through the novel, which Bakhtin would call images of the bodily lower stratum. Food and excrement are linked in the way that they are used to parody anything that claims to be spiritually elevated. The cross, the symbol of the puritan work ethics, is degraded into what is left behind from Ignatius' grotesque feasting. Once again, the purely idealistic, religious, and mystic have been transformed into the lower strata by being robbed of their abstract qualities. The power of the grotesque, in this case the power of food and drink, liberates the abstract spirit and gives it a concrete quality. Free play with the sacred – be it God or capitalism – turns out to be one of the essential qualities of the novel.

After completing his "corrective" project with the office, Ignatius sets an eye on the factory, which looks like the combination of "the worst of *Uncle Tom's Cabin* and Fritz Lang's *Metropolis*" (130), and decides to lead a revolt in Levy Pants by the company's largely black workforce while using his experiences as the basis for a memoir titled "The Journal of a Working Boy, or, Up from Sloth" (111).

Writing in his journal, he admits having devoted himself to a progressive cause, and celebrates this decision vigorously praising the militancy, depth and strength involved in it: "Too long have I confined myself in Miltonic isolation and meditation. It is clearly time for me to step boldly into our society, not in the boring passive manner of the Myrna Minkoff school of social action, but with great style and zest" (139).

---

4 It is interesting to note here that nothing in the novel is immune to carnivalistic degradation and debasing, even Ignatius' spiritual mentor Boethius. His *Consolation of Philosophy* keeps changing hands in the course of the novel; it first appears in a bus station public rest room, and finally ends up in the hands of a pornography queen posing naked holding the book – the references both reflecting the downward movement and involving the recurrent themes of the grotesque: excrement and sexual organs.

The rally scene that follows this declaration has a particularly entertaining quality with Ignatius turning into a real jester being followed half-heartedly by the black workers waving broomsticks and chanting spirituals. The carnivalesque quality of the scene reaches its peak when Ignatius urges them to march beneath a banner that turns out to be one of his badly stained bed sheets: "Among the yellow stains the word FORWARD was printed in high block letters in red crayon. Below this *Crusade for Moorish Dignity* was written in an intricate blue script" (149).

All the details concerning Ignatius' adventures at Levy Pants present the character of a popular festive performance: they are part of a gay and free play, but they are also full of deep meaning (Bakhtin, *Rabelais* 207). Ignatius degrades the whole culture behind the idea of progress when he raises the stained bed sheet and says: "I'm holding before you the proudest of banners, an identification of our purpose, and a visualization of all that we seek." (149) As an anti-hero, as the fool, he uncrowns, covers with ridicule, kills the old world (the old authority and truth) and at the same time gives birth to the new in the form of fearless laughter.

As Bakhtin emphasizes in *Rabelais and his World*, material bodily principle is the concept of grotesque realism (18). In grotesque realism the bodily element is truly positive, because, unlike the spiritual or the mental element, it is not devoid of content. The spiritual, the ideal, the supposedly 'absolute,' on the other hand, is just an abstraction. Being presented in a private and egoistic form, being cut off from 'the other,' and at the same time claiming to be the universal, it is doomed to fall short of representing all people. The bodily principle, however, does not refer to a single body, but has a cosmic character, and possesses the power to represent all that there is; the total of human existence.

> The material bodily principle is contained not in the biological individual, not in the bourgeois ego, but in the people, a people who are continually growing and renewed [. . .] This exaggeration has a positive, assertive character. The leading themes of these images of bodily life are fertility, growth, and a brimming-over abundance. Manifestations of this life

> refer not to the isolated biological individual, not to the private, egotistic 'economic man,' but to the collective ancestral body of all the people. (*Rabelais* 19)

The power that carnival laughter possesses lies in its dynamic quality of going beyond the rigidity of binary oppositions. As opposed to the seriousness of authority that bases its essence on the definition of a subject/object dichotomy, laughter overcomes any such definition by its constant gesture of reversal. By turning things upside down, by reversing the upper strata with the lower, it objectifies any idea that claims to be the absolute. It fills the vacuum, and gives it content. As Bakhtin repeatedly underlines, it is only through carnival laughter that "the world is seen anew, no less (and perhaps more) profoundly than when seen from the serious standpoint" (66).

The material bodily principle embedded in laughter is, therefore, liberating. It brings anything that is idealized, romanticized, stabilized into the realm of the tangible and material. It brings the heavenly down to earth and makes it real. By familiarizing the unfamiliar it annihilates the fear involved in it. It is the antidote for dogmatism, for anything that induces fear and pity. It purifies and liberates us "from fanaticism and pedantry, from fear and intimidation, from didacticism, naïveté and illusion, from the single meaning, the single level, from sentimentality" (123).

With the banner/bed sheet equation, Toole transfers the image of progress from the high mythical level (upper strata) to the gay level of popular festive degradation (lower strata). The typically grotesque image of bodily fluids and the stains on the sheet are related to the bodily lower stratum. They are remains of Ignatius' body, which grows to monstrous dimensions in the course of the novel. As cosmic matter that can be interpreted bodily, the stains provide the reversal of the spiritual with the material, humanizing and transforming that which claims to be the absolute.

The act of crowning and uncrowning works in both ways in this scene. It is not only the banner, as the heavy and monolithically serious symbol of progress that is being debased by Ignatius' carnivalistic gesture. It is also Ignatius himself who is subjected to the grotesque swing. Once he declares himself the leader of the progressive movement, he is bound to go down – the downward movement always being reflected in curse and abuse. When the chanting workers finally turn against him at the end of the riot scene, Ignatius becomes the Fool-king of the carnival, whose attributes are ambivalent from the very start since "decrowning always glimmers through the crowning." The king's attributes are turned upside down in the clown; now he is "the king of a world turned inside out" (370).

In Toole's *A Confederacy of Dunces*, in the very person of Ignatius we see the toppling down of the modernist ideal of progress, which has established itself as the absolute. He presents us with the carnivalistic crowning and uncrowning of 'sacred texts' of modernity. Any political movement or cultural institution that takes itself too seriously falls prey to laughter; anything that claims to be the absolute is brought down to earth by the carnivalistic gesture of profanation: civil rights movement, modern psychology, gay rights, college education, law enforcement, modern commerce, and leftist social reform efforts. Ignatius reminds us that the essential problem with modernity is not inequality or lack of justice, but a failure to understand the fact that the modernist project offers nothing but a tedious uniformity since it can not stand the presence of 'the other' fearing that it might challenge the validity of its own ground. And uniformity does not pass as true equality, as a tamed and polished humanist understanding of liberty does not pass as real freedom. In this sense, Toole seems to be echoing Bakhtin saying, "Fear is the extreme expression of narrow-minded and stupid seriousness, which is defeated by laughter [. . .] Complete liberty is possible only in the completely fearless world" (*Rabelais* 41).

Works Cited

Bakhtin, Mikhail. *Problems of Dostoevsky's Poetics*. Ed. and trans. Carly Emerson. Minneapolis: U of Minnesota P, 1984.

Bakhtin, Mikhail. *Rabelais and his World*. Trans. Helene Iswolsky. Bloomington: Indiana UP, 1984.

Calinescu, Matei. *Five Faces of Modernity*. Durham: Duke UP, 1987.

Danow, David K. *The Spirit of the Carnival: Magical Realism and the Grotesque*. Kentucky: The UP of Kentucky, 1995.

Dentith, Simon. *Bakhtinian Thought*. New York: Routledge, 1996.

Derrida, Jacques. *Writing and Difference*. Trans. Alan Bass. Chicago: U of Chicago P, 1978.

Toole, John Kennedy. *A Confederacy of Dunces*. New York: Grove, 1987.

How to Be a Victim: Politics and Language in David Mamet's *Oleanna*

Sırma Soran Gumpert
Haliç University

Abstract: In David Mamet's 1992 play *Oleanna*, the male college instructor John and his female student Carol discuss the problems Carol has in her course. The conversation between teacher and student proves to be fateful, and the play turns into a war between mechanisms of power, language and abuse. Although both manage to assert one kind of power over each other, they are destroyed by the end of the play. Both John and Carol are self-absorbed and are searching for understanding and power. They eventually become victims of the languages they choose to use on one another. John's pedantic use of specialized academic language turns Carol into a "feminist" equipped with the appropriate discourse that goes with it. However both are trapped in their own linguistic mechanisms. In *Oleanna, language* is portrayed as an inescapable prison which determines the characters' fate and sets the boundaries of their world. Thus, the focus of this paper is on the way David Mamet's play *Oleanna* treats the inextricable relationship between man's fate and his use of language.

When discussing the theater of Mamet, perhaps what we are really dealing with is a theatre of language, or a theatre of speech, in which *language* is granted the leading role. Language is so much the subject of Mamet's plays that it is almost impossible to analyze their thematics without dealing explicitly with their language. In this sense, David Mamet is surely not alone, he fits into a larger group of post-war playwrights on both sides of the Atlantic – namely Samuel Beckett, Eugène Ionesco, Edward Albee, Sam Shepard, and the like – who treat *language* not as a vehicle serving character, but as the central locus of the action.

Language might be Mamet's central character but it is not exactly a protagonist; rather we might say it is in the manner of a dramatic force, which destroys the characters or obliges them to conform with its pre-given structures and rules; or else it is portrayed as an inescapable prison which determines the characters' fate and sets the boundaries of their world. Thus the focus of this paper is on the way Mamet's play *Oleanna* treats the inextricable relationship between man's fate and his use of language. The fates of the college professor John and his student Carol in the 1992 play *Oleanna* have in a sense been entirely molded by the discourses they have chosen to communicate with each other.

All three acts of the play take place in John's office. John is trying to advise his twenty-year old student Carol, who has dropped by at office hours. In Act I, Carol has come to John for help with his course which she is failing; she simply does not understand what is being discussed in class, nor the texts she is assigned, nor why she has received a low grade on her paper assigned for John's class. Carol's major complaint is that she does not understand anything:

> **Carol:** Nobody *tells* me anything. And I *sit* there . . . in the *corner*. In the *back*. And everybody is talking about "this" all the time. And "concepts" and precepts" and, and, and, and, and, WHAT IN THE WORLD ARE YOU TALKING ABOUT? And I read your book. And they said, "Fine go in that class." Because you talked about responsibility to the young. I DON'T KNOW WHAT IT MEANS AND I'M *FAILING* . . . (14)

As Carol ironically, incomprehensible on the whole, tries to explain her problems, John is distracted by a series of phone calls concerning the house he is buying in expectation of receiving tenure within the week. But, in spite of the distraction John does try to sympathize with her, and even tells her about his own personal struggles. Towards the end of the first act, as each character becomes increasingly frustrated with the other, an exasperated John makes the mistake of offering Carol an ''A'' in the class, if she will just meet him in his office a few times during the semester to discuss her problems. He does this because he ''likes'' Carol and thinks they might have things in common. She protests, only to have John tell her to "[f]orget about the paper,'' for ''[w]hat is The Class but you and me?'' (25-26).

Carol: You're buying a new house.

John: That's right.

Carol: Because of your promotion.

John: Well, I suppose that that's right.

Carol: Why did you stay here with me?

John: Stay here.

Carol: Yes. When you should have gone.

John: Because I like you.

Carol: You like me.

John: Yes.

Carol: Why?

John: Why? Well? Perhaps we're similar. (*Pause*) Yes.

(*Pause*)

Carol: You said "everyone has problems."

John: Everyone has problems.

Carol: Do they?

John: Certainly.

Carol: You do?

John: Yes.

Carol: What are they?

John: Well. (*Pause*) Well, you're perfectly right. (*Pause*) If we're going to take off the Artificial *Stricture*, of "Teacher," and "Student," why should *my* problems be any more a mystery than your own? Of *course* I have problems. (20-21)

This dialogue will prove fateful; it is one of the exchanges Carol will use in the next two scenes to accuse John of making a pass at her. In the following scene we discover that Carol has charged John with sexual harassment. Meanwhile John's tenure committee is investigating the charge. Carol explains how she and her unidentified "group" believe John to have "misused" his position. Carol has apparently joined a certain group which has shaped her, almost overnight, into a "feminist." John tries hard to dissuade Carol from pressing charges. In the third and final act John is on the point of being fired, but still makes one last attempt to come to an agreement with Carol. Carol will not change her mind; instead she lectures John about his misbehavior, armed with a new language she previously lacked:

> **Carol:** My charges are not trivial. [. . .] A *joke* you have told, with a sexual tinge. The language you use, a verbal or physical caress, yes, yes, I know, you say that it is meaningless. I understand. I differ from you. To lay a hand on someone's shoulder.
> **John:** It was devoid of sexual content.
> **Carol:** I say it was not. I SAY IT WAS NOT: Don't you begin to *see* . . . ? Don't you begin to understand? IT'S NOT FOR YOU TO SAY. (70)

Carol goes as far as offering a list of demands including a list of books that she and her group wish to have removed from the curriculum. On the list is John's book as well. At the play's end we learn that John is being charged with rape; motivated by the end of scene two in which John tries to physically prevent Carol from leaving the office before they settle matters. And Carol *reads* this act as an attempted rape. In the final moments of the play, after overhearing a phone call John makes with his wife, Carol tells John not to call his wife "baby." It is the last straw; John explodes in a sudden flare of violence;

> **John**: You vicious little bitch. You think you can come in here with your political correctness and destroy my life?
> (He knocks her to the floor.)
> After how I treated you . . .? You should be . . .
> Rape you . . . ? Are you kidding me . . . ?
> (He picks up a chair, raises it above his head, and advances on her.)
> I wouldn't touch you with a ten-foot pole. You little *cunt* . . . (79)

The play ends with Carol repeating her response twice: "Yes. That's right" looking at John, and again, "Yes. That's right" (80), her head lowered this time, looking away from John. What does this mean? Has Carol changed her mind; is she now in agreement with the adversary? Ironically, this moment of convergence occurs as John and Carol are on the point of destroying each another. The ending scene validates both of the charges they have leveled at each other. She consents to him (and perhaps herself), and John to her.

Carol's use of what has been referred to as "political correctness" as a weapon, her apparently sudden feminist voice, John's abrupt retreat to misogynist behavior has created so much polemic among critics and viewers that the play's aesthetic merit has become almost irrelevant.

At just about the same time there was also a very popular court case being held about one Clarence Thomas who was accused of sexual harassment and was appointed to the Supreme Court. Again in the 1990s the new cultural concept of "political correctness" was gaining power. Because the play was premiered simultaneously with the court hearings and the rise of political correctness, many people thought the play was about political correctness in academia.

Few would disagree that the play is about political correctness in academia, although, in the 1990s, during its first stagings, the critical literature about *Oleanna* saw it as a fable about gender and sought to evaluate the play purely in terms of sexual politics. Of course any attempt to say what a play is *about* is bound to be reductive. Mamet resisted these interpretations pointing out that his play was "structured as a tragedy [. . .] about power" (Kane 125).

Contemporary criticism has offered more political and more rhetorical approaches to the play, focusing on issues of power linked to language. *Oleanna*, from this perspective, is not a play about gender, but about how gender becomes an issue when *and only when* Carol discovers the rhetorical strategies of sexual politics to change her position in the hierarchy. It is a matter of tactics, says Christine MacLeod, "of deploying to the best advantage the best available weapons" (207). In a way *gender*, in this play, becomes a sort of pragmatic strategy. Mamet himself in several of his interviews dismisses the idea of the play as being a polemic about gender written from the "male" point of view, stating that

> [t]he points [Carol] makes about power and privilege – I believe them all. If I didn't believe them, the play wouldn't work as well. It is a play about two people, and each person's point of view is correct. Yet they end up destroying each other. (Norman 52-53)

I would say that *Oleanna* is about that which has always fascinated Mamet: the use and abuse of specialized languages. His extensive experience in academia, for example, has given him sufficient material with which to work in *Oleanna.* Just as Mamet uses ruthless salesmen language in *Glengary Glen Ross*, or macho masculine discourses in *Sexual Perversity in Chicago.*

John speaks the discourse of academia, his status depends on his ability to utilize that discourse. In the academic world "language," according to linguist Robin Lakoff is the most important semiotic system. "[. . .] university people love to talk," she says and continues:

> [. . .] the discourse of academe seems especially designed for incomprehensibility, [t]oward the outside world [the special languages of the academy] are elitist: we know, you cannot understand, you may not enter. But for insiders they are a secret handshake. When I encounter my profession's term of art in a piece of writing or a talk, I am obscurely comforted: I am at home among friends. (Lakoff, qtd. in Badenhausen 4)

To have access to special linguistic communities (in *Oleanna* there is the discourse of law, real estate, academia, and feminism) means you also have power within a social group, which can also be used to subordinate or marginalize those who are outside it. John has the skills and the authority to use his linguistic power to marginalize Carol by excluding her from his verbal sphere. And Carol's utter lack of access to this discourse puts her at a great disadvantage.

Mamet wants to highlight this subordination from the start, for the play opens with John talking on the phone in Carol's presence, a conversation physically closed to the student. Likewise, Carol's first words are in the form of a question: ''What is a "term of art"?'' she asks John to explain a phrase he has just employed on the phone. John explains, "It seems to me a *term*, which has come, through its use, to mean something *more specific* than the words would, to someone *not acquainted* with them . . . indicate" (2-3). This exchange not only draws attention to the play's focus on specialized discourse as its main point but discloses Carol's failure to participate properly in this language-centered society.

The more Carol and John talk, or rather try to talk, the farther apart they are driven. Mamet is drawing attention to the problems that result from certain false impressions held by members of the academy concerning the ability of different discourses to communicate meaning.

To set a theoretical approach to the play the work of the reader response theorist Stanley Fish and in particular his idea of the "interpretive community" proves to be useful here. Within Stanley Fish's concept John and Carol belong to different institutes or communities which means they belong to different groups of readers. Carol's *mis-reading* of John can be explained by the fact that she does not belong to this community. Fish's argument is that *readers* make meanings, not subjectively but by reference to the group they are members of. Carol's model of reading therefore, is formulated within the feminist community of readers with whom she shares a set of interpretive strategies.

Fish's work was initially criticized for the power it gave the reader over the text, but Fish makes it clear that not all readers are equal. Criticism for Fish is a mode by which certain powerful readers persuade others of the nature and meaning of the text they are reading. Likewise, Carol is led inevitably (by the powerful readers or critics in her group) to *interpret* John in a certain manner: John as an oppressor, a misogynist, a rapist and so on. In Fish's model "meanings are not extracted but made, [;] what utterers do" according to Fish, "is give hearers and readers the opportunity to make meanings (and texts) by inviting them to put into execution a set of strategies" (220). This can also explain, to a certain extent, why Carol returns in the next two acts, having realized that, as C. S. Walker puts it,

> the meaning of what she has experienced is to be determined, not on some communicative basis of shared values, but in the context of the assertion of one kind of power or another; and that there is no source outside of the systems of material power by which the moral sense of action can be measured. (160)

From this perspective what Carol says in her central speech seems more understandable:

> Why do you hate me? Because you think me wrong? No. Because I have, you think, *power* over you. Listen to me. Listen to me, Professor. *(Pause)* It is the power that you hate. So deeply that, that any atmosphere of free discussion is impossible. It's not "unlikely." It's *impossible.* Isn't it? [. . .] Now. The thing which you find so cruel is the selfsame process of selection I, and my group, go through *every day of our lives.* In admittance to school. In our tests, in our class rankings. . . . (68-69)

Michel Foucault theorizes this relationship between discourse, power and knowledge. Foucault argues that *discourses* impose, even demand, a particular kind of identity for those who use them. Of course, the fact that institutions and their discourses demand that you be a particular sort of person was not unknown before poststructuralist theory, but Foucauldian theory argues further that we don't just *play roles* in such cases, but our very identity, the notion we have of ourselves, is at issue when we are affected by discourses of power. From the Foucauldian point of view, therefore, the conclusion of *Oleanna* shows not John's true *nature*, but rather what John has truly *become*. For Foucauldians it is not so much the individual who does dreadful things as the discourse of power that flows through him or her (Butler 49). Thus, Mamet's play encourages its viewers to question whether *discourse* or *language* represents identities that already exist or whether it produces them.

Regarding the radical change in identity and therefore in discourse of both Carol (from weak, lost and inarticulate to aggressive, accusative, articulate and feminist) and John (from authoritative, pedantic and articulate to inarticulate, victimized, powerless, and from there to abusive, violent and misogynist) it would not be wrong to state that the two are being "dispersed among the interstices of language, enmeshed with and finally lost among the endless relay of signification," thus, a human being on this view is "not a unity, not autonomous, but a process, [is] perpetually in construction, perpetually contradictory, perpetually open to change" (Belsey, qtd. in Butler 53).

The notion of the human being as a "process" always "in construction" allies with the poststructural criticism that makes political discussions in relation to the nature of the self, or rather, the *subject.* One of these is that the conflicting languages of power moving through individuals in fact construct the subject; persons are seen as undergoing an internal conflict between systems (Butler 53). Seyla Benhabib's words strengthen this argument:

> The subject is replaced by a system of structures, oppositions and differences which, to be intelligible, need not be viewed as products of a living subjectivity at all. You and I are the mere 'sites' of such conflicting languages of power, and the self is merely another position in language. (Benhabib, qtd. in Butler 51)

In this respect, once again John and Carol can be viewed as individuals torn or worn between "conflicting languages of power," which in the end posits them as victims of these power games rather than masters of their language. Mamet's *Oleanna* therefore may very well be holding an almost deterministic position of the human being as a creature at the mercy of the brutal forces of hegemonic language. Carol and John are crushed by the discourses they choose to exploit on one another; this may be the real tragedy of Mamet's play.

Works Cited

Badenhausen, Richard. "The Modern Academy Raging in the Dark: Misreading Mamet's Political Incorrectness in *Oleanna*." *College Literature* 25.3 (Fall 1998):1-19.

Belsey, Catherine. *Critical Practice.* New York: Routledge,1980.

Benhabib, Seyla. *Situating the Self: Gender, Community and Postmodernism in Contemporary Ethics.* New York: Routledge, 1992.

Bigsby, Christopher, ed. *A Cambridge Companion to David Mamet.* Cambridge Companions to Literature. Cambridge UP, 2004.

Butler, Christopher. *Postmodernism: A Very Short Introduction.* Oxford UP, 2002.

Fish, Stanley. "Interpretive Communities." *Literary Theory: An Anthology.* Ed. Julie Rivkin and Michael Ryan. 2nd ed. Malden, MA.: Blackwell, 2004. 217-221.

Kane, Leslie, ed. *David Mamet in Conversations.* Ann Arbor: U of Michigan P, 2001.

Lakoff, Robin Tolmach. *Talking Power: The Politics of Language.* New York: Basic, 1990.

Malkin, Jeanette R. *Verbal Violence in Contemporary Drama: From Handke to Shepard.* Cambridge UP, 1992.

Mamet, David. *Oleanna.* New York: Vintage, 1992.

Norman, Geoffrey and John Rezek. "David Mamet: A Candid Conversation with America's Foremost Dramatist about Tough Talk, TV Violence, Women and Why Government Shouldn't Fund the Arts." *Playboy* April 1995: 52-53.

Walker, Craig Stewart. "Three Tutorial Plays: *The Lesson, The Prince of Naples,* and *Oleanna.*" *Modern Drama* 40.1 (Spring 1997): 149-161.

Rewriting Fairytales from a Feminist Perspective: *Transformations* by Anne Sexton

Gülfer Göze
Boğaziçi University

Abstract: Fairy tales contain secret messages. Modern psychology accounts for this in its observations of the genre. Parents take this fact into consideration when they read these tales to their children. And many adults accept the influence of fairy tales on their children's development. But are these messages thoroughly beneficent? Or are they just one of the invisible constituents of a system preparing the children for a patriarchal system of stereotyped people with no originality, controlled by a set of rules established long ago in favor of the male and authority? In *Transformations* Anne Sexton gives an answer to the latter question and exemplifies the negative effects of these messages on children. She criticizes society for creating such fairy tales which in their turn created generations of commanding fathers, brothers and husbands, dutiful housewives and daughters, and, while promoting patriarchal values, debased the role and power of women. Concentrating on the issue of gender in the light of the work of child psychologist Bruno Bettelheim, this paper investigates the transformations Anne Sexton carries out in her interpretation of fairy tales.

Talking about logocentrism and phallocentrism, the prominent French feminist Hélène Cixous assumes that "subordination of the feminine to the masculine order is the condition for the functioning of the machine," the patriarchal system of society and its effects on practically every field of our lives. And she asks: "What would become of logocentrism, of the great philosophical systems, of world order in general if the rock upon which they founded their church were to crumble? [. . .] Then all the stories would have to be told differently, the future would be incalculable, the historical forces would, will, change hands, bodies; another thinking as yet not thinkable will transform the functioning of all society" (289). However, until the way power is shared changes, women can struggle to attain it, until the way we think changes, women can begin to construct a new thinking and until the way the stories are told changes, women can read them in a different way and play with the significances of the texts in feminist readings.

Twentieth-century American poet Anne Sexton is one of the women who re-read the stories told to her in her childhood and then rewrote them from a woman's perspective. As a poet who grew up, read poetry and found her voice in a poetic environment dominated by male poets, Sexton could begin to write more freely of authority only in the 1960s, with the renaissance of women writers who questioned the traditional gender roles. She found another self inside her, repressed under the pressure of her role as a wife and a mother, and of her psychotherapy sessions encouraging her to assume the traditional gender roles and comply with cultural expectations. This new self was the "witch," as many critics name it. The witch seems to be the strongest female character she introduced in her poetry. This witch, the voice of the independent, disobeying and rebelling female, left her mark on poems like "Her Kind" and "The Black Art," but especially on her book *Transformations,* a collection of transformed fairy tales.

Sexton wrote *Transformations*, published in 1971, in one year. The volume is composed of seventeen transformed tales, the first of which, "The Gold Key," serves as a general prologue. The remaining poems are composed of a prologue of one or two stanzas and then the tale itself. The prologue is where the poet speaks directly to the reader, presents the thematic focus of the tale and attunes the reader to that theme rather than the theme of the original tale. The tale itself is exceedingly different from the version of the Grimm Brothers although it shares the same plot. In this paper I'm going to focus on the transformations Sexton carried out in the fairy tales by giving examples from the poems, contrasting them with the originals, and arguing the difference of Sexton's fairyland from that of the previous tellers of the tales. Moreover, I'll take a look at the theories of psychologists and analysts on the fairy tales, especially those of child psychologist Bruno Bettelheim.

According to Bettelheim, the fairy tale is the only form of art that is fully comprehensible to the child and "unlike any other form of literature, direct[s] the child to discover his identity and calling, and [. . .] also suggest[s] what experiences are needed to develop his character further" (24). Although fairy tales teach little about the specific conditions of modern life due to the fact that they were composed a long time ago, children can learn about their problems and solutions to the issues treated no matter what society they live in. The themes of the fairy tales, in fact, reflect the inner conflicts the child is still unable to detect. As psychoanalyst Mark Dean points out, "fairy tales express universal states of regression which all children experience when faced with the traumata and conflicts of growing up. Children can identify with the heroines and heroes of fairy tales and vicariously struggle through their ordeals. Most importantly they learn that there are ways out of these dilemmas, that with perseverance and courage, the challenges and conflicts of growing up can be overcome"(qtd. in Hall 95).

Besides helping the children deal with their problems, fairy tales have another purpose. Bettelheim says that they "convey at the same time overt and covert meanings [. . .] speak simultaneously to all levels of the human personality, communicating in a manner which reaches the uneducated mind of the child as well as that of the sophisticated adult [. . .] Applying the psychoanalytic model of the human personality, fairy tales carry important messages to the conscious, the preconscious, and the unconscious mind, on whatever level each is functioning at the time" (5-6). According to psychologists, one of the most important functions of these messages is to transmit the cultural heritage to the children. Developed within the Western European oral tradition, recorded and overlaid with nineteenth-century didacticism, these tales express the underlying values of Western culture. They help many traditions and customs to survive and teach children to live in harmony with them.

While the children receive these messages and store them in their unconscious, they are also programmed by them. The colorful fairy tales become merely black and white when we look into their hidden meanings. There is always the good and the bad. Good wins out, bad loses. We empathize with the good, not caring for the bad, and at the end the bad is burnt or dead or left alone. While we see the wolf as a deceiver and cause of distress in "Little Red

Riding Hood," we don't feel a bit shocked by the cold-blooded girl and the grandmother who, to quote from Sexton, remembered "nothing naked and brutal / from that little death" (80). Besides, there are always the males and the females, whose sex roles determine their roles in the fairy tale. All the "damsels in distress" are saved by handsome princes, strong hunters or powerful kings. And mostly the reason for the distress is a witch or a stepmother: women. Fathers and husbands are never the cause of a problem. I could find only "Bluebeard" in which it was the husband that caused all the distress to the wife but even here, rather than celebrating the courage and wisdom of Bluebeard's wife in discovering the dreadful truth about her husband's murderous deeds, the tellers of the tale disparage her unruly act of insubordination. Furthermore, it ends with two stanzas, each of which is called "Moral," that accuse the wife for her curiosity rather than the husband. These stanzas address women telling them that the bad husband Bluebeard is an exception. So it is apparent that fairy tales are written from a male perspective and reflect a powerful bias of male-oriented society. All female characters are classified into two groups: good and bad. Evil women are mostly witches and they are always hideous, scheming, and tricky, and they try to change the lives of the innocent. On the other hand, good women, generally beautiful princesses, are quiet and submissive. They do whatever their fathers or husbands tell them to do, and if they disobey, they pay for it. Then a male rescues them from the predicament they find themselves in, and at the end they repent their disobedience and live happily ever after with their princes. So the messages that help the children tackle problems, as Bettelheim argues, seem to tell the girls to respect authority, to obey, to be a good wife, not to be curious, and to live quietly ever after. The message for the boys, contrary to that, directs them to act and conveys to them the idea that the opposite sex is weak and vulnerable and that they are the ones to protect the girls.

What Sexton does in her transformations is to show that she is aware of these messages, and to render these tales in the version of the witch, her powerful woman voice, to whom the creators of the previous fairylands gave no opportunity to defend herself. Now it is time for the witch to justify herself and deconstruct the identity of woman as it had been forced into our unconscious. It is, in fact, the confessional poet Anne Sexton who chose the exact fairy tales and transformed them according to her own needs and created a new fairyland that is extremely different from that of the Grimm Brothers. However, as Suzanne Juhasz comments, "much of the strength comes from the way in which the personal gets expanded so that she comes to tell a tale of her tribe – women [. . .]. The witch poet of *Transformations* is Sexton at her best, because she draws on the stuff of a powerful female identity to speak on behalf of" all women (317). And in creating this identity, Sexton breaks down the feminine archetypes (and stereotypes) prevalent in myth and fairytale. From Snow White to Sleeping Beauty, Sexton reexamines the stepmother, the wicked witch, the dutiful wife, and the innocent maiden, changing them from mere archetypes into real characters.

The tales Sexton chose to reinterpret for our modern culture also seem to form a cycle of poems that observes all the periods of the life of a woman. We see the pre-puberty girl child in "Snow White" and "Red Riding Hood," her wish to be accepted in "One-Eye, Two-Eyes, Three-Eyes," then we witness the pressures on her in her puberty in "Rapunzel," her sexual awakening in "The Frog Prince" and "Rapunzel," her contact with the outside world in "Hansel and Gretel," her motherhood in "Snow White" and her old age in "Rapunzel." And in all of these periods, Sexton finds things to criticize and mock in society. One of her most prominent critiques is directed at the ubiquitous perfect "happily ever after" fairy tale ending. For the heroine, the end of most of the Grimm tales coincides with marriage. The princesses always get married to the handsome prince or king. "Cinderella," "Rapunzel," "Snow White and the Seven Dwarves," "Sleeping Beauty" and "The Frog Prince" are some of the many examples. This, of course, is to make little girls envious of the heroines and sneak the concepts of marriage, wife, wedding, children and family into their unconscious. However, in Sexton's versions, marriage is never a happy ending. It's a complete self-denial of the heroine, a self-imprisonment. In "Cinderella," the prince brings the glass slipper and instead of fitting it onto Cinderella's foot, "This time Cinderella fit into the shoe." From now on she is going to live in the prison of marriage into which she fitted.

> Cinderella and the prince
> lived, they say, happily ever after,
> like two dolls in a museum case
> never bothered by diapers or dust,
> never arguing over the timing of an egg,
> never telling the same story twice,
> never getting a middle-aged spread,
> their darling smiles pasted on for eternity. (58)

Although she has married a prince and begun to live in a palace, the heroine doesn't seem to have achieved anything at all; besides, now she is a captive in marriage. She gets married and her life is over. What follows is nothing more than the life of a doll. This is the inevitable end the order of society prepares for women.

Another example showing Sexton's attitude towards marriage is "Twelve Dancing Princesses." In this tale, the king, who wants to know why his daughters' shoes are worn out each morning even though he locks the door of their dormitory, promises one of his daughters to the man who finds the answer. For years no one is able to do this until a worn-out soldier with the aid of magic finds out that the girls have a secret passage out and dance from midnight until dawn with handsome princes. When he tells this to their father, the king allows the soldier to marry any of the girls he wants, and the soldier chooses the eldest. In the original tale we are told nothing about the daughters after their hidden life is revealed:

> Then the king called for the princesses, and asked them whether what the soldier said was true: and when they saw that they were discovered, that it was of no use to deny what had happened, they confessed it all. And the king asked the soldier which of them he would choose for his wife; and he answered, 'I am not very young, so I will have the eldest.' – And they were married that very day, and the soldier was chosen to be king's heir. (Brothers Grimm 48)

However, the conclusion of Sexton's version focuses on the princesses and the readers empathize with them:

> He had won. The dancing shoes would dance
> no more. The princesses were torn from
> their night life like a baby from its pacifier.
> Because he was old he picked the eldest.
> At the wedding the princesses averted their eyes
> and sagged like old sweatshirts.
> Now the runaways would run no more and never
> again would their hair be tangled into diamonds,
> never again their shoes worn down to a laugh [. . .] (92)

The princesses will never be free again. Their carefree days are over, and they are imprisoned by the main components of patriarchal order, their father, the soldier who later turns into the husband, and the institution of marriage. They will continue to live under authority, have children, read them fairy tales which will enhance the bombardment of their young and clean unconscious with patriarchal values, and watch them lose, too.

The alternative Sexton gives is the case of Rapunzel, the bravest fairy tale heroine of all. Rapunzel's difference from other heroines is not so apparent in the original tale. Sexton's Rapunzel is different, in fact, she is a rebel. More important than the fact that she marries the prince and gives birth to twins, she has sex with him and is liberated from the tower, from the authority of her godmother. Even in the Grimms' version she never tries to return to the tower, manages to live alone and has the power to cure the blind eyes of the prince. In addition to this, Sexton gives her an identity, which all the other fairyland heroines lack, and she makes her heroine choose the prince not because he is a prince but because "he dazzled her with his answers" and "he dazzled her with his dancing stick," and she took pleasure from this relationship:

> They lay together upon the yellowy threads,
> swimming through them

like minnows through kelp
and they sang out benedictions like the pope. (Sexton 41)

Sexton's Rapunzel is a modern woman and almost a feminist. Her relationship with the prince is highly sexual. Sexton focuses on Rapunzel's final blossoming into a rose, a sexual entity, independent of the stem, her godmother, which once fought to enclose her completely. At the end Rapunzel doesn't ride off to the kingdom of the prince to be his wife. She doesn't hold court. She is free and that's all. She is not like the other heroines who wait for the kiss of the prince to be awakened just in order to begin a new sleep. And her daughters, free in the forests where their mother lives, will not be read fairy tales in the way the other children are. They will, without intervention of authority in their unconscious, be among those who pave the way for a freer life equal to that of the males.

Through her transformations, Sexton criticizes society for its fairy tales which in their turn helped to shape generations of commanding fathers, brothers, husbands, dutiful housewives and daughters and masses of ordinary stereotypes. She tries to eliminate the hidden messages in the fairy tales which are invisible constituents of a system preparing the children for a patriarchal system of people with no originality, identity or individuality, controlled by a set of rules established long ago in favor of the male and authority. Instead of telling the tales to us as our grandmother, Sexton chooses to be the wolf in grandma's clothes. However, this wolf, rather than deceiving, tries to awaken us, especially women, from the sleep to which the order put us. A complicated life as opposed to a black and white universe, the bitter end as opposed to the happy end, and the liberty of women as opposed to the kiss of the prince; these are Sexton's transformations.

Works Cited

Bettelheim, Bruno. *The Uses of Enchantment: The Meaning and Importance of Fairy Tales.* London: Thames and Hudson, 1976.

Cixous, Hélène. "Sorties." *Modern Criticism and Theory*. Ed. David Lodge. New York: Longman, 1988.

Grimm, Jacob and Wilhelm. *Grimm's Fairy Tales*. Berkshire: Penguin, 1996

Grimm, Jacob and Wilhelm. *Selected Tales*. Trans. David Luke. New York: Penguin, 1982.

Hall, Caroline King Barnard. *Anne Sexton*. Twayne's United States Authors Series 548. Boston: Twayne, 1989.

Juhasz, Susanne. "Anne Sexton." *Modern American Women Writers*. Ed. Elaine Showalter et al. New York: Collier, 1993. 309- 320.

Sexton, Anne. *Transformations*. New York: Mariner, 2001.

On the Intrinsic Value of the Land: Terry Tempest Williams' *Refuge: An Unnatural History of Family and Place*

Ufuk Özdağ
Hacettepe University

Abstract: Since the times of Henry David Thoreau, American nature writing has emphasized the intrinsic value of nature and of wildlife. And yet, the political discourse still retains an anthropocentric stance and confers utilitarian value to the land and to nonhuman life on earth. Leading American conservationist and nature writer Terry Tempest Williams' *Refuge: An Unnatural History of Family and Place* (1991), draws attention to this paradox in the conception of the land. Williams, in *Refuge*, chronicling the devastation inflicted on human life and on the intrinsically valuable land by the atmospheric nuclear testing between the years 1951-1962, and the underground nuclear testing after 1963 in the Nevada Test Site, revolts against her culture that lacks a "land ethic." The argument derives from the fact that the work upholds a Leopoldian expanded community concept that changes the role of man in the biota "from conqueror of the land-community to plain member and citizen of it."

> "Give me the ocean, the desert, or the wilderness!"
>
> Henry David Thoreau "Walking"

Thomas Cole, the father of American landscape painting, in the tradition of all Hudson River School painters in the early decades of the nineteenth century, calls attention to the holy qualities of the land. Among his landscape paintings that promote feelings of sublimity, one particular painting, *The Oxbow: View from Mount Holyoke, Northampton, Massachusetts, after a Thunderstorm* (figure1), emerges as having a distinct place in the social history of American art owing to its symbolic overtones. Once interpreted as a "spectacular bend in the Connecticut River" (Stokstad 975), the painting, now, assumes new significance with the advent of mounting interest in the environment: Indeed, *The Ox-*

bow is, and has always been, a bitter critique of man's attitude toward nature and of his presumption that he is the rightful owner of the land.

Figure 1
Thomas Cole. *The Oxbow: View from Mount Holyoke, Northampton, Massachusetts, after a Thunderstorm.* 1836.
The Metropolitan Museum of Art, New York

Nevertheless, Thomas Cole had given his spectators the clues for a truthful interpretation of the painting: a river, in the shape of a question mark, streching over the inhabited landscape next to the yet untouched wilderness areas, pointed at the wrong of perceiving land as resource waiting to be exploited for human benefit. An "oxbow" also stood for "a yoke, a symbol of control over raw nature" (Hughes 146). What is more, the word "Shaddai" [the Almighty] inscribed on the slopes of the hill in the background, cried out the sacred nature of the land. Cole was, indeed, anticipating environmental degradation by western business that would transmute holy land into territory to be conquered. As Robert Hughes reveals, "Cole saw that the rhetoric of American nationhood was fatally entangled with greed" (146), a conception Hughes defends with reference to the following verses by Cole,

> Each hill and every valley is become
> An altar unto Mammon, and the gods
> Of man's idolatry – its victims we. (Qtd. in Hughes 146)

Today, in view of the magnitude of the destruction of the land around the globe, and of the ongoing rhetoric that downplays it, an "ecological necessity"[1] arises to expand the boundaries of ethical considerability to the land, and to realize that the "victims" of environmental degradation are no longer solely human communities. Indeed, the "victims" are both human communities and the land – soils, waters, plants, and animals – and their victimization best surfaces in Terry Tempest Williams' unequaled nature writing, *Refuge: An Unnatural History of Family and Place* (1991), a work that protests the land-denying atmospheric and underground nuclear testing of the American government in the Nevada Test Site for decades, and calls for a Leopoldian "land ethic," an expanded community concept that includes the land.

In *Refuge: An Unnatural History of Family and Place,* Terry Tempest Williams conceives of the land as intrinsically valuable space. The unprecedented victimization of the human and nonhuman communities in *Refuge,* on the other hand, arises from the ongoing practice of regarding the land as territory to be conquered. A glimpse at Cole's *The Oxbow,* therefore, reveals that Williams' plea, in *Refuge*, for an ethical relation to the land is the culmination of a long tradition in America that cries out the sacred nature of the land. Indeed, her plea for a land ethic has its roots in early American nature writing. The two polar opposites in the conception of the land – land as resource for the use of man and land as sacred space – surfaces in the nature writing of Thoreau, and his warning, at this early date, for the potential victimization of the holy land if men are not heedful of it, is taken up more forcefully by the next generation of nature writers.

Thoreau is, indeed, one of the first nature writers to articulate an ethical relation to the land, for he had "the brilliance to recognize, before Darwin pub-

---

1 In *A Sand County Almanac*, Aldo Leopold regards "[t]he extension of ethics" to the land as "an evolutionary possibility and an ecological necessity" (239).

lished his theory of evolution, an organic connection between Homo Sapiens and nature" (Oelschlaeger 133). Living for two years and two months on the shore of Walden Pond, making the acutest observations on the land and its species, Thoreau comes to the conclusion that the most meaningful life is one in which man leaves aside material encumbrances and lives in harmony with sacred nature which nourishes both human and nonhuman life. In *Walden or, Life in the Woods* (1854), in the section "The Bean-field," Thoreau complains,

> By avarice and selfishness, and a grovelling habit, from which none of us is free, of regarding the soil as property, or the means of acquiring property chiefly, the landscape is deformed, husbandry is degraded with us, and the farmer leads the meanest of lives. He knows Nature but as a robber. (114)

In the section "Solitude," to heal the division between man and land, Thoreau redefines the concept of society and acknowledges kinship with nonhuman species:

> As I walk along the stony shore of the pond [. . .] all the elements are unusually congenial to me. [. . .] I experienced sometimes that the most sweet and tender, the most innocent, and encouraging society may be found in any natural object [. . .] In the midst of a gentle rain [. . .] I was suddenly sensible of such sweet and beneficient society in Nature [. . .] in every sound and sight around my house, an infinite and unaccountable friendliness all at once like an atmosphere sustaining me, as made the fancied advantages of human neighborhood insignificant, and have never thought of them since. (90-92)

Thoreau's long essay, "Walking" (1862), regarded as "one of the gospels of the conservation movement" (Finch and Elder 170), is the account of a symbolic walking away from anthropocentrism to ecocentrism. In this essay, Thoreau declares that all the land is "Holy," and that he is the true "discoverer" of the land, with an awareness of all its sentient beings that have a right to continued existence. In this respect, Thoreau states, "neither Americus Vespucius nor Columbus, nor the rest were the discoverers of it" (2161). Thoreau's awareness that he is "a part and parcel of Nature, rather than a member of society" (2157) leads to his famous dictum that "in Wildness is the preservation of the world" (2167). After all, it is a moral wrong and also a sacrilege to harm wilderness in view of this expanded community concept, an understanding which naturally necessitates "the preservation of the world."

The idea of intrinsic value in the land, so forcefully declared in the early decades of the 19th century, is reiterated by the next generation of American nature writers, by the disciples of Thoreau. The preservationist and nature writer, John Muir, furthers the biocentric view of the world and is the first to articulate "species rights." A frequent crusader to the wilderness, to Yosemite, which he refers to as "holy" land (Muir 16), and tirelessly involved in nature study for his botanical interests, Muir comes to the conclusion that the land is to be respected regardless of human interests. In *A Thousand-Mile Walk to the Gulf* (1916), an epic account of his journeying, on foot, from Indiana to the Gulf of Mexico in 1867, Muir takes a Thoreauvian stance and celebrates an expanded concept of society that includes the land and its species:

> The world, we are told, was made especially for man – a presumption not supported by all the facts. A numerous class of men are painfully astonished whenever they find anything, living or dead, in all God's universe, which they cannot eat or render in some way what they call useful to themselves. [. . .] Now, it never seems to occur to these far-seeing teachers that Nature's object in making animals and plants might possibly be first of all the happiness of each one of them, not the creation of all for the happiness of one. Why should man value himself as more than a small part of the one great unit of creation? (Qtd. in Scheese 63)

A generation after Muir's plea for species rights, philosopher, scientist and nature writer, Aldo Leopold, openly declares the need for a "Land Ethic" in his now classic *A Sand County Almanac* (1949). In this work, Leopold takes a decisive stance against human preeminence and proposes instead "a land ethic [that] changes the role of Homo sapiens from conqueror of the land-community to plain member and citizen of it" (240). The land ethic that Leopold formulates is, at base, an expanded community concept that "include[s] soils, waters, plants, and animals, or collectively: the land" (239). Journeying into the wilderness in the tradition of earlier nature writers – to the Wisconsin countryside – for long years, making close observations on "the land community" and realizing intrinsic value in the "biota," Leopold declares that "[a] thing is right when it tends to preserve the integrity, stability, and beauty of the biotic community. It is wrong when it tends otherwise" (262). In a well-known essay in *A Sand County Almanac,* in "On a Monument to the Pigeon," Leopold understands humanity as sharing "the odyssey of evolution" with other species, an understanding which has affinities with a new field of study, today, dedicated to animal minds, emotions and cognition.[2] Leopold states,

> It is a century now since Darwin gave us the first glimpse of the origin of species. We know now what was unknown to all the preceding caravan of generations: that men are only fellow-voyagers with other creatures in the odyssey of evolution. This new knowledge should have given us, by this time, a sense of kinship with fellow-creatures; a wish to live and let live; a sense of wonder over the magnitude and duration of the biotic enterprise. Above all we should, in the century since Darwin, have come to know that man, while now captain of the adventuring ship, is hardly the sole object of its quest, and that his prior assumptions to this effect arose from the simple necessity of whistling in the dark. (116-117)

---

2 The reference is to "cognitive ethology" – a field of study that has its roots in the theories of Charles Darwin. In Mark Bekoff's words, cognitive ethology is "the comparative, evo-

In short, the sacred nature of the land and the rights of species to "continued existence" are forcefully expressed in the ecologically informed works of prominent American nature writers over the years, and reaches a culmination in the formulation of "the land ethic" by Aldo Leopold, who lays bare "the complexity of the land organism," an "outstanding scientific discovery of the twentieth century" (190) that necessitates the preservation of every part in the web of life. In the words of Stewart, "[s]oil, mountains, rivers, atmosphere, plants, and animals all needed one another to exist, and the elimination of the smallest part had unpredictable consequences throughout the interrelated system" (147).

However, it was during the formulation of the land ethic by Aldo Leopold that the very conception of the land as sacred space was forgotten. Land became property, raw material, territory – more than ever – exclusively for human use. These were the Cold War years and the idea of expanding the boundaries of community to include the land was no man's concern. When "national security" was the most pressing issue, countries looked for "uninhabited" lands to test lethal weapons. As revealed by Clive Ponting in his *A Green History of the World: The Environment and the Collapse of Great Civilizations* (1993), the land was shaken by 458 atmospheric nuclear explosions in the world between the years 1945-1985. But the greatest sacrilege took place in the southwestern United States when Tonopah Gunnery Range near Las Vegas was chosen as the site for exploding atomic bombs – a land-denying activity of the military that would go on for decades – with both underground and aboveground testing. Over a hundred atmospheric nuclear tests were detonated in the Nevada Test Site, from January 1951 through July 1962, only 65 miles away to Las Vegas. After a Test Ban Treaty was signed in 1963, more than one thousand nuclear tests were conducted underground, in the same area.[3] The landscape chosen as the "test site" was reduced to utilitarianism and the "Holy Land" faced the biggest assault in the history of the world.

---

lutionary, and ecological study of animal minds and mental experiences." (86).

3 Studies reveal that more than 2000 nuclear tests have been conducted in various parts of the world, by a number of countries, since 16 July 1945 when the US exploded the first nuclear bomb, 'Trinity.'

In the totally anthropocentric official rhetoric of the Atomic Energy Commission – the United States government agency that owned the test site at that time – the country north of the test site was "virtually uninhabited desert terrain" (Williams 287). An official from the AEC described the desert between St. George, Utah, and Las Vegas, Nevada as "a damn good place to dump used razor blades." As for the people living downwind of the Nevada Test Site, they were described by the AEC as "a low-use segment of the population" (Gallagher xxiii). And yet, the desert, so irreverently described as "uninhabited" space, is thriving with life in Edward Abbey's *Desert Solitaire: A Season in the Wilderness* (1968). A much-celebrated nature writing that emerged out of Abbey's experience as a park ranger in Arches National Monument in Utah, in "a sanctuary for wildlife" (20), it seems that *Desert Solitaire* was specifically written to overturn the official rhetoric of the Atomic Energy Commission that declared the desert as "virtually uninhabited terrain."[4]

An even more significant attempt, on the part of American nature writing, to overturn the land-denying official rhetoric of the American government is Terry Tempest Williams' *Refuge*. Written at a time when underground nuclear testing was still going on in the Nevada Test Site, *Refuge* chronicles the magnitude of the environmental degradation that went far beyond the limits of the 1,350-square-mile Nevada Test Site. Williams protests her government's testing of nuclear weapons in the "virtually uninhabited desert terrain" by exposing the devastation inflicted on human life and on the holy land – on the Bear River Migratory Bird Refuge in Great Salt Lake – by the testing that went on for decades. In *Refuge*, in "The Clan of One-breasted Women" – the last part of the book that exposes the causes of the devastations – Williams declares, "[w]hen the Atomic Energy Commission described the country north of the Nevada Test Site as 'virtually uninhabited desert terrain,' my family and the birds at Great Salt Lake were some of the 'virtual uninhabitants'" (287).

---

4 In "Cliffrose and Bayonets," Abbey makes an inventory of the flora of "the slickrock desert," and concludes saying, "[s]o much for the inventory. After such a lengthy listing of plant life the reader may now be visualizing Arches National Monument as more a jungle than a desert. Be reassured, it is not so" (35).

Terry Tempest Williams, recognized by the Utne Reader as a "visionary," one of the Utne 100 "who could change your life," is from Salt Lake City, Utah. This is an area where fallout often drifted into, causing many radiation-induced cancers during, and after, the years of atmospheric nuclear testing.[5] The people living in these areas in the west – in Utah, Nevada, and Arizona – under the trajectories of blast clouds, were referred to as "downwinders." As a nature writer with a Leopoldian expanded community concept, Williams not only laments the tragedies of the "downwinders" in her immediate family in Salt Lake City, Utah. The devastation of the Bear River Migratory Bird Refuge at Great Salt Lake, caused by the unusual amount of precipitation and snowmelt and the resultant rise of water level to record heights, due to underground nuclear testing at the Nevada Test Site as implied by Williams, is equally tragic for Williams, and she laments the losses at the Bird Refuge, the sacred space that hosted millions of birds in a season.[6]

Williams, as a writer whose holistic concern embraces ecosystems as well as species, starts *Refuge* with an account of the sacred nature of the Bear River Migratory Bird Refuge, and refers to it as a "sanctuary" (15). Her journeying into this sacred space as a birdwatcher, ever since a child of nine, taught her the intrinsic value of the land, and of each member of the 208 species of birds who use the Refuge. It is the sacred space where Williams came to a realization of the rights of species to "continued existence"[7] and acquired a Leopoldian expanded community concept. In *Refuge*, in the essay, "Whimbrels," Williams

---

5 Ortmeyer and Makhijani state, "[o]n August 1, the National Cancer Institute (NCI) revealed that as a result of U.S. nuclear tests conducted at the Nevada Test Site (NTS), American children were actually exposed to 15 to 70 times as much radiation as had been previously reported to Congress [. . .] The National Cancer Institute estimates that around 160 million people – virtually everyone living in the U.S. at that time – received some iodine dose from fallout. But those most at risk, according to a peer-reviewed 1995 study, are people who were exposed while under 15 years of age who received a radiation dose of 10 rad or more. The risk is greatest for those exposed before the age of five."

6 For a connection between underground nuclear testing and unusual weather patterns, see the article by Jay Mayer.

7 In "The Land Ethic," Leopold affirms the "right" of the land to "continued existence in a natural state" (240).

narrates with profound ecological literacy her connectedness to this land and its intrinsically valuable species of birds.

> The birds and I share a natural history. It is a matter of rootedness, of living inside a place for so long that the mind and imagination fuse. [. . .] Of the 208 species of birds who use the Refuge, sixty-two are known to nest here. Such nesting species include eared, western, and pied-billed grebes, great blue herons, snowyegrets, white-faced ibises, American avocets, black-necked stilts, and Wilson's phalaropes. Also nesting at Bear River are Canada geese, mallards, gadwalls, pintails, greenwinged, blue-winged, and cinnamon teals, redheads, and ruddy ducks, It is a fertile community where the hope of each day rides on the backs of migrating birds. These wetlands, emeralds around Great Salt Lake, provide critical habitat for North American waterfowl and shorebirds, supporting hundreds of thousands, even millions of individuals during spring and autumn migrations. The long-legged birds with their eyes focused down transform a seemingly sterile world into a fecund one. It is here in the marshes with the birds that I seal my relationship to Great Salt Lake. (21-22)

Williams, in the thirty-six essays that touch upon the natural history of the major bird species that had inhabited the Bird Refuge, celebrates the intrinsic value of the members of the biotic community. To reflect her conviction in the analogous lives of human and nonhuman communities, and in the equally sentient lives of bird communities, Williams, in the essay "Killdeer," very much like a cognitive ethologist, refers to a "killdeer [that] feigns a broken wing, dragging it around the sand in a circle" (119). Williams explains the killdeer's behavior as "a protective device," for she and her company may be close to its nest. The killdeer, explains Williams, is "trying to distract" the intruders in its habitat to protect her young.[8] Thus, the essay "Killdeer" and many others in *Refuge,* respond to Leopold's call to extend ethics to the natural world. Williams, in the manner of Leopold, implies "[a] thing is right when it tends to preserve the integrity, stability, and beauty of the biotic community. It is wrong when it tends otherwise" (Leopold 262). Thus, she rejects a "conqueror role" in the Nevada test site for exclusively human benefit, as it backfires. As a nature writer taking up Leopold's key ideas, Williams wishes to change the role of man "from conqueror of the land-community to plain member and citizen of it" (Leopold 240), and, in her resultant narration, she gives equal weight to the tragedies lived in both human and nonhuman environments, caused by nuclear testing.

Terry Tempest Williams' holistic outlook in *Refuge,* that embraces human communities, ecosystems and species, contrasts decidedly with the "conqueror role"[9] of the Atomic Energy Commission during the decades of nuclear testing. In the totally anthropocentric official rhetoric of the AEC, there were frequent assurances, preceding the nuclear tests, that it was all very safe, and that no danger was posed to the local people.[10] Besides, there were frequent cover-ups regarding damage to nonhuman populations.[11] And yet, in the following dec-

---

8 A similar account exists in the cognitive ethologist Mark Bekoff's *Minding Animals: Awareness, Emotions, and Heart* Bekoff reveals, "[d]eception is observed in adult birds who are protecting their young. Carolyn Ristau discovered that female piping plovers feign a broken wing and hobble away from nests to distract a predator's attention. After the predator has been lured away, the mothers rush back to their chicks" (91).

9 The phrase "conqueror role" belongs to Aldo Leopold who states, "[i]n human history, we have learned (I hope) that the conqueror role is eventually self-defeating" (240).

10 The assurances were so convincing that back in Las Vegas-which became a tourist attraction to watch the flashes from each nuclear test-people would watch the mushroom clouds from the roof of their hotels, and celebrate the blasts with parties in the streets. Thousand of troops would be sent to trenches only a short distance from "ground zero." Shortly after the atomic blasts, they were ordered to walk under the radioactive clouds to ground zero. Decades later, they died tragically from fallout related illnesses. In fact, in the 1950s, The AEC was aware of the hazards of fallout but went on conducting the tests thinking they were necessary to US security.

11 A startling example of such cover-up is provided by Keith Schneider in his foreword to Gallagher's *American Ground Zero* Schneider reveals, "[o]f 14,000 sheep on the range east of the Nevada Test Site, roughly 4,500 died in May and June of 1953." Schneider

ades, after the secrets – the suppressed information related to nuclear testing – were made public in Federal Courts, Congress, and the press, the people came to the realization that "the conqueror role is eventually self-defeating."

During the years of nuclear testing, in an AEC booklet, one statement was, "[y]our best action is not to be worried about fallout" (Williams 284). However, virtually the entire continental United States was exposed to radiation of fallout. As revealed by Richard L. Miller in his *Under the Cloud: The Decades of Nuclear Testing* (1986), a most comprehensive study of atmospheric nuclear testing in Nevada, "every person alive during the 1950s and early 1960s lived under the atomic cloud" (9). As Miller explains, detonations produced mushroom clouds that extended 30,000-40,000 feet into the air, and the clouds of highly radioactive debris from each detonation "passed not only over Utah, Nevada, and Arizona, but over the entire continent" (Miller 8). The nuclear clouds travelled for thousands of miles and sprinkled the whole country with radioactive rain (figure 2).[12]

As documented by Miller, with reference to 82 maps of fallout trajectories, the radioactive clouds from each blast travelled east as far away as the Atlantic coasts, and even went beyond the borders of the United States. Sometimes, the clouds "circled the globe" and re-entered the United States, adding to the radioactivity of new blasts from the Nevada Test Site.[13] Countless people, exposed to

---

gives a detailed account of the ranchers' efforts for the compensation of their losses and refers to the decision of Judge A. Sherman Christensen, in 1982, for a new trial, stating, "[i]n granting the ranchers a new trial, Christensen said the government scientists and lawyers had deliberately concealed documents, given false testimony, and withheld information" (xvii-xviii).

12 Miller compiled his map, "Areas of the Continental United States Crossed by More Than One Nuclear Cloud from Aboveground Detonations," with the maps of fallout trajectories for the United States. Miller explains that he "produce[d] a locus of points where at least THREE nuclear clouds had passed overhead. So, what you see are actually lines associated with three or more trajectories" (personal communication).

13 Miller's reference is to an occurrence in the "Tumbler-Snapper series. Miller reveals, "[o]n May 5, [1952], Dog's [the fourth shot in the series] 18,000-foot trajectory crossed Philadelphia at 10:00 A.M. local time. On the same day, while much of the rest of the nuclear cloud was hovering north of Lake Superior, the western states again began to record increased fallout. But Dog was not the culprit. The radioactivity was from shot

nuclear fallout, contracted cancer, leukemia, and thyroid illnesses.[14] As indicated in an article in the *The Bulletin of the Atomic Scientists,* the tests were a serious health risk even to those people who were living far away from the test site, as fallout travels to distant places:

> Although areas near the Nevada Test Site were most often contaminated, the newly released data show that virtually the entire continental U.S. was affected, and "hot spots" occurred in unpredictable places far from the site. These hot spots occurred because rainstorms sometimes caused locally heavy deposits of fallout. As a result, some children in large portions of the Midwest, parts of New England, and areas east and northeast of the test site (Idaho, Montana, and the Dakotas), received doses of iodine 131 as high as 112 rad. (Ortmeyer and Makhijani)

As for the devastation wrought to the sacred land, it was totally dismissed by the AEC.[15] The harm to soils, waters, plants, and animals was downplayed or ignored, and cover-ups such as "malnutrition" (Gallagher xxiv) for the dead and deformed sheep that grazed on fallout-contaminated pastures were frequent. During the fourth series of Nevada tests in 1953, one "Army expert on atomic energy," addressing the troops, "cheerily" referred to the test site as "the valley where the tall mushrooms grow" (Miller 160). Earlier, in the detonations of 1952, AEC chairman Gordon Dean, adressing the newsmen who were permitted to the test site for media coverage, stated,

---

Charlie, which had circled the globe and now returned to drizzle activity onto the West Coast" (150).

14 For comprehensive information on the association between fallout levels and cancer rates in the U.S., see Richard L. Miller's *The U.S. Atlas of Nuclear Fallout.*

15 Keith Schneider states, "[a]ccording to tests conducted in secret by the Public Health Service and the Atomic Energy Commission, the government's atomic assault in Nevada poisoned milk in New England, wheat in South Dakota, soil in Virginia, and fish in the Great Lakes." (xv).

> What you will see tomorrow will be a bomb. It will be a bomb dropped from an airplane. The energy release of that bomb will be considerable. For example, it is planned to give a slightly larger energy release than the bombs exploded at Hiroshima, Nagasaki or Bikini. But it will not be the largest bomb that we have exploded. If it were, we would not be exploding it here within the continental limits of the United States. We would, instead, be exploding at Eniwetok. (Qtd. in Miller 145)

After each blast, the once sublime landscape lost its integrity. As Samuel W. Matthews, a reporter with *National Geographic* magazine, after having seen one of the detonations,[16] revealed,

> Here the landscape had a strange look. I realized suddenly that all vegetation had vanished – greasewood and creosote bush, cactus and yucca. Only bare sand remained. Ahead, where the tower had been, a disc of black scarred the earth. (Qtd. in Miller 162)

Detonations, poisoning human and non-human life, went on until 1962, and a Test Ban Treaty was, finally, signed in 1963. Finally, "downwinders," unaware of the deadly illnesses of the near future, were relieved of atomic debris carried by the winds. However, the sacred land – soils, waters, plants, and animals – continued facing assault with the underground nuclear testing that started in 1963, in the same area, and went on until 1992. Noone could predict the magnitude of the victimization of the non-human communities in the coming decades by the desecration of the "virtually uninhabited desert terrain" through underground nuclear testing.

---

16 For the first detonation of the Upshot-Knothole series in 1953, reporters were allowed on site to view the event from News Nob, which was about 7 miles away from the tower (Miller 159).

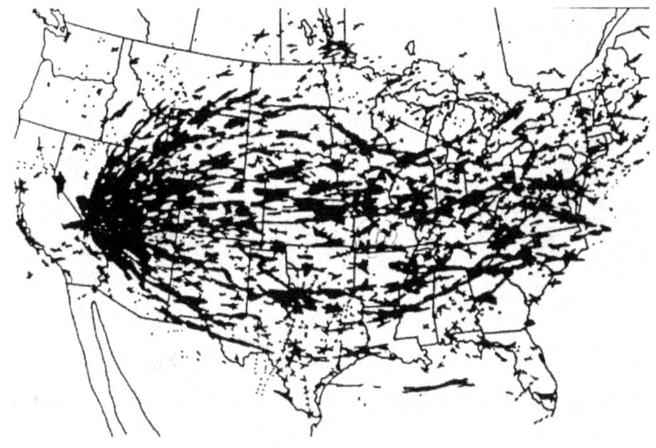

Figure 2.
Richard L. Miller. Areas of the Continental United States
Crossed by More Than One Nuclear Cloud from Aboveground Detonations (444).[17]

In *Refuge*, Terry Tempest Williams' emphasis on her government's atmospheric and underground testing of nuclear weapons can be taken as a reflection of her disillusionment over the lack of a land ethic – a community concept that extends to the natural world. The driving force behind *Refuge* is Williams' confrontation with a mushroom cloud, herself, when she was only a child. Her father, in the last part of *Refuge*, "The Clan of One-breasted Women," narrates,

> We were driving home from Riverside, California. You were sitting on Diane's [Williams' mother] lap [. . .] September 7, 1957 [. . .] We were driving north, past Las Vegas. It was an hour or so before dawn, when this explosion went off. We not only heard it, but felt it. I thought the oil tanker in front of us had blown up. We pulled over and suddenly, rising from the desert floor, we saw it, clearly, this golden-stemmed cloud, the mushroom. The sky seemed to vibrate

17 Permission received through personal communication with Richard L. Miller on March 14, 2005.

> with an eerie pink glow. Within a few minutes, a light ash was raining on the car. (Williams 283)

As Williams explains, "the flash of light" she remembers was "part of Operation Plumbbob, one of the most intensive series of bomb tests to be initiated" (286) in 1957 in the Nevada test site. Williams and her family, "downwinders" of Salt Lake City, Utah, were some of tens of thousands of people exposed to intense radiation during nuclear testing in the 1950s and early 1960s.[18] The cancers in Williams' immediate family, therefore, require no explanation. As revealed in *Refuge*, Williams "belongs to a Clan of One-Breasted Women. [Her] mother, [her] grandmothers, and six aunts have all had mastectomies. Seven are dead. The two who survive have just completed rounds of chemotheraphy and radiation" (281). Terry Tempest Williams, thus, attributes cancer in her family to unhealthy human/land relations. "I realized the deceit I had been living under," says Williams referring to ionizing radiation that entered their bodies from 1951 to 1962, "Children growing up in American Southwest, drinking contaminated milk from contaminated cows,[19] even from the contaminated breasts of their mothers, my mother-members, years later, of the Clan of One-Breasted Women" (Williams 283).

In *Refuge*, Williams couples the tragedy of human communities, caused by environmental degradation, with the tragedy of the bird communities in the Great Salt Lake area. Deeply attached to a Leopoldian expanded community concept, Williams also laments for the losses at the Bear River Migratory Bird Refuge caused by its flooding. Williams' detailed account of the "cyclic" nature of the Great Salt Lake, earlier in *Refuge*, and its disruption, in the later essays, hints at the far-reaching effects of underground nuclear testing. In the first essay, "Burrowing Owls," Williams explains,

---

18 Studies, in early 1980s, by radiation physicists, revealed that the residents of Salt Lake City " received greater exposures than most Utah residents who lived far closer to the Nevada Test Site" (Miller 382).

19 According to Ortmeyer and Makhijani, "[a]s cows and goats grazed in fallout-contaminated pastures, iodine 131 contaminated their milk. Children received higher thyroid doses because they drank much more milk than adults, and because their thyroids were smaller and still growing" ("Let Them Drink Milk").

> Great Salt Lake is cyclic. At winter's end, the lake level rises with mountain runoff. By late spring, it begins to decline when the weather becomes hot enough that loss of water by evaporation from the surface is greater than the combined inflow from streams, ground water, and precipitation. The lake begins to rise again in the autumn, when the temperature decreases, and the loss of water by evaporation is exceeded by the inflow. (6-7)

During the years 1982-1987, however, the cyclic nature of the lake is disrupted, and the water level of Great Salt Lake – the sacred space that "hosts millions of birds in a season" – continuously rises, flooding the Bird Refuge. In "Whimbrels," in the essay that marks the rise of Great Salt Lake, Williams narrates the unusual weather patterns. "It is raining. And it seems as though it has always been raining," says Williams, and goes on explaining, "[e]very day another quilted sky rools in and covers us with water. Rain. Rain. More rain. The Great Basin is being filled. It isn't just the cloud's doing. The depth of snowpack in the Wasatch Mountains is the highest on record. It begind to melt, and streams you could jump over become raging rivers with no place to go. Local Canyons are splitting at their seams as saturated hillsides slide. Great Salt Lake is rising" (29-30).

In the essay, "Redheads," during the time when the lake level goes on rising, causing the destruction of the wetlands of Great Salt Lake, Williams provides striking information on the sharp decrease of bird species visiting the Bear River Bay:

> Before the rise of Great Salt Lake, thousands of whistling swans [. . .] descended on Bear River Bay each autumn. As many as sixty thousand swans have been counted at the Bear River Migratory Bird Refuge during mid-October and mid-November, making it the single largest concentration of migrating swans in North America. In November, 1984, only

> two hundred fifty-nine whistling swans were counted at the Refuge. One year later: three. (112)

The extent of devastation to wildlife leads to a renewed understanding of man's place in the biota. Man is no longer a "conqueror" of the land-community," but a "plain member and citizen of it." Thus, Williams affirms intrinsic value of each member of the biotic community. In the essay, "Whistling Swan," on her return from a " funeral" [of a possible downwinder], Williams narrates the funeral she had for a dead swan, "a late migrant from the north slapped silly by a ravenous Great Salt Lake." Williams' caring "preparation of the swan," echoes a Leopoldian expanded community concept:

> I knelt beside the bird, took off my deerskin gloves, and began smoothing feathers. [. . .] I lifted both wings out from under its belly and spread them on the sand. [. . .] The small dark eyes had sunk behind the yellow lores. [. . .] I looked for two black stones, found them, and placed them over the eyes like coins. They held. And, using my own saliva as my mother and grandmother had done to wash my face, I washed the swan's black bill and feet until they shone like patent leather. I have no idea of the amount of time that passed in the preparation of the swan. (121)

In the last part of *Refuge*, the previous references to the unnatural amount of precipitation and snowmelt, and the eventual flooding of the Bird Refuge, gain new meaning with Williams' reference to the ongoing underground nuclear testing in Nevada – the testing that made the "rocks [. . .] hot from the inside out:"

> A few miles downwind from the fire circle, bombs were being tested. Rabbits felt the tremors. [. . .] Rocks were hot from the inside out and dust devils hummed unnaturally. And each time there was another nuclear test, ravens

> watched the desert heave. Stretch marks appeared. The land was losing its muscle. (287-288)

Williams, in an effort to show how a Leopoldian expanded community concept might guide people today, weaves the tragedies of the two landscapes, and narrates the "rise" of water in Great Salt Lake and the eventual flooding of the Bird Refuge in relation to the "rise" of tumor "on the left side of [Williams'] mother's abdomen" (23). With the advent of years, the Migratory Bird Refuge ceases to be a refuge for the many species of birds, and Williams' mother undergoes chemotherapy and surgeries for her ovarian cancer which follows the cancer of the breast. Thus, the slow death of the mother due to ovarian cancer becomes synonymous to the cancer of Great Salt Lake which "consumes slowly and secretly"[20] the abundance of life in the Bird Refuge. In Leopolds's words, "the integrity, stability, and beauty of the biotic community" slowly vanishes in the Bird Refuge, and Williams suffers for the losses there just as she suffers for the losses in her immediate family.

At the end of *Refuge*, Williams narrates an act of "civil disobediance" in the Nevada Test Site, in the "uninhabited desert," committed by Williams, herself, and nine other Utah women to protest the ongoing nuclear tests and "to reclaim the desert." As she explains, they were arrested "for trespassing on military lands" (289). At the time, the American government was still conducting underground nuclear tests. During an interview, published in the February 2005 issue of *The Progressive*, Williams was asked to comment on a previous remark that she had made, that "our language has been taken hostage." In this interview, Williams explains what she had earlier meant. She states,

> [n]ot only has our language been taken hostage, but individual words like 'patriot,' 'patriotism,' 'democracy,' and 'liberty' have been bound and gagged, forced to perform indecent acts through the abuse of slogans like 'Liberty and free-

20 Significantly, Williams reveals the meaning of cancer with reference to the Oxford Dictionary. Cancer is "anything that frets, corrodes, corrupts, or consumes slowly and secretly" (Williams 43).

> dom will prevail.' As a writer, I cannot in good conscience use the word 'prevail' anymore because I keep hearing the cliches circling around it [...] cliches circling around it." With the present concern of the United States government to resume nuclear testing in Southern Nevada, it seems that the language will be taken hostage again, and in the official rhetoric, the sacred lands will be reduced to "virtually uninhabited desert terrain. (Williams "Interview")

Nuclear testing is a terrifying chapter in the history of the United States, and yet, there are preparations for the potential resumption of nuclear testing in the Nevada Test Site. An expanded community concept is still missing in the rhetoric of political power. American nature writing, instead, contrasts decidedly with such rhetoric of conquest. Ever since American Nature writers' journeying into the wilderness, to the "sanctuaries" of their home towns and their inspiring writing on the "holy" land, man has had a chance to renounce the "conqueror role" and realize profound nonhuman life on every corner of the earth. Thoreau's long walks in the woods in Walden Pond near Concord, Massachusetts, Muir's travellings to the Yosemite, in California, Leopold's journeying into the Wisconsin countryside, Abbey's tours in the Arches National Monument, in southeast Utah, and Williams' pilgrimage to The Bear River Migratory Bird Refuge near Salt Lake City have taught us what we had forgotten. The question is whether their passionate accounts of the land and of its intrinsically valuable species can still give hope to a planet in peril.

Works Cited

Abbey, Edward. *Desert Solitaire: A Season in the Wilderness.* New York: Ballantine, 1971.

Bekoff, Marc. *Minding Animals: Awareness, Emotions, and Heart.* New York: Oxford UP, 2002.

Cole, Thomas. *The Oxbow: View from Mount Holyoke, Northampton, Massachusetts, after a Thunderstorm.* 1836. The Metropolitan Museum of Art,

New York. 24 July 2005 <http://www.artchive.com/artchive/C/cole/cole_oxbow.jpg.html>.

Finch, Robert & John Elder. Ed. The *Norton Book of Nature Writing*. New York: W. W. Norton, 1990.

Gallagher, Carole. American *Ground Zero: The Secret Nuclear War*. New York: Random House, 1993.

Hughes, Robert. *American Visions: The Epic History of Art in America*. New York: Alfred A. Knopf, 1997.

Leopold, Aldo. *A Sand County Almanac*. New York: Ballantine, 1970.

Mayer, Jay. "Is There a Connection Between Nuke Testing and Weather?" *Coastal Post* November, 1999 <http://www.coastalpost.com/98/11/12htm>

Miller, L. Richard. *Under the Cloud: The Decades of Nuclear Testing*. Woodlands, TX: Two-Sixty, 1991.

Miller, L. Richard. *The U.S. Atlas of Nuclear Fallout: Total Fallout, 1951-1962*. Woodlands, TX: Two Sixty, 2002

Muir, John. *My First Summer in the Sierra*. New York: Penguin, 1997.

Oelschlaeger, Max. *The Idea of Wilderness: From Prehistory to the Age of Ecology*. New Haven: Yale UP, 1993.

Ortmeyer, Pat and Makhijani, Arjun. "Let Them Drink Milk." *Bulletin of the Atomic Scientists* November/December 1997. 28 February 2005 <http://www.ieer.org/latest/iodnart.html>.

Scheese, Don. *Nature Writing: The Pastoral Impulse in America*. New York: Twayne, 1996.

Schneider, Keith. Foreword. *American Ground Zero: The Secret Nuclear War*. Carole Gallagher. New York: Random House, 1993. xv-xxii.

Stewart, Frank. *A Natural History of Nature Writing*. Washington D.C.: Island, 1995.

Stokstad, Marilyn. *Art History*. New York: Harry N. Abrams, 1995.

Thoreau, Henry David. *Walden or, Life in the Woods*. New York: Signet Classic, 1980.

---. "Walking." *The Heath Anthology of American Literature*. Vol. 1. Ed. Paul Lauter. New York: Houghton Mifflin, 1998.

Williams, Terry Tempest. *Refuge: An Unnatural History of Family and Place*. New York: Pantheon, 1991.

---. Interview. *Progressive*. February 2005. 15 February 2005 <http://www.progressive.org/feb05/intv0205.html>.

Beloved, Bewept, Bereft: Nationhood as Melancholia in Toni Morrison's *Beloved*

Trevor Hope
Ankara University

Abstract: In this paper, Toni Morrison's novel *Beloved* is considered in relation to questions of nationhood and memory, according to models suggested by Ernest Renan, Hortense Spillers and Homi Bhabha. Freudian libido theory permits an account of the quintessential woundedness of national community in its melancholic constitution. The ethical problems of therapeutic notions of reclamation and restoration are considered in relation to the question of the wound, the victim and the "join" and "disjointure" of national belonging.

> Beyond right, and still more beyond juridicism, beyond morality, and still more beyond moralism, does not justice as relation to the other suppose on the contrary the irreducible excess of a disjointure or an anachrony, some *Un-Fuge*, some "out of joint" dislocation in Being and in time itself, a disjointure that, in always risking the evil, expropriation, and injustice (*adikia*) against which there is no calculable insurance, would alone be able to *do justice* or *to render* justice to the other as other?
>
> Jacques Derrida, *Specters of Marx* 27

> To live in the unhomely world, to find its ambivalences and ambiguities enacted in the house of fiction, or its sundering and splitting performed in the work of art, is also to affirm a profound desire for social solidarity: 'I am looking for the join . . . I want to join . . . I want to join.'
>
> Homi K. Bhabha, *The Location of Culture* 18 (quoting Toni Morrison's *Beloved*)

Toni Morrison's novel *Beloved* is notoriously a novel of woundedness and of collective victimization. It is also about memory, trauma, and the limits of the narrativizability of wounds both individual and collective, psychic and social as well as the material scars of the brutality of slavery. Indeed, it may well be seen as an exploration of the relationship between the corporeal marks left historically on the body of individual African Americans and the entry of those scars into contemporary American symbolization. While many previous critics have worked very productively to clarify these issues in the text, I hope to raise some at least partially original questions by considering the relationship between the narration specifically of nation, the maternal body as a figure of national collectivity and the Freudian economics of libido.[1]

As my title, "Beloved, Bewept, Bereft," indicates, my reading will tend to resist the temptation to resolve or dissolve the traumas of the flesh into a syntax of reclamation, reparation and restoration in favor of a consideration of the way in which the novel insists on the paradoxical open-endedness of grief: to recognize ourselves as bereaved and bereft is to experience a rift, a join or disjoin which traverses any attempt to conceive the ego or the collectivity as totalizable and thus opens the way for an ethics of alterity. But as the novel constantly reminds us, this rift, the condition of our joining an ethical community (which thereby remains disjoined), can also be the site of an avaricious hunger for difference – racial, sexual, temporal – which tends towards a kind of sentimental vampirism incessantly introjecting a loss on which it feeds in an orgy of narcissistic national self-pity: the postmodern banquet of difference may turn out to be a paradoxically solipsistic feast in which alterity is devoured, digested and dissolved back into the imaginarily de-differentiated logic of identity.[2]

---

1 Kathleen Brogan, in her reading of the novel, refers to the traumatic nature of slavery and its resistance to the "integrative powers of narrative" (71). Valerie Smith deals extensively with memory and forgetfulness and the manner in which it is both impressed on the body and also in some sense "inaccessible" in narrative. She also offers a valuable perspective on the novel's demands on its readers.

2 See Lawrence Chua, "The Postmodern Ethnic Brunch: Devouring Difference." Kathleen Brogan writes, "Most emphatically, Morrison does not invite whites to the funeral to engage in a national version of what Mary Louise Pratt calls the postcolonial mode of 'anti-

"Let's face it, I am a marked woman," begins Hortense Spillers' "Mama's Baby, Papa's Maybe: An American Grammar Book," "but not everybody knows my name [. . .] I describe a locus of confounded identities, a meeting place of investments and privations in the national treasury of rhetorical wealth. My country needs me, and if I were not here, I would have to be invented" (65). Spillers goes on to investigate the exaction of a national symbolic surplus from the flesh of black female bodies in a mode of analysis that owes much to the French psychoanalytic feminist critique of Lacan and Lévi-Strauss while arguing that the "investment" in bodies which are trafficked across the threshold of the Middle Passage is at least partly secured by the occlusion of the paternal function within kinship and the interruption of the workings of sexual difference in favor of the property relations of slavery. Invoking the crack of the whip as part of what she calls ironically the "national treasury of rhetorical wealth" and for which I would also proffer the term national archive, she states,

> These undecipherable markings on the captive body render a kind of hieroglyphics of the flesh whose severe disjunctures come to be hidden to the cultural seeing by skin color. We might well ask if this phenomenon of marking and branding actually "transfers" from one generation to another, finding its various *symbolic substitutions* in an efficacy of meanings that repeat the initiating moments? (67)

The return of Beloved, the ghostly figure at the center of Morrison's novel, the child killed by its mother in order to save it from the social death of slavery, seems to represent just such a repetition.

Beloved is also a text that revisits the marking of the black female body as the flesh through which the symbolic investment of the master's mark is repaid at such high symbolic dividends.

While Benedict Anderson locates the privileged join between narrative and the imagining of national community in the "empty homogenous time" of the

---

conquest,' in which Europeans seek a sentimental identification with the colonized that barely masks the continued (even strengthened) assumption of superiority" (92).

novel within whose ambit we experience ourselves as existing in a state of temporal simultaneity with our fellow citizens, Homi Bhabha has challenged the model of simultaneity, emphasizing the disjoint nature of national narration. For Bhabha, national temporality is fundamentally riven between what he calls the pedagogical time of the inherited past and the performative time through which the national community constantly reaffirms itself in the present. We might see this interaction as one of reiterative re-collection, but the past for Bhabha is not a treasure house or archive of signs in their positivity. Rather, the irrecoverable horizon of the immemorially ancient ungrounds the collectivity of the present. Rather than suturing the past seamlessly to the present, recollection disaggregates the national archive back into those sundered acts of collection and re-collection that Bhabha punningly calls "dissemiNation."[3]

It might be useful, in order to understand what I am thus calling the national archive, to remember Bhabha's debts to Ernest Renan's classic essay, "What Is a Nation." Renan at one point provides a distinctly idealist description:

> A nation is a soul, a spiritual principle. Two things which in truth are one, constitute this soul or spiritual principle. One lies in the past, one in the present. One is the possession of a rich legacy of memories; the other is present-day consent, the desire to live together, the will to perpetuate the value of the heritage that one has received in an undivided form. (19)

So far so good for the logocentric project of national collectivity in which riven temporality seems nevertheless to resolve itself through an effort of consensual will into an ultimately "undivided form," but then we remember that Renan sees sacrifice, the consent to collective loss, and forgetfulness, as *more* important than what he calls the social capital of a heroic past, great men and glory:

---

3 See the eighth chapter of *The Location of Culture*, entitled "DissemiNation: Time, Narrative and the Margins of the Modern Nation" (139-170).

> Forgetting, I would even go so far as to say historical error, is a crucial factor in the creation of a nation, which is why progress in historical studies often constitutes a danger for [the principle of] nationality. Indeed, historical enquiry brings to light deeds of violence which took place at the origin of all political formations, even of those whose consequences have been altogether beneficial. Unity is always effected by means of brutality [. . .] (11; parenthesis in original)

Memory, here, does not effect the rallying of signs into the positive archive of identity, but rather opens the archive up to rivenness through the logic of supplementarity.

It is not difficult to locate in *Beloved* a central image of the marking of the black woman's body, but in what ways exactly can we link it to Spillers' "national treasury of rhetorical wealth" or what I am calling the national archive? The first reference to the scar on Sethe, Beloved's mother's, back, follows almost immediately after the evocation of the principle of willful forgetting whereby she "worked hard to remember as close to nothing as was safe":

> The picture of the men coming to nurse her was as lifeless as the nerves in her back where the skin had buckled like a washboard. Nor was there the faintest scent of ink or the cherry gum and oak bark from which it was made. (6)

The deeds of violence constitutive of nationality here coincide directly, in the image of the morbidified flesh, with their forgetting. In fact, if Renan leaves us with the paradox of a forgetfulness which must take a strangely objectified and transmissible form – to be French is to inherit the burden of forgetting the massacres of St. Bartholomew – this passage surely reveals the answer provided by the Freudian concept of melancholy identification according to which the lost object is internalized or swallowed, preserved and petrified. I would suggest that the compulsion to participate in periodic shared rituals of national commemoration is only the visible surface of a much more thoroughgoing collectivization of loss which makes of national identification the disciplinary imposition on the individual body of the marks and signs of bereavement.

National identification renders us all the petrified victims of unavowable loss, but Freud's essay "Mourning and Melancholia" appears to offer mourning as the therapeutic obverse of pathological grief, suggesting that the ego must sever its cathexes to the object and thus liberate or unbind libido for new productive ends, and indeed the novel repeatedly offers images for the possibility of such a libidinal unfreezing and therapeutic reclamation. Under questioning from her daughter Denver, Sethe reveals what she has come to know of this frozen memory-image that she herself must bear without being able to witness or read it:

> "What tree on your back? Is something growing on your back? I don't see nothing growing on your back."
> "It's there all the same."
> "Who told you that?"
> "Whitegirl. That's what she called it. I've never seen it and never will. But that's what she said it looked like. A chokecherry tree. Trunk, branches, and even leaves. Tiny little chokecherry leaves. But that was eighteen years ago. Could have cherries too now for all I know." (18)

The fact that the scar takes the form of a tree is highly suggestive. The terribly alliterative chokecherry evokes Sethe's earlier involuntary memory of the trees of Sweet Home, the plantation which she has fled with her children, trees whose beauty she treacherously remembers (or rather her treacherous memory remembers) before she recollects the "strange fruit" of the lynched boys hanging in them. Sweet Home becomes a twisted re-working of the national fantasy of the American Eden, a place from which African Americans are on the one hand exiled and barred (since the scars will later seem to be transformed into wrought-iron gates) and in which they provide the labor; indeed, the female slave body *is* the tree that bears the fruit of reproductive labor which the mother will then see choked by hanging from its branches. Given its encryptment in the deadened nerves of Sethe's back, this is a tree not of knowledge, but of a sanctified forgetfulness that sustains the fiction of American prelapsarian innocence.

Later, in this fragmented and repetitive narrative, we will revisit the scene in which Amy, the white girl she has run into on her flight from the plantation, tends to Sethe's body:

> "It's a tree, Lu. A chokecherry tree. See, here's the trunk – it's red and split wide open, full of sap, and this here's the parting for the branches. You got a mighty lot of branches. Leaves, too, look like, and dern if these ain't blossoms. Tiny little cherry blossoms, just as white. Your back got a whole tree on it. In bloom. What God have in mind, I wonder.
> [. . .]
> Maybe I ought to break them blossoms open. Get that pus to running, you think? (93-94)

There is a hint of the possibility of a libidinal reclamation here. The hands of the carer – and it is at one level a gesture of ethical generosity, I think, that these hands are figured as white in the text – might heal by liberating the living sap-pus that lies frozen and encrypted within the corporeal symptom, just as the psychoanalytic talking cure might attempt to disencrypt the buried and encoded meaning behind the symptom through its release into the discursive flow of narrative. The implications of this are described in another feature of the corporeal encounter between Sethe and Amy:

> Then she did the magic: lifted Sethe's feet and legs and massaged them until she cried salt tears.
> "It's gonna hurt, now," said Amy. "Anything dead coming back to life hurts." (42)

It is perfectly logical, of course, within the Freudian opposition between mourning and melancholia, that the unfreezing of the melancholic symptom would require the experiencing afresh of the pain associated with the acknowledgment of a loss previously foreclosed from consciousness. Indeed, Freud suggests that the cathexes that tie the ego to the lost object must be relived and, as the English has it, "hypercathected," in order finally to be relinquished. What, in larger terms, might it mean for the corporeally borne crypt to be re-awoken, for the blood/sap/pus/tears to flow once again, and for sensation to return to the disremembered back or limb? When Sethe's mother-in-law Baby Suggs avers that there's "barely a house in the country ain't packed to the rafter's with some dead Negro's grief," we become justified in suspecting that Sethe as melancholic mother bears not just her own pain but suffers the pangs of a murderous labor for the nation as a whole to which slavery is a violent and foreclosed yet foundational part of its historical and fleshly constitution (6). To tend the symptom of this foreclosed history through a therapeutic anamnesis is thus to revivify the frozen national archive, to make *its* blood, sap, tears, pus and, indeed, semen, run freely once again. And it is surely also, therefore, to re-member *as* living limb and member of the national body those – the slaves of the past, but also their descendants in the present – who have been amputated from the national imaginary. To unfreeze the libidinal assets of the nation is potentially to transform a collective libidinal deficit – the shame of racism – into the dividends of an enlarged collectivity into which African Americans are thus unproblematically re-integrated. But things, of course, cannot be quite so simple, as Freud himself averred later in his work when, for example, in *The Ego and the Id*, he came to see melancholia not as absolutely pathological but rather as the very basis of the constitution of the ego through identification.[4]

4 In *The Ego and the Id*, incorporation (on the model of oral introjection) be-comes not the obverse of object-loss but the mechanism that enables it: "When it happens that a person has to give up a sexual object, there quite often ensues an alteration of his ego which can only be described as a set-ting up of the object inside the ego, as it occurs in melancholia [. . .] It may be that this introjection, which is a kind of regression to the mechanism of the oral phase, the ego makes it easier for the object to be given up or renders that process possible. It may be that this identification is the sole condition under which the id can give up its objects." (368) Far from entertaining a vision of therapeutic reintegration of lost members, then, this later model suggests that a melancholic encryptment of loss – what in Renan's terms we might see as an archive of forgetfulness – is the uneasy bedrock of identity: "[it is possible to suppose] that the character of the ego is a precipitate of abandoned object-cathexes and that it contains the history of those object-choices" (368).

Let us come back once again to that first evocation of Sethe's tree-like scar:

> The picture of the men coming to nurse her was as lifeless as the nerves in her back where the skin buckled like a washboard. Nor was there the faintest scent of ink or the cherry gum and oak bark from which it was made. (6)

The liberation of frozen libido makes ink run like tree sap, and the symptom seems thus happily to be dissolved into narrative, but it is important that we recall that in the text it is Sethe who, on the plantation, has performed the labor of producing ink, and with this ink one of her masters, the schoolteacher, has been writing a book on the slaves. The point, of course, is that the very national narrative that forecloses the memory of slavery is dependent upon the labor of slaves. In the political economy of national sentiment, surplus value is exacted from the slave body. Indeed, the ink of the American grammar book is the blood, sweat and tears of African Americans, and to imagine that to make it run freely is to cure or dissolve the national melancholic symptom is potentially to desire that black women once again bear the pain of national (re-)birth and regeneration.

A source of possible revival is suggested by Paul D., another sometime resident of Sweet Home who catches up with Sethe and becomes her lover. It is strongly suggested that making love with Paul D. has the *potential* to effect a redemption of Sethe's frozen libido:

> He rubbed his cheek on her back and learned that way her sorrow, the roots of it; its wide trunk and intricate branches. Raising his fingers to the hooks of her dress, he knew without seeing them or hearing any sigh that the tears were coming fast [. . .] And he would tolerate no peace until he had touched every ridge and leaf of it with his mouth, none of which Sethe could feel because her back skin had been dead for years [. . .] Though she could remember desire, she had forgotten how it worked. (20)

The flowing of tears suggests only an incomplete mourning, for she remains unable to feel his mouth, and he experiences the tree finally as "the decorative work of an ironsmith too passionate for display" (21).

But even to insist on the priority of the scar on Sethe's back is to do a certain violence to her own understanding of what to her has been important – and traumatic – in the experience of slavery. Even as she tells Paul D. the story of how she was whipped, Sethe insists on the significance of the one detail Paul D., with his focus on her back, seems unwilling or unable to acknowledge:

> "We was talking 'bout a tree, Sethe."
> "After I left you, those boys came in there and took my milk. That's
> what they came in there for. Held me down and took it [. . .] Them boys found out I told on em. Schoolteacher made one open up my back, and when it closed it made a tree. It grows there still."
> "They used cowhide on you?"
> "And they took my milk."
> "They beat you and you was pregnant?"
> "And they took my milk!" (19-20)

Where Paul D. sees only violence, Sethe insists on the violence of the appropriation, as we might say, of her milk/ink to the treasury of narrative and libidinal wealth. The desire simply to dissolve the melancholic symptom back into the flow of narrative, to set the libidinal sap coursing through the body once again may disturbingly echo the very act by which Sethe is most traumatized: the theft of her milk. The hunger for national sentiment, the desire to feel the sap of national sensibility coursing once again through the morbidified members of the national body may in fact constitute black women as the forced nurturers of an only apparently enlarged and egalitarian collectivity. In suggesting the risk of such an avaricious demand for the sadistic and appropriative incorporation of the other, the novel may also generate a certain caution about utopian projects that imagine a liberating *écriture féminine* that would be written in mother's milk.[5] If this represents an optimistic hope within feminist psychoanalytic theory of *liberating* an occluded feminine/maternal body within signification, we perhaps need to remember the implications of the fact that, as Luce Irigaray has demonstrated, the maternal body in many ways finds itself already deeply encrypted within the symbolic order, if only as the flesh which subtends patriarchal exchange and yet which has no symbolic coinage of its own.[6] How can the novel rewrite the American grammar book in a manner which doesn't simply remark a nation born out of female and slave labor in some newly triumphant form?

In the limited space available, I would like to return, in albeit rather an abbreviated manner, to the "join," disjuncture and the ethics of joining as suggested by the passages cited above from Derrida's discussion of ghosts, Spillers' attention to the hieroglyphics of the slave body and Bhabha's reading of community in *Beloved.* An important element of our understanding of the wound on Sethe's back should, I would argue, be the fact that, if she is required to bear on her back the foundational lack which projects the nation into narration, she is also required to suture the nation's wound. The mother to whom reparation, to move into a more Kleinian register, is owed, the mother upon whose breast sadism has been enacted, is the same mother from whom reparation – the work of reconstituting the national body as once again united – is required. Sethe is potentially caught between the desire that her body be wrenched open, become once again unsutured, so that the nation can feed vampirically at her breast, and the demand that she bear the responsibility for the encryptment precisely of such violence, that she numb her flesh and nerves against the pain that the re-opening of the national archive entails. The demand that Sethe *be* the join in the social, that she suture the narrative of nation into some seamless ideal form, is precisely what the text refuses, however, and it is

5 Anne E. Goldman, on the other hand, has argued that the novel does permit Sethe a reclamation of the power to tell her own story, which she links to maternity and mother's milk.

6 See Irigaray's *This Sex Which Is Not One*, and especially the essay, "Women on the Market."

perhaps thus that we can understand the possibility that the text thereby imposes an ethics of joining on its *readers*.

The text is, in the most obvious and thoroughgoing way, unsutured. Fragmentary and repetitious, the past constantly leaks back into the present in a manner which I will suggest, however, resists the dissolution of the symptom in favor of libidinal freeflow. It would be too sadistic for words to wish that Amy had tended Sethe's body in the supposedly therapeutic manner she proposes, but which at some other level begins to sound like a cannibalistic rape: "Maybe I ought to break them blossoms open. Get that pus to running, you think?" (94).[7]

The text will not let us happily consume, digest and incorporate the strange fruit of the national totemic feast, but neither can its recollection of the preserved signs of a cryptic archive leave the national body frozen over, sutured by the numbing scar of race.[8] Rather, it mobilizes the wound which, by demanding that we join without foreclosure, that we re-collect as members which will never constitute a pristine national body, makes of us a readerly body responsive to the ethical call of alterity, and it is in this passing on of the responsibility of joining, I would submit, and not in the politics of redemption, that the possibility of justice lies.

Works Cited

Anderson, Benedict. *Imagined Communities: Reflections on the Origin and Spread of Nationalism*. London: Verso, 1983.

Bhabha, Homi K. *The Location of Culture*. London: Routledge, 1994.

Brogan, Kathleen. *Cultural Haunting: Ghosts and Ethnicity in Recent American Literature*. Charlottesville: UP of Virginia, 1998.

Chua, Lawrence. "The Postmodern Ethnic Brunch: Devouring Difference." *Muae 1*. Ed. Walter K. Lew. New York: Kaya, 1995.

---

7 It thus seems to me that Amy – or Aimée? – is the double of both Beloved and the white boys who confound the notions of rape, theft and nursing.

8 This is my understanding, I should state, of Spillers' assertion that the disjunctures of the flesh "come to be hidden to the cultural seeing by skin color" (67).

Derrida, Jacques. *Specters of Marx: The State of the Debt, the Work of Mourning, and the New International.* Trans. Peggy Kamuf. New York: Routledge, 1994.

Freud, Sigmund. *The Ego and the Id.* In *On Metapsychology: The Theory of Psychoanalysis.* Ed. and trans. James Strachey. Pelican Freud Library 11. Harmondsworth: Penguin, 1984. 339-401.

---. "Mourning and Melancholia." *On Metapsychology: The Theory of Psychoanalysis.* Ed. and trans. James Strachey. Pelican Freud Library 11. Harmondsworth: Penguin, 1984. 245-268.

Goldman, Anne E. "'I Made the Ink': (Literary) Production and Reproduction in Dessa Rose and Beloved." *Feminist Studies* 16.2 (Summer 1990): 313-320.

Morrison, Toni. *Beloved.* New York: Alfred A. Knopf, 1998.

Irigaray, Luce. *This Sex Which Is Not One.* Trans. Catherine Porter. Ithaca: Cornell UP, 1985.

Renan, Ernest. "What Is a Nation?" *Nation and Narration.* Ed. Homi K. Bhabha. London: Routledge, 1990.

Smith, Valerie. "'Circling the Subject': History and Narrative in Beloved." *Toni Morrison: Critical Perspectives Past and Present.* Ed. Henry Louis Gates, Jr. and K. A. Appiah. New York: Amistad, 1993. 342-355.

Spillers, Hortense. "Mama's Baby, Papa's Maybe: An American Grammar Book." *Diacritics* (Summer1987). 65-81

The Role of "Gaze" in the Formulation of Black Female Subjectivities in Toni Morrison's *The Bluest Eye*

Ayşe Ece
Marmara University

Abstract: This study aims to analyze the role of the "white gaze" in the formulation of black female subjectivities as reflected in Toni Morrison's *The Bluest Eye*, which focuses on the destructive effects of the dominant white ideology on the black community. The mechanics of the controlling "white gaze" is foregrounded particularly in the encounters of the black female characters with both black and white people. During these encounters, the black female subjectivities are questioned and most of the time rejected by the people who have already internalized the dominant white ideology. The black female characters of *The Bluest Eye* finally lose their self-esteem and develop tragically shattered personalities as a result of the dominant "white gaze" which denies them their subjectivities.

The prerequisite condition of initiating any kind of social relation is the formulation, internalization and acceptance of an "identity." The identity we strive to realize is located in the blurred area where our personal history confronts the structures of belief developed by the dominant ideology based on gender, race, ethnicity and social class. In other words, the "I" comes into being when it meets and tries to fit in the constructed standards of possible ways of existence in a given society. While trying to establish social relations with others, we first perceive these ways of existence and choose one of them to conform to. Thus, others are the ones to inform us about the possible ways of existence, or more precisely about the only way of existence in the society in accordance with the standards imposed on us by the dominant ideology. In the process of formulation of the "I," we end up finding ourselves in a vicious circle. The circle begins and ends at the same point which is occupied by the "other." One struggles to formulate an identity as it is the basis of any social relation with the "other" and this identity can only be grasped through relations with the "other." During the identification process, identity is perceived as a present entity which is, in fact, absent and temporarily deferred to be obtained in the course of the relations with the "other." The relations with the "other," then, have a decisive influence on the process of formulation of an "identity." In an encounter with the "other," the first contact is obviously established through eyes. The "I," who is in pursuit of an identity, looks at the other; and the "other" looks back at the "I," or refuses to set eyes on him/her. Hence, "gaze" plays a crucial role in the initiation and development of the relationship between the "I" and the "other."

In Toni Morrison's debut novel *The Bluest Eye*, a significant number of scenes are devoted to the encounters of the black female characters with others. Apparently, the black female characters are aware of the necessity of an exchange of gaze with others in order to exist as an individual in the society they live in. During these encounters, they are sometimes looked back into the eye and sometimes partly or completely ignored. Thus, their subjectivities are all the time questioned by the people they meet at school, in the streets, at hospitals, at parks, and even in their own houses. They seem to be the ones who are influenced by the process of being looked at. However, the action of looking clearly needs two parties: the one who looks at and the one who is looked at. This process engenders different experiences for both parties: The owner of the gaze reacts to what s/he sees either by following the norms of the dominant ideology or by reconsidering these norms and eventually questioning them; on the other hand, the one who is looked at responds to the gaze with a view to either confirming his/her identity or negating it thoroughly. The present study aims to analyze the mechanics of the controlling gaze of a racially oppressive society which regards whiteness as the norm while viewing African-Americans as "the other." The focus will be on the experiences of both the black female characters of *The Bluest Eye* who are looked at and of the other characters who set eyes on them. The former desperately seek to come to terms with the dominant white ideology while the latter look at them to question the probable presence or absence of their subjectivities.

The Bluest Eye illustrates the destructive effects of the dominant white ideology on the black community by revealing the origins of the dominant "white gaze" which literally destroys the black people's self-esteem. The construction and function of this gaze can easily be discerned by exploring the novel's principal victim, a twelve-year old black girl named Pecola Breedlove. As the novel opens, the reader comes to understand that Pecola, being born into a violent, impoverished underclass home environment, does not get much of a start in life. Her low birth is compounded, moreover, by a crushing sense of inferiority and ugliness inherited from her family. She attempts to ease her misery by retreating more deeply into a confused, and finally shattered and psychotic self-image. However, Pecola is not the only black girl suffering from the white gaze in the novel. Claudia MacTeer too, who undertakes to narrate Pecola's story in many parts of the novel, experiences various encounters with the gaze and reacts to it in different ways. Mrs. Pauline Breedlove, Pecola's mother, and Frieda, Claudia's sister, are also trapped in that gaze most of the time.

The MacTeers, a relatively well-off black family, rent one of their rooms to a black man named Mr. Henry (15-16). The roomer's first encounter with the MacTeer girls Claudia and Frieda, who are respectively nine and ten years old, represents the effects of the dominant white gaze on the ways black people perceive and comment on the identities of their own folk. Being introduced to the girls, Mr. Henry looks at them and says: "Hello there. You must be Greta Garbo, and you must be Ginger Rogers" (16). The girls are likened to white movie stars by a black man who wants to flatter them. The white culture's definition and symbols of beauty are adopted as they are by Mr. Henry without feeling the need to find a way of adjusting them to the characteristic physical properties of black people. For Mr. Henry beauty is associated with a white skin the MacTeer girls do not possess. However, Claudia and Frieda do not recognize the incompatibility of this compliment with the color of their skin and react to it as Claudia describes: "We giggled. Even my father was startled into a smile" (16). The compliment makes both the girls and their father happy because they overlook the dangers of identifying beauty with whiteness just like the other members of the black community who unquestioningly agree with them.

In another episode of the novel, Frieda, the elder daughter of MacTeers, offers Pecola some milk in a blue-and-white Shirley Temple cup (19). Claudia narrates Pecola's encounter with Shirley Temple's face: "She was a long time with the milk, and gazed fondly at the silhouette of Shirley Temple's dimpled face. Frieda and she had a long conversation about how cu-ute Shirley Temple was" (19). The colors of the cup – white and blue – reflect two basic norms of beauty that the black girls perceive as prerequisites of female charm: a white skin and blue eyes. Pecola and Frieda have already internalized the standards of white, middle class American definitions of beauty just like their black friends and relatives. They need to accept these standards in order to adjust to the structures determined by the dominant white ideology. Hence, their admiration for white beauty is rooted in their desire for approval in the white society. This approval is crucially important as it is the only means which would provide them with an identity. The reason for this is that self-esteem and self-love are obtained through the eyes of the others who justify the subjectivity of the self. Claudia, on the other hand, feels uncomfortable at the sight of Shirley Temple. When she confesses her hatred towards Shirley Temple, Pecola and Frieda give her "a puzzled look" which Claudia finds difficult to understand at the age of nine (19). She is angered by the injustice which favours white beauty while triggering black people's confused feelings such as self-hatred and self-negation. She feels threatened by the standards of beauty that glorify Shirley Temple while ignoring black children. She also wants to dismember the white babydolls given to her as a Christmas present (22). Her wish to dismantle them rather than herself (as Pecola wished to do) renders her a figure of resistance against the social forces which provoke a contempt for anything which is black, including black beauty. However, this anger and resistance do not last long. Claudia comments that her hatred towards Shirley Temple would turn into admiration in time: "Younger than both Frieda and Pecola, I had not yet arrived at the turning point in the development of my psyche which would allow me to love her" (19). The black children adopt the white standards of beauty while playing with blonde dolls, watching Hollywood movies and witnessing black people acknowledging the beauty of white children as well as of the light-skinned black children. The standards of beauty are internalized through socialization in various environments including home, school, church, streets, cinemas, parks, and other places where the inner dynamics of the dominant ideology are imposed upon individuals subconsciously. To use Louis Alt-husser's words, the ideological apparatuses shape the individuals' value-judgements long before they are at the age of contesting any given truth (125). Claudia calls the change of her feelings towards Shirley Temple "adjustment without improvement" (23). In a way, she recognizes the need to subscribe to a false white standard of beauty, but at the same time she is aware that this adoption will not result in an "improvement" of black people's condition in the society, it will only result in burying black identities following an unhealthy path of self-hatred rather than self-love.

Pecola Breedlove's trip to buy candy and the way she is treated by the white shopkeeper Mr. Yacobowski is indicative of the role gaze plays in the formulation of identity. Mr. Yacobowski "does not see her [Pecola], because for him there is nothing to see" (48). To see her would be to see her as a person, to encounter her subjectivity. Mr. Yacobowski rather prefers to follow the norms of the white master narrative which has already dictated him to deprive black people of their subjectivities by avoiding setting eyes on them. Homi Bhabha formulates three conditions that underlie an understanding of the process of identification. The first one states, "to exist is to be called into being in relation to an otherness, its look or locus" (44). Pecola tests her "otherness" by trying to see a light in Mr. Yacobowski's eyes which would justify her identity as "a subject" rather than "an object" in the society she lives in. She wants desperately to be looked at by Mr. Yacobowski's blue eyes which stand for the dominant white gaze in order to be able to see herself as an individual because she cannot conceive of her own worth if no human being looks at her. Bhabha's second condition of acquiring an identity is again related to a gaze, which is "caught in the tension of demand and desire" (44). Pecola tries hard to see a gaze loaded with demand and desire to acquire her subjectivity; however, she only faces a "total absence of human recognition" which leads her to lose her own basic sense of identity (48). The sense of identity is so vulnerable that it can disappear thoroughly in the absence of others who have to support its presence all the time. In his third condition of acquiring an identity Bhabha suggests that the process of identification is a never-ending one: "The question of identification is never the affirmation of a pre-given identity, never a self-fulfilling prophecy" (44). Pecola's encounters with others who either completely or partially refuse to look back into her eyes result in the negation of self which tragically leads to insanity at the end of the novel. Pecola finally manages to let herself be seen by somebody who is her imaginary friend. Her dialogues with her imaginary friend provide her with a space where she can exist as "a subject" in the most twisted way possible.

One of Pecola's most devastating encounters in the novel takes place in a black household. Junior, a black boy attending the same school as Pecola, invites her to his house out of sheer boredom (88). Junior's aggressive and humiliating behavior toward Pecola results in the accidental death of his mother's beloved cat. When Geraldine, Junior's mother, comes in, she sees a black girl in her tidy, clean and well-kept house. She sets eyes on the black girl unlike the white shopkeeper Mr. Yacabowski. She does see something in Pecola's eyes but what she sees fills her with revulsion and fear. Geraldine sees in Pecola's eyes a type of black: "She had seen this little girl all her life" (91). This type of dirty, poorly dressed black is exactly what Geraldine despises most. Although, unlike Mr. Yacabowski, Geraldine sees something, she does not see Pecola, the individual. She sees instead an abstracted representative of a whole social class, a social class she hates; consequently, she is merciless and cruel to Pecola. Internalized racism manifests itself in Geraldine's gaze to all the black people she meets, including Pecola. She even distinguishes between "colored people" and "niggers" and forbids her son to play with niggers. In her opinion, "colored people were neat and quiet; niggers were dirty and loud" (87). She struggles to remove what is black about herself by striving to lead a life aspiring towards bourgeois respectability. However, she pays for internalizing the white standard of life and denouncing her black identity by her unhappy marriage and her inability to show affection to her son. Being insulted by Geraldine and held responsible for the death of her cat, Pecola leaves the black family's house – the cleanest house she has ever been in – with the sense of a thorough negation of her identity and self-hatred. Her encounter with Geraldine acquaints her with a different type of victimhood: She becomes the victim of other black people's cruelty which displays the process of the internalization of hatred by the hated.

Claudia, Frieda and Pecola's visit to the Fishers' house where Mrs. Breedlove works as a servant manifests the significance of the gaze in shaping one's identity by introducing another scene pervaded by eye imagery (107-109). Surprisingly, the three black girls "are seen" this time by a smaller and younger white girl who happens to enter the kitchen hoping to see Mrs. Breedlove whom she calls "Polly." The white girl establishes eye contact with the black girls which enables them to confirm their subjectivities. However, this confirmation is not a simple and pure one; it is accompanied by fear as the white girl is afraid when she sees them. Claudia narrates this scene in the following way: "When she saw us, fear danced across her face for a second. She looked anxiously around the kitchen" (108). Thus, "fear" and "anxiety" become inseparable parts of the white girl's experience of looking into the black people's eye. Frantz Fanon describes a similar scene between self and other in *Black Skin, White Masks*: "Mama, see the Negro! I'm frightened! Frightened! Frightened!" (111). In Fanon's scene, a black man comes across a white girl and thus becomes the spectacular object of the white gaze. The black girls' experience in *The Bluest Eye* is not different from the black man's; whether male or female, all the black people might encounter this white gaze loaded with fear in similar situations. The white girl's experience with the other results in fear that is shaped by the dominant white ideology's presentation of black people in legends, stories and history. The white gaze inhabited by fear leads black people to question their status in the society and eventually to consider their racial identity from a white point of view. Carl Plasa, who devotes a chapter of his book entitled *Textual Politics from Slavery to Postcolonialism* to the analysis of *The Bluest Eye* with the aim of "feminizing" Fanon's work, comments on the effects of the white gaze on black people as follows:

> It is this internalization of the white gaze which produces the dramatic and ruinous shift from the 'corporeal' to the 'racial epidermal schema'. The black subject is no longer able to experience his body merely as something he neutrally inhabits, but as something that is racialized – assailed and layered with 'legends, stories, history, and above all historicity'. (102)

The internalization of the white girl's gaze by Claudia, Frieda and Pecola alienates them from their own body and each one reacts to this alienation in different ways. Claudia is angry with the owner of the white gaze, Frieda accepts alienation as her inescapable destiny and Pecola wishes to change physically as her longing to have the bluest eyes ever seen on this world clearly shows. Mrs. Breedlove's comment while she is talking to the little white girl later is also relevant here. When the little white girl begins to cry and asks her who the black girls were, she says "Don't worry none, baby" (109). The black girls' partly acknowledged and feared identity is once more erased by one of their own folks who preferred to call them "none."

Mrs. Breedlove narrates how she gave birth to Pecola by presenting another scene dominated by the white gaze as an indicator of the complete negation of black female subjectivities (124-125). A group of white doctors approach Mrs. Breedlove who is about to deliver Pecola and the oldest one starts to lecture about childbirth as follows: "When he got to me he said now these here women you don't have any trouble with. They deliver right away and with no pain. Just like horses" (124-125). The white doctor separates black women from white women by attributing to them a property that they do not obviously possess. Unlike white women, who suffer and need care and attention in childbirth, the black women can endure any kind of physical pain and deserve no help. This tragic discrimination highlights the so-called "success" of the dominant white ideology in shaping the society's value-judgements concerning black women. White doctors avoid looking into Mrs. Breedlove's eyes during the examination:

> They looked at my stomach and between my legs. They never said anything to me. Only one looked at me. Looked at my face, I mean. I looked right back at him. He dropped his eyes and turned red. He knowed, I reckon, that maybe I weren't no horse foaling. But them others. They didn't know. They went on. (125)

All the doctors except one prefer to adopt the dominant white ideology by dehumanizing Mrs. Breedlove. The dehumanization is partly realized by likening her to a horse and partly by refusing to look into her eyes. If they looked into her eyes, they would see her looking back at them, and encounter Mrs. Breedlove's undeniable humanity and her status as a subject as opposed to purely an object. One doctor, however, performs the forbidden act and looks into her eyes. Mrs. Breedlove, finally managing to attract the gaze of the doctor, immediately looks back at him. Having reconsidered the norms of the dominant ideology and consequently recognized the black woman's presence, the courageous white gaze feels ashamed. Hence, Mrs. Breedlove's subjectivity is confirmed by the white doctor only temporarily. Afterwards, she is again denied the status of a subject with no one comforting her by looking into her eyes.

In *The Bluest Eye*, Toni Morrison demonstrates the destructive effects of the white gaze on the formulation of black female subjectivities. Pecola, Claudia, Frieda and Mrs. Breedlove all suffer from a deep feeling of inferiority which originates in the absence or partial presence of the white gaze. Either launched by black people who have internalized the dominant racist ideology, or by white people who tend to negate black presence completely – except the white doctor who dares to look into Mrs. Breedlove's eyes – the white gaze functions as a reminder of the black female characters' inability to acquire an identity in a racially oppressive society. Deprived of an identity which would grant them their subjectivity, they lose their self-esteem and develop tragically shattered personalities.

Works Cited

Althusser, Louis. "Ideology and Ideological State Apparatuses." *Lenin and Philosophy and Other Essays*. Trans. Ben Brewster. New York: Monthly Review, 2001. 85-126.

Bhabha, Homi K. *The Location of Culture*. London: Routledge, 1994.

Fanon, Frantz. *Black Skin, White Masks*. Trans. Charles Lam Markmann. London: Pluto, 1993.

Morrison, Toni. *The Bluest Eye*. New York: Plume, 1994.

Plasa, Carl. *Textual Politics from Slavery to Postcolonialism*. New York: St. Martin's, 2000. 98-121.

Representations of Victimhood in Toni Morrison's *Song of Solomon*

Banu Özel
Haliç University

Abstract: Throughout human history, there have always been the powerful and the powerless, the rulers and the ruled, and, usually, victimization has been discussed in terms of binary oppositions. However, as it is represented in Toni Morrison's *Song of Solomon*, victimization is a multifaceted phenomenon and a discussion of it should be in the light of multiple approaches and standpoints. This paper aims to explore the dynamics of victimhood, and to demonstrate that victimhood is not necessarily a permanent condition for a particular community or a person – especially in a "contact zone" where different ethnicities, classes, and values compete and interact with each other. In *Song of Solomon*, Morrison portrays a "contact zone" where values of whites and blacks, the middle class and the working class meet. Their co-existence creates ambivalence over the question of who is victim and who is victimizer.

In general terms, Toni Morrison's *Song of Solomon* is a novel that treats the African-American migration from Africa to America, and within America, from South to North. Morrison depicts African-American life both in the American North and South between the 1930s and 1960s, while compelling our attention to an assortment of issues such as culture, history, identity, racism, slavery and inevitably, violence and victimhood. In *Song of Solomon* these notions are not represented as solid and permanent, but as transitory and evolving. In the course of the novel, we observe how the African-American community evolves in time –transforming from passive sufferers of racism or victims of slavery into perpetrators who – in different ways – actively respond to the system. And we also notice how both the "collaborative and dialogical" and the "antagonistic, conflictual" values, interests and perceptions formulate the differences in subjectivities even within the same race and community (Bhabha 2). In this paper, I speculate on the blurred notions of the victim and the victimizer – particularly focusing on the characters Macon Dead Jr. (Milkman), Macon Dead Sr., Pilate,

Hagar, and Milkman's friend Guitar since they experience the most striking conditions of "in-betweenness." Questions of race, class, and history are central to my examination of the socio-economic, political and cultural contexts in which African-American subjects position themselves in their community as victims and victimizers.

Before the Civil Rights Movement in the 1970s, the white-dominated political and social system in the United States, especially in the American South, provided the ground for the victimization of African Americans. For African Americans, the issue of identity and heritage became more and more complicated due to socio-economic and political practices. Dan McAdams states, "The problem of identity is the problem of arriving at a life story that makes sense – providing unity and purpose – within a socio-historical matrix that embodies a much larger story" (18). As *Song of Solomon* demonstrates, slavery and migrations rendered it almost impossible for many African Americans to acquire a life story that has unity. When black people were captured and brought to America, they lost their connection with Africa. Under slavery, they were given names that detached them from their African identity. When they were released, various factors (such as illiteracy and errors in implementation of laws) made them unable to recover their original names and therefore their ancestral history. Moreover, the oral tradition that was at the core of the transmission of traditional black values, culture, and history was destructed by migrations from the American South to the North.

Song of Solomon narrates a story of partial recovery of ancestral and cultural knowledge which was concealed as a consequence of generational resettlement; or, more specifically, it tells us the story of Milkman and his quest for his self and community identity. Milkman – the first black child born in Mercy Hospital in Michigan – grows up in a middle-class African-American family that holds materialistic values, a family whose members neither have intimate relationships with each other nor with their community. Accordingly, Milkman and his father Macon Dead Sr. have conflicting and competing positions in society: sometimes as victims (of slavery and racism), sometimes as victimizers (as members of the middle class), and from time to time both.

The Dead family's history was obscured by slavery, migration, and nonexistent or unavailable records, just as that of many African Americans. In *The Location of Culture*, Homi Bhabha points out that displacement forces upon subjects "a vision that is as divided as it is disorienting" (9). Due to resettlements, Macon's vision of life is divided and disorienting as Bhabha suggests. Macon does not have clear memories about his family's past. He does not know and care about who his grandparents are and where they come from. His mother passed away when she was giving birth to his sister Pilate. When he and his sister Pilate were kids, their father Jake (who was an ex-slave) was killed over an argument about land. Macon's way departed from Pilate's a short time after their father's death. Macon came to Michigan from Pennsylvania, leaving behind his past. He married Ruth (daughter of Dr. Foster, who was the first black doctor in the town), and built a middle-class life in which he aims to make more money.

The Dead family's life style and upper social class alienate them from most people of their race. In accordance with the stratification of colonial social production that Gayatri Spivak provides in her eminent "Can the Subaltern Speak?" they can be considered as one of the "dominant indigenous groups at the regional and local levels" (284).[1] The people of Virginia regard Milkman as an outsider:

> His manner, his clothes were reminders that they had no crops of their own and no land to speak of either. [. . .] They looked at his skin and saw it was as black as theirs, but they knew he had the heart of the white men who came to pick them up in the trucks when they needed anonymous, faceless laborers. (266)

Despite the fact that materially Milkman is no different from people of his race, he has been an "Other" in his own community as he is in some ways associated with the white man, i.e., with the oppressor. Milkman's best friend Guitar "was

1 See "Can the Subaltern Speak" 284 for information about other levels.

constantly chafing Milkman about how he lived" (106). A dialogue between the two develops as follows:

> "There are things that interest me that don't interest you."
> "How you know they don't interest me?"
> "I know you. Been knowing you. You got your high-tone friends and your picnics on Honoré Island and you can afford to spend fifty percent of your brainpower thinking about a piece of ass." (103)

Guitar's words reveal the fact that the Dead Family's economical situation is a lot better and their interests are different from those of most other black people in the town. Macon is a materialist whose priority in life is to "own things," and even to own "other people" (55). In the course of the narrative, we witness his attempts to be more like a white man (wealthier and more cultivated than people of his own race). Macon's never-ending lust for property, his ignorance of the poor, and his mercilessness make one of his tenants say, "A nigger in business is a terrible thing to see. Terrible. Terrible" (228). Having been brought up in such an environment and spending some time working for his father, Milkman is highly influenced by his father's vision. In this respect, we see Milkman as a victimizer in his own community: As he collects the rent from his father's tenants, Milkman sees how poor and desperate these people are. However, "He didn't concern himself an awful lot about other people" (107). While most of the people in his community are trying hard to get by, Milkman and his family are enjoying their Sunday rides in their American car and thinking of constructing beach houses for the wealthy black folks. Nevertheless, it is at this point where the line between the victim and the victimizer is obscured. Wealth is not a real source of joy and comfort for Milkman because, as Valerie Smith states, "Milkman appears to be doomed to a life of alienation from himself and from others" (33). Milkman's estrangement from the other people in his community, his lack of spiritual fulfillment in his life make him a victim of his own social class.

Milkman's disappointment with his life comes to a climax in his thirties, when he eventually realizes that life should be more than what he has had. One of the things that paved the way for Milkman's quest for some sort of cohesion in his life is his occasional visits to his estranged aunt Pilate – whom Macon hates. Pilate has developed self-awareness and "tackled the problem of trying to decide how she wanted to live and what was valuable to her" (149). However, Milkman was still troubled with the meaning of his life: "All he knew in the world about the world was what other people had told him" (120). Everything was boring to Milkman: "The city was boring. The racial problems [. . .] were the most boring of all" (107). Milkman sees that life in Pilate's house is quite different from his family's life. Pilate, her daughter Reba, and Reba's daughter Hagar have intimate relationships. Their home is a place where people talk, share, laugh, and sing together, whereas it is almost impossible to have pleasant conversations at Macon's home. Unlike Macon, Pilate is not money-oriented (she is just making enough money to get by from wine-selling); she regards spirituality and cultural wisdom as real richness. Milkman finds happiness in the times he spends with these people; at the same time he comes to an understanding that Pilate's and Macon's perspectives on social relations and life standards fluctuate greatly. Macon's and Pilate's perceptions of history are also antithetical. Macon usually avoids thinking and speaking about his past; thus he provides little ancestral or cultural knowledge to his children. "He had not said any of this for years. Had not even reminisced much about it recently. [. . .] For years he hadn't had that kind of time, or interest" (51). On the contrary, Pilate imparts cultural knowledge and sensitivity to Milkman through their talks, discussions, and all sorts of sharing. Unlike Macon's linear conception of time that makes him disregard his past and ancestors while concentrating fully on future endeavors, Pilate's appreciation of time is circular; in other words, she believes that one's identity cannot be considered without a fusion of past experiences and present insight. Morrison has a similar stance regarding creating a cohesion between African history and the present. In an interview, Morrison states:

> The reclamation of the history of black people in this country is paramount in its importance. [. . .] There's a great deal

> of obfuscation and distortion and erasure, so that the presence and the heartbeat of black people has been systematically annihilated in many, many ways. You have to [. . .] identify those who have preceded you – resummoning them, acknowledging them is just one step in that process of reclamation. (224-225)

Pilate's resisting, rather than repressing or ignoring, white oppression in the way of reclaiming her heritage and carrying it with her in the form of songs, stories, and her sack of bones, can be considered as an implementation of Morrison's statement. Pilate rejects victimization in her own humanistic way and inspires Milkman as he sets out to trace his family history and roots in the American South, in Pennsylvania and Virginia. On the other hand, keeping himself aloof from African traditions and being so obsessed with white values, Macon seems to be a victim of his own success.

A different perspective on the victimization of African Americans – one that also challenges the binary of victim and victimizer – is presented in the narrative through Milkman's friendship with Guitar. Guitar takes a harsh stance to life, and his philosophy is highly affected by his disturbing childhood memories. All his life, Guitar has been marginalized economically. As a member of the working class, Guitar believes that the white-dominated system in the United States does not offer true justice to black people: "Where's the money, the state, the country to finance our justice?" (160). Guitar thinks that he has to do something for his race because "the earth is soggy with black people's blood" (154). What he comes up with is joining "The Seven Days," which is a secret group of black men that aims to murder whites who are not sentenced by white courts:

> There is a society. It is made up of a few men who are willing to take some risks. They don't initiate anything; they don't even choose. [. . .] But when a Negro child, Negro woman, or Negro man is killed by whites and nothing is done about it by their law and their courts, this society se-

> lects a similar victim at random, and they execute him or her in a similar manner if they can. If the Negro was hanged, they hang; if a Negro was burnt, they burn; raped and murdered, they rape and murder. If they can. If they can't do it precisely in the same manner, they do it any way they can, but they do it. (154-155)

Guitar's perspective evokes African-American activist Malcom X's views: "If it must take violence to get the black man his human rights in this country, I'm for violence" (qtd. in Medoro 367). Like Malcom X, unlike Pilate, Guitar believes that – under the circumstances they lead their lives – violence for violence is the inevitable response for white oppression, the most effective way to end victimization. Guitar justifies his deadly actions as attempts "to make a world where white people will think before they lynch" (160). With those words Guitar also alludes to historical lynchings and murders. The Ku Klux Klan, which according to Guitar kills African Americans for fun, was founded in Kentucky in 1866. The Klan was the most prominent and widespread of racist groups:

> The organization [. . .] robed itself in secrecy – concealing the faces of members during 'night rides' in which they dispensed vigilante justice and conducted lynchings, communicating with secret hand signals and coded language during silent parades. [. . .] These tactics had the added effect of creating fear through mystery. (Wright 396)

In Morrison's account, African-American violence emerges in relation to the violent acts of whites. "The Seven Days" is founded against white racist groups such as the Ku Klux Klan. Yet, the idea of counterattack does not legitimize crime and the victimization of (innocent) whites.

In *Song of Solomon*, Milkman cannot come to grips with the idea of "revenge"/"justice" that "The Seven Days" is built on. As Guitar continues blaming Milkman for not being sensitive to community matters and taking action, their mutual friendship transforms into a deadly tension. Towards the end of the story, Guitar wants to shoot Milkman, yet he kills Pilate. Once more in the story a black becomes a victim of another black. The conflicts between Milkman and Guitar symbolize the problematic relationships between the middle class and the working class that lead to the victimization of one party.

Last but not least, in *Song of Solomon*, Hagar's self-destruction represents another kind of victimization. When Milkman breaks off their relationship, Hagar first tries to kill him because of "the sight of Milkman's arm around the shoulders of a girl" with a light skin and silky copper-colored hair. She strongly believes that Milkman left her because of her ugliness. "I look awful," "I look terrible," "I look like a groundhog," she says (308-309). Not being able to achieve self-definition and live peacefully with her African-American identity, Hagar looks at herself through European eyes. She believes that a light-skinned woman comes closer to looking like a European lady, and that therefore such a woman is more beautiful than her. Hagar tries to make herself beautiful with cosmetics and new clothes, insisting that Milkman prefers silky penny-colored hair, "lemon-colored skin," "gray-blue eyes," and a "thin nose" (316). Pilate's claim that Milkman cannot hate her hair because he has the same kind of hair does not calm Hagar. Hagar's attempt to make herself beautiful ends with her death. In *The Souls of Black Folk*, W. E. B. Du Bois states that "The American world *yields the black* no true self-consciousness, but only lets him see himself through the revelation of the other world" (10). Hagar's negative self-perception and internalized racism underscore Du Bois' claim. Black people in the U.S have been so detached from their racial and cultural heritage, and some of them have internalized racism so deeply, that in a way they have become their own destruction.

Throughout *Song of Solomon* Morrison questions the meaning and the conditions of victimization. Who is a victim? Is it he who suffers from a profound identity problem, from an obscured past? Or is it he who is economically marginalized? What about those who are physically abused, those who destroy themselves because of internalized racism? The examples of victimization in *Song of Solomon* can be multiplied. However, what is crucial is not to come up with a definition of victim but rather to realize that the conditions and definitions of victimhood alter in the "liminal spaces" between competing cultural traditions and historical periods (Bhabha 1). "Cultures are never unitary in themselves, nor simply dualistic in the relation of Self and Other" (Bhabha 35-36). Therefore the notion of culture and identity should not be discussed in the oversimplifying context of binary oppositions such as victimizer – victimized, dominant – dominated, elite – subaltern, oppressor – oppressed, etc. As Morrison eloquently demonstrates, whom we regard as a victim can be a victimizer at the same time or turn into one in time.

Works Cited

Bhabha, Homi K. *The Location of Culture*. London: Routledge, 1994.

Du Bois, W. E. B. *The Souls of Black Folk: Authoritative Text, Contexts, Criticism.* Ed. Henry Louis Gates and Terri Hume Oliver. Norton Critical Editions. New York: W. W. Norton, 1999.

Malcom X and Alex Haley. *The Autobiography of Malcom X (As Told to Alex Haley).* New York: Grove, 1966.

McAdams, Dan P. *Power, Intimacy and Life Story: Personological Inquiries into Identity*. New York: Guilford, 1988.

Medoro, Dana. "Justice and Citizenship in Toni Morrison's *Song of Solomon*." *Canadian Review of American Studies* 32.1 (2002): 1-12.

Morrison, Toni. "An Interview with Toni Morrison." Christina Davis. *Conversations with Toni Morrison*. Ed. Danille Taylor-Guthrie. Literary Conversations. Mississippi: UP of Mississippi, 1994. 223-233.

---. *Song of Solomon*. New York: Alfred A. Knopf, 1994.

Smith, Valerie. "The Quest for and Discovery of Identity in Toni Morrison's *Song of Solomon*." *Toni Morrison's Song of Solomon: A Casebook*. Ed. Jan Furman. Casebooks in Criticism. New York: Oxford UP, 2003.

Spivak, Gayatri Chakravorty. "Can the Subaltern Speak?" *Marxism and the Interpretation of Culture*. Ed. Cary Nelson and Lawrence Grossberg. Urbana: U of Illinois P, 1988. 271-313.

The Master Changed: The Victimization of the Ex-colonizer in Derek Walcott's *Pantomime*

Eda Dedebaş
Boğaziçi University

Abstract: Derek Walcott's play *Pantomime*, a postcolonial adaptation of Defoe's *Robinson Crusoe,* is centered on the change of roles between the master and the servant. Abandoning his wife and career in England, Harry tries to construct a new life for himself in Tobago with his factotum Jackson. However, as the play proceeds, he appears as the real servant, who unquestioningly obeys Jackson. Being stripped of his socio-political power due to decolonization, he is exposed to Jackson's brutality and becomes vulnerable. This paper discusses both Harry's reversed position as the victim – both socio-politically and sexually – his standpoint as an abortive master trying to vindicate himself in an ex-colony and the new master Jackson and his psychological harassment of Harry. Moreover, while analyzing their positions, it discusses the master-slave dialectics in the light of some twentieth-century critics such as Fredric Jameson and Albert Memmi. Finally, it examines the impact of the genre – the dialogue form instead of Defoe's single narrative voice – and the metatheatrical elements in the play on Harry's losing his single narrative voice as the colonizer and being subject to Jackson's offending remarks.

Western civilization has been deeply influenced by a colonialist perspective which makes clear-cut distinctions between the two sides of the colonial encounter, namely the oppressor and the oppressed. Moreover, this distinction is bolstered by binary oppositions attributed to both sides. However, contemporary literary criticism has sought to redress these firmly grounded adjectives about the relationship between the master and the slave. With the help of deconstruction, the last century witnessed the overthrowing of established concepts and questioned the relationship between the oppressor and the victim. One of the significant critics of the century, Fredric Jameson, comments on the Hegelian analysis of the master-slave relationship in this way: "Two equals struggle each for recognition by the other. [. . .] The Master – now the fulfillment of a baleful and inhuman feudal-aristocratic disdain for life without honor – proceeds to enjoy the benefits of his recognition by the other, now become his humble serf or slave" (85). According to Jameson, the relationship between the master and the slave should be reconsidered in the light of the fact that they are mutually dependent on each other rather than one side being more independent.

The outcries from the colonized countries started to emerge with the decolonization period. As a response to the Western dominant ideology, post-colonial Caribbean poet and playwright Derek Walcott states in his essay "What the Twilight Says": "Centuries of servitude have to be shucked; but there is no history, only the history of emotion. Pubescent ignorance comes into the light, a shy girl, eager to charm, and one's instinct is savage: to violate that ingenuousness, to degrade, to strip her of those values learnt from films and books" (5). Hence, Walcott regards it necessary to dismantle the binaries and to "unlearn" what has been dictated to the colonized. Besides, he states the urgency for the young generation to be courageous enough to subvert Western ideology: "The children of slaves must sear their memory with a torch. The actor must break up his body and feed it as ruminatively as ancestral story-tellers fed twigs to the fire. Those who look from their darkness into the tribal fire must be bold enough to cross it" (5-6).

Walcott, being one of the "children of the slaves," carries the courage to sear history so as to rewrite it from a different perspective. In his plays, Walcott reveals this courage to revise learned assumptions. His two-act play, *Pantomime* (1980), which is a rewriting of *Robinson Crusoe,* is mainly based on the master-slave dynamics. The play is about an Englishman, Harry Trewe, who abandons his home and acting career in England to run the "Castaways Guest House" in Tobago with his servant, Jackson Philips, who is a retired calypso singer. The plot unfolds itself with the insistent demand of Harry the master to stage a different version of the Crusoe story in which Jackson plays Crusoe and Harry the white slave Friday for the Western tourists. However, as the play proceeds, it becomes apparent that due to Jackson's antagonism to present a naive pre-colonial background, it is not as easy as Harry envisions to perform an entertaining, light pantomime.

The most remarkable aspect of the play is the change of roles between Harry and Jackson. The disruption in the master-slave relationship is advantageous for Jackson, who, with Harry's consent, plays the role of the black master. The childlike, retired actor and ex-colonizer Harry is scolded and instructed by the rational, assertive, black servant, who commands his master how to behave. With the help of the symbolic Crusoe hat which Harry hands over to him, Jackson becomes the instructor inverting the binary oppositions (136). Besides, although Harry starts writing a play about Crusoe and Friday for the hotel customers, in the end, Jackson turns out to be the director of the play with his "stage directions." As the subtle director of the play, he subverts Harry's text to his own wish. That reversal could be explained by the Caribbean setting since "[p]eople who come out to the Caribbean from the cities and the continents go through a process of being recultured" (Walcott, "The Art of Poetry" 74). With his intentional decision to settle in Tobago and allow himself to be recultured, Harry paves the way for the change of power relations. He hands over the former colonial power which he stands for. Relinquishing his power, he, thus becomes susceptible to harassment and psychological pressure. Now his former colonial power has to fight against the rebirth of the colonized. In addition to his agreement with Hegel, Jameson takes this problematic relationship a step further:

> [T]he slave is called upon to labor for the master and to furnish him with all the material benefits befitting his supremacy. But this means that, in the end, only the slave knows what reality and the resistance of matter really are; only the slave can attain some true materialistic consciousness of his situation; since it is precisely to that that he is condemned. The Master, however, is condemned to idealism – to the luxury of a placeless freedom in which any consciousness of his own concrete situation flees like a dream, like a word unre-

> membered on the tip of the tongue, a nagging doubt which the puzzled mind is unable to formulate. (85)

It is this acquaintance with reality which makes Jackson tip the balance over Harry, who is constricted within his colonial fantasies and dreams.

In addition to the loss of his powerful political background, Harry's living in Tobago in a solitary hotel – which, according to Jackson, is actually a hospital hosting casualties rather than guests – and his being estranged from his wife and occupation consolidate his being more prone to victimization. He reveals his desperate situation by saying: "[T]here's absolutely no hearth for Crusoe to go home to" (145). Therefore, his colonial fantasy to stage the pantomime is the only thing left him. Moreover, when Jackson asks why he puts so much emphasis on the pantomime, he answers back resolutely: "I'm determined to make this place work. I gave up the theater for it. [. . .] Flopped at too many things, though. Including classical and Creole acting. I just want to make this place work, you know. And a desperate man'll try anything" (143). The imbalance is furthered on the social level since Harry is presented as a solitary, unsuccessful man who has to give up theatre and his life in England, whereas his servant is more powerful in having the privilege to make a choice between working for Harry and living with his family.

Besides Harry's political and social disadvantages, there is also his inability to maintain his rational attitudes. This encounter with the colonized leads him to lose his stiff upper lip. This interaction process is explained by Walcott in the following way:

> There is that stolid façade, that mask of the Englishman, that wall behind which there is much horror and fear and trembling. The cracks appear and it is where these cracks appear that Jackson darts in and widens. The play is about Jackson besieging and darting in and out until the whole thing crumbles, the wall is broken down and we look into his room and see Trewe naked and exposed. (Interview with Christopher Gunnes, qtd. in Gunness 290)

When his proper façade is shattered, his servant fills the gap since "Jackson has a profound motive for opposing Trewe and his ideas. Through the conflict, Jackson brings Trewe to self-knowledge. He sees further and further into Trewe, dragging his old inhibitions to the surface and in forcing him to recognise them" (Gunness 290). It is this cathartic impulse of Jackson that reverses the balance.

This renunciation of his political and social power transforms Harry into a pitiable man who tries to vindicate himself on a small Caribbean island away from his cultural roots. Furthermore, the servant, who repudiates the submissive role assigned to him, defies his position and transforms into a tyrant. When Harry wants to break free from the reality of the colonial background, Jackson summarizes their dependency in a trance-like mood by using the metaphor of the child who is afraid of the shadow he creates. In his own creole, Jackson states:

> After a while the child does get frighten of the shadow he make. He say to himself, That is too much obedience, I better hads stop. But the shadow don't stop, no matter if the child stop playing that pantomime, and the shadow does follow the child everywhere, [. . .] until it is the shadow that start dominating the child, it is the servant that start dominating the master. (137)

Jackson's awareness of being a shadow and, thus, having the privilege to reverse the order enables him to break free from being the follower. However, "[even] if the servant does manage to reverse the psychohistorical act enabling himself to start dominating the master, giving victory to the shadow, the servant may indeed be freed of his problems to some extent but not necessarily totally freed from a general world of madness" (Peters 160). Likewise, despite his having the upper hand in the relationship, Jackson sometimes bursts out, appears mad and cannot avoid imitating Harry.

Jackson, when analyzed separately from Harry, reveals a tendency to irritation and violence. The story with the ice pick that he recounts to Harry seems not to be convincing enough for Harry, so towards the end of the play, in a moment when his contempt for the parrot is at the pinnacle, he cruelly kills the parrot (148). His hatred for the parrot is a sign of his desire to dissociate himself from mimicking the white man; therefore the reminder of his mimicry has to be wiped away. Finally, his severity and violence come to an unbearable point causing a psychological breakdown in Harry.

Jackson's harassment of Harry extends to another dimension when he makes him confess his past. Playing the role of Harry's ex-wife Ellen, whose reputation has surpassed that of Harry as an actress, Jackson causes Harry to confess how he has missed his wife, and how he actually envies her acting ability. From that imaginary but confessional conversation, Jackson also learns that the couple had played *Robinson Crusoe* before, Ellen playing Crusoe and Harry the submissive Friday (149-150). Deeply influenced by his own confessions, Harry quotes from *Robinson Crusoe*: "But what is paradise without a woman? [. . .] I miss the voice of even one consoling creature, the touch of a hand, the look of kind eyes," (151). Being alone on the island and having a family outside that specific space solidify both the impossibility of the insertion of a third subject in the colonial encounter, and the homoerotic undercurrent implied throughout the play. However, even when there are homoerotic implications, the traditional roles of a heterosexual relationship are already assigned; the powerful servant triumphs over his subject who has been submissive throughout his life. In other words, Jackson strips Harry of his manhood.

At this point, it would be useful to examine the motives for Jackson's inclination towards violence. According to Albert Memmi, after colonization the colonized gains self-assurance and self-consciousness which leads him to transform his negative parts and mythologize the positive ones. "Suddenly, exactly to the reverse of the colonialist accusation, the colonized, his culture, his country, everything that belongs to him, everything he represents, become perfectly positive elements". Later on, however, being doubtful about his actions "he gives in to the intoxication of fury and violence" (138-139). However, Jackson's inclination to oppression does not fit into such a clear statement since there is one particular scene – the scene in which he mends the sun deck – in which he obeys the master without objection (*Pantomime* 142). Probably because he is fed up with being labeled, Jackson defies any kind of categorization.

With this role reversal prevalent in the play, questions of authority come to the foreground as well. The vulnerability of the master and the empowerment of the servant build up simultaneously. The more open Harry is towards harassment, the more of a tyrant Jackson becomes. However, there is also one significant aspect, namely the genre, which should be remembered when considering Jackson's gaining authority.

In the rewritten version, the novel *Robinson Crusoe*, which is narrated by the master in Defoe, is transformed into a play, which signifies a dialogic relationship between Crusoe and Friday as opposed to the monologic and single narrative voice in Defoe's novel. Therefore, Jackson, unlike his ancestor Friday, literally and metaphorically gains a voice. It is time for him to speak against the colonial discourse. However, with his aggressive demands and offending remarks he rather turns the play into a monologue.

Apart from the genre, the fact that the play carries metatheatrical elements, and that it puts emphasis on role-playing draws attention to the assigned roles in a colonial encounter. Both of the characters share multiple roles; for instance, Jackson is a servant who plays either Crusoe or Friday during the rehearsals and who appears as the real master of the play *Pantomime.* Likewise, the master Harry acts sometimes as Crusoe and sometimes as Friday in the rehearsals and is exposed to Jackson's oppression. Such blurred role divisions refute the exact reversal of roles and clear-cut distinctions. With that in-betweenness, Walcott seems to endorse the complexity of the post-colonial situation.

The reconstruction that Jackson puts forth cannot avoid being another construction. His acts of violence and offending remarks to Harry do not carry him to a position so different from the colonizer. When given the chance and the power, he acts as brutally as the colonizer. The power relations are still dominant in the play. In *The Empire Writes Back*, Bill Ashcroft discusses the relationship between power relations and post-colonial text in the following way:

> The post-colonial text is always a complex and hybridized formation. It is inadequate to read it either as a reconstruc-

> tion of pure traditional values or as simply foreign and intrusive. The reconstruction of 'pure' cultural value is always conducted within a radically altered dynamic of power relations. (110)

Therefore, power relations and their representations become an intrinsic part of post-colonial discourse. Since it is not possible to return to a pre-colonial period, and the rewriting of Western canonical texts provides a possibility to analyze the European discourse from within, it is almost unavoidable for the rewritten texts not to deal with power relations (Ashcroft et al. 195-196). However, this idea of change in power relations while maintaining them in different hands may fall into the trap of transforming reconstructions into new constructions.

In order to avoid those new constructions, Walcott proposes an alienation from the Western understanding of history and progress. In his article "The Muse of History," he points out:

> [T]he vision of progress is the rational madness of history seen as sequential time, of a dominated future. Its imagery is absurd. In the history books the discoverer sets a shod foot on virgin sand, kneels, and the savage also kneels from his bushes in awe. Such images are stamped on the colonial memory. [. . .] These blasphemous images fade, because these hieroglyphs of progress are basically comic. (Qtd. in Peters 168)

With the example of a tyrant such as Jackson, the image of the colonized has been revealed as absurd and irritating. Jackson's being a detached, unsympathetic character urges the reader to reconsider the colonial background. Furthermore, his re-narrating history imprisons him within history and post-colonial biases. As Erskine Peters puts it, "[o]bsession with history pushes the slave toward revenge and the master toward remorse. Both lead to anguished existence, foregoing the opportunity to turn loss into rebirth, renewal, or redemption" (11). Likewise, Jackson and Harry, the former obsessed with revenge and the latter with repentance, cannot avoid being other stereotypes for the new post-colonial constructions.

In regarding Derek Walcott's plays, Patrick Taylor makes a distinction between a "mythologizing narrative" and a "liberating narrative". He draws attention to the fact that in any attempt to deconstruct the mythology and to reveal the oppression, there is the danger of mythologizing the oppressed. The fact that Jackson and Harry become stereotypes in the play may suggest the play's being a "mythologizing narrative." However, this deliberate attempt on the part of their author to depict them as sequestered within a colonial history liberates the reader and the text from establishing new constructions. Thus, the reader has the privilege to witness the biases of both characters and their tendency to mythologize. The characters serve as a foil so as to enlighten the reader and help him or her to peruse the text with a critical eye. Derek Walcott's *Pantomime,* therefore, with the help of its characters, proves to be a "liberating narrative."

Works Cited

Ashcroft, Bill, Gareth Griffiths and Helen Tiffin. *The Empire Writes Back: Theory and Practice in Post-Colonial Literatures*. London: Routledge, 1989.

Gunness, Christopher. "White Man, Black Man." Hamner 288-297.

Hamner, Robert D., ed. *Critical Perspectives on Derek Walcott.* Critical Perspectives. Boulder: Lynne Rienner, 1997.

Jameson, Fredric. "Third-World Literature in the Era of Multinational Capitalism." *Social Text* 15 (1986): 65-88.

Memmi, Albert. *The Colonizer and the Colonized.* New York: Orion, 1965.

Peters, Erskine. "The Theme of Madness in the Plays of Derek Walcott". *CLA Journal* 32.2 (December 1988): 148-169.

Taylor, Patrick. "Myth and Reality in Caribbean Narrative: Derek Walcott's *Pantomime*." Hamner 293-299.

Walcott, Derek. "The Art of Poetry." Interview with Edward Hirsch. Hamner 74-76.

---. *Pantomime*. In *Post-Colonial Plays: An Anthology*. Ed. Helen Gilbert. London: Routledge, 2001. 128-153.

---. “What the Twilight Says: An Overture.” *Dream on Monkey Mountain and Other Plays*. Ed. Robert Hamner. London: Jonathan Cape, 1972. 3-40.

Silence Before Apartheid:
J. M. Coetzee's *Foe*

Oya Berk
Haliç University

Abstract: This paper aims to analyze J. M. Coetzee's *Foe* from the standpoint of its relationship to the colonizing texts of the past on the one hand and to the history of apartheid on the other, with a focus on the colonizing power of the pen which absorbs and subjugates the voice of the Other. The first part of the study uncovers how *Foe* invades and deconstructs the economic utopia of Daniel Defoe's *Robinson Crusoe* while the second part explores the relationship between the colonizer's exploitation of the colonized and the colonial author's exploitation of the Other by trying to speak for him. The last section of the paper aims to account for Coetzee' s refusal to verbalize the history of apartheid via addressing the broader issue of whether it is possible to give the Other voice in fiction without denying him his subjectivity.

J. M.Coetzee's novels seek to bear witness to the suffering engendered by apartheid and more broadly by the history of colonialism, the larger context within which South African apartheid must be understood. Like the novels of Kafka and Beckett, Coetzee's novels remain speechless before history and draw attention to their own incompletion, to the silence at their core.

As a white South African writer, Coetzee is painfully aware of the gap between the privileged position of the narrator and the oppressed position of an Other the narrator seeks to narrate. In his Jerusalem speech in 1987, Coetzee said: "You cannot resign from the [master] caste. You can imagine resigning, you can perform a symbolic act of resignation, but short of shaking the dust of the country off your feet, there is no way of actually doing it" (*Doubling the Point* 96). This awareness of his own implication in the oppression of Black South Africa opens up an irreducible gap in his narratives between the privileged positions of the narrators and the oppressed position of the figures of alterity whose lives the narrators so desperately want to relate. Coetzee's figures of alterity remain radically incommensurable with the narrative in which they find themselves because they embody the material history of suffering that the narrative is unable to represent. Coetzee's own status as a writer is best explained by Mrs. Curren's words in *The Age of Iron*. When asked to describe the violence of the government security forces in Guguletu, a township in Capetown, Mrs. Curren first "waves a hand over the bush, the smoke, the filth littering the path, and says: "To speak of this [. . .], you would need the tongue of a God" (91). Like Mrs. Curren, Coetzee remains speechless before the history of apartheid – a history of racial oppression, barbarity and suffering.

In addressing apartheid, Coetzee's novels do not make direct references to history; that is, rather than providing a direct relation with the history of apartheid, they provide a way of relating to that history. As Sam Durrant puts it, "The truth-telling aspect of Coetzee's narratives consists not in the presentation of factual information but in the attempt to demonstrate a "true grief," a grief that acquires a certain materiality or historical weight despite the insubstantial fictional context" (24).

In his essay, "The Novel Today" Coetzee distinguishes between two types of novels: The supplementary novel, one that is colonized by the historical present, "aims to provide the reader with vicarious first-hand experience of living in a certain historical time" (3). This novel is documentary, reportorial and provides a camera-eye's view. The novel as rival, however, "operates in terms of its own procedures and issues in its own conclusions, it does not operate in terms of the procedures of history. [It] evolves its own paradigms and myths [. . .] perhaps going so far as to show the mythic status of history" (3). Hence, as Susan Gallagher points out in "History and the novel in post-apartheid South Africa" Coetzee sees historical discourse as a "constructed text of what has happened, a myth, a metanarrative, which might be resisted or even destroyed by the rival discourse of the novel" (378). Much of Coetzee's own fiction operates in this fashion, rivalling historical discourse, revealing its mythic qualities and undercutting its authority, such as in *Foe*'s revisionary account of *Robinson Crusoe*. Moreover, as Tiffin points out, "*Foe* succeeds in 'writing back' not just to an English canonical text, but also to the whole of the discursive field within which such a text operated and continues to operate in post-colonial worlds" (17).

The present study aims to analyse *Foe* from the standpoint of its relationship to the colonizing texts of the past on the one hand and to the history of apartheid on the other with focus on the colonizing power of the pen which absorbs and subjugates the voice of the Other.

In *Foe,* the narrator, Susan Barton, leaves England and goes to Brazil in search of her daughter who has been abducted by an English slave-runner. After two fruitless years of searching, she boards a ship to Lisbon and becomes the captain's mistress. The crew mutinies, kills the captain and sets her adrift with the corpse. Susan abandons the boat and swims to an island inhabited by a white man named Cruso and a black native called Friday whose tongue has been severed in an act of mutilation. The three are eventually rescued but Cruso dies on board the ship to England and Susan Barton arrives in England accompanied by Friday. She writes letters to Daniel Foe to persuade him to write a book about her adventures on the island. However, Foe is much more interested in the story of Susan's lost daughter than in her story of the island. When Foe goes into hiding in order to avoid being imprisoned for debt, Susan and Friday move into his abandoned house and she continues to plead with him to write their story. Later, Susan and Friday visit Foe in his hiding place and Susan has a long talk with him about the difficulties of writing after which they sleep together. Susan and Foe find it very difficult to write about Friday as he is silent and cannot recount the events leading up to his arrival on the island, especially the story of his mutilation. The novel ends in a brief chapter containing the dream vision of an unnamed speaker who visits Susan and Foe's room as they sleep and imaginatively descends into the sea.

In her article "Theory in the Margin: Coetzee's *Foe* Reading Defoe's *Crusoe/Roxana*," Gayatri Chakravorty Spivak has noted the incompatibility of the three negative segments that make up *Foe* and the resulting indeterminacy of the work as a whole (166). The island story remains nothing more than an opaque fragment, hiding more than it reveals. Susan refuses to tell Foe the story of her lost daughter because she wants him to write the story of the island. The third, Friday's story, remains a mystery, as Barton puts it, "a hole in the narrative" (*Foe* 121). We are left with silence, emptiness and a fragmentary story which Susan Barton describes as "a sorry limping affair" (47).

Foe offers a contemporary rereading of Daniel Defoe's *Robinson Crusoe*, the originating text for the myth of economic individualism. Regardless of whether they have read it or not, most people know the amazing story of the man cast away on a desert island for twenty-eight years, who not only survives but conquers his harsh environment, building shelters, fashioning clothing, setting up plantations and cattle herds, even crafting that ultimate symbol of civilization – an umbrella. He is forced to invent himself from nothing on his island, building from the ground up his self, his culture, his history, spelling out, as many critics have noted, a powerful Puritan lesson of individual self-making. Crusoe also has ink and parchment for keeping a diary which equips him with the power of discourse.

Robinson Crusoe rescues a native prisoner from cannibals, names him Friday and remakes him into a Christian manservant. He teaches Friday to call him "Master" and teaches him English so that he can understand his orders. Friday is the prototype of the successful colonial subject. He learns his master's speech, does his master's work, happily swears loyalty and believes that the culture of his master is superior to his.

In traditional Defoe scholarship, *Robinson Crusoe* was read as the 18th-century testament to the superiority of rational civilization over nature and savagery as well as an Ur-text for a widely proliferated myth of economic individualism. However, 20th-century critics such as Ian Watt tended to view the novel as a central cultural text extolling the myth of civilization based on oppression. Particularly within the context of South African literary criticism, *Robinson Crusoe* is seen as an embodiment of the great myth of Western Imperialism, a narrative of the project of colonizing and oppressing indigenous peoples. Lewis Nkosi, one of the leading black South African novelists and critics, claims: "In *Robinson Crusoe,* the element of myth regarding the painstaking industry of building a civilization [. . .] is inseparable from the story of colonization, of subjugation, exploitation and finally Christianisation" (154).

There are marked differences between Defoe's *Robinson Crusoe* and Coetzee's *Foe.* While Defoe's text epitomizes Western Imperialism, in Coetzee's *Foe*, the mythic legitimization of economic individualism collapses. Coetzee empties the colonial message of *Robinson Crusoe* by invading and deconstructing its economic utopia.

Whereas Defoe's Crusoe is the archetypal imperialist, Coetzee's Cruso is concerned merely with survival and sterile work. Accordingly, Cruso feels no need for tools whereas Defoe's Crusoe makes repeated trips to his wrecked ship to recover his tools and guns. Among his activities are planting his two "plantations," as he calls them, animal husbandry, crafts and manufacturing and a defence infrastructure. Cruso, unlike his literary model, makes no table or chair, no lamp or candle; he has no desire to keep a journal or build a boat. His "improvement" of nature consists of a Sysiphus-like labour of carrying stones up the island's hills to build gigantic terraces walled by stone which stand empty and barren because he has no seed. He thinks that perhaps later explorers will be able to use them as garden plots. As he puts it, "The planting is reserved for those who come after us and have the foresight to bring seed. I only clear the ground for them" (33). Cruso's useless terraces deconstruct the myth of economic individualism by laying bare the emptiness which lies at the core of empire building.

In *Foe,* Friday is transformed from the light-skinned, European native into a woolly-haired, thick-lipped, dark-complexioned Negro (5) which suggests his kinship with the indigenous people of South Africa. Moreover, in Defoe's original narrative, Friday can speak but Coetzee's text marks him as forever silenced, as unable to speak because his tongue has been ripped out of his mouth. The deformed and speechless Friday shatters the optimistic myth of *Robinson Crusoe* by underscoring the violence done to the Other by the colonizer.

In rewriting the myth of Robinson Crusoe, Coetzee focuses on the relationship between authority and authorship and the related question of who will write and who will remain silent, which are of central importance in *Foe*. When Coetzee was asked why *Foe* was radically removed from contemporary South African life, he said:

> *Foe* is a retreat from the South African situation, but only from that situation in a narrow temporal perspective. It is not a retreat from the subject of colonialism or from questions of power. What you call 'the nature and process of fiction' may also be called the question of *who writes*? Who takes up the position of power, pen in hand? ("Two Interviews with J. M. Coetzee" 462)

Coetzee challenges and deconstructs the hegemony of male consciousness in the patriarchal Robinson myth by telling the story from the perspective of a female character – Susan Barton – who has been omitted from and silenced in Defoe's novel. He accounts for his inclusion of a female narrator in *Foe* in the following way: "How can one question power ('success') from a position of power? One ought to question it from its antagonist position, namely the position of weakness" (Morphet 461).

Coetzee's examination of the power of the pen from the female stance enables him to explore the link between authorship and authority on the one hand and between the colonizer and the colonized on the other. The association of authorship with patriarchal authority is made throughout *Foe* particularly when Foe links the idea of God with writing: "We are accustomed to believe that our world was created by God speaking the Word; but I ask, may it not rather be that he wrote it, wrote a Word so long we have yet to come to the end of it?" (143).

The assumption that authorship is a male domain can be found throughout the Western culture. As Sandra Gilbert and Susan Gubar point out in *The Madwoman in the Attic*, in the Western world, "the text's author is a father, a progenitor, a procreator, an aesthetic patriarch whose pen is an instrument of generative power like his penis" (6). Condemned by her gender to silence, Susan must also turn to the more adequately equipped male, the professional writer Foe, to write her story.

Coetzee's use of the original form of Defoe's name, Foe (Defoe's birth name was Foe. He added the prefix "De" to his name later), with its denotation of enemy, reveals the patriarchal author's adverse stance to Susan. Foe is the enemy of the female voice which he seeks to suppress. He is the patriarchal colonizer/author figure who takes control of, marginalizes and silences the female voice. As Foe works on the story, he manifests his desire to control and direct it. Susan wants him to write the story of the island but he insists on writing about her adventures in Bahia in search of her lost daughter. Although Susan wants her story to reflect the truth ("I will not have any lies told," she says (40)), Foe wants to make it more interesting by adding imaginary details such as a threat of cannibals landing on the island (94). Susan also fears that Foe may exclude her from the island story altogether, thinking that the story would be better if it included only Cruso and Friday, "better without the woman" (72).

Susan, on the other hand, wants to be both "the goddess and begetter" and the "father" (123) of her story, not just the Muse or mother. She tries to assume a masculine position of dominance by refusing to take on the traditionally subservient role of the female Muse. She says, "I am a free woman who asserts her freedom by telling her story according to her own desire" (131). Foe ignores her remarks and says, "Wait to see what fruit I bear" (152). The fruit is the total silencing and subjection of Susan and bits of fiction that cannot articulate a story.

Coetzee's use of a woman narrator attempting to control her version of events also allows him to explore the links between the exploitation of women by man, especially by patriarchal authors like Defoe, and the colonizer's exploitation of the Other represented by Friday. Both Foe and Susan Barton try to impose words upon Friday to colonize him via language as the original Crusoe had done on the island in order to make him a useful functionary. Susan wishes "to build a bridge of words" for Friday so that she can subject him to her will (60). "We must make Friday's silence speak," Foe says (142). He is confident that he can penetrate into Friday's silence by his realistic texts and his formula of writing: "It is thus that we make up a book: loss, then quest, then recovery; beginning, then middle, then end" (117).

Susan also assumes the role of the colonizing author when she says, "It is for us to descend into [Friday's] mouth. It is for us to open Friday's mouth and hear what it holds" (142), making Friday the "helpless captive" of her "desire to have their story told" (150). Her very desire to turn Friday into a story parallels Foe's desire to reduce her to a character in her story.

Nevertheless, as Susan views the act of writing from the female perspective, from the position of the oppressed and the silenced, her model of authorship is less authoritarian than Foe's. She is more aware of the difficulties of speaking for the Other and less confident about how it can be done: "Who will do it? [. . .] Who will dive into the wreck?" she asks (142), echoing Coetzee's question "Who writes? Who takes up the position of power, pen in hand?". However, this does not prevent her from seeing the pen and the narrative as instruments that can make Friday speak: "The true story will not be heard till by art we have found a means of giving voice to Friday" (118). Foe's and Susan Barton's efforts to penetrate Friday's silence foreground the important questions of how the Other can be given voice in fiction and how we can speak for the Other without becoming oppressors ourselves.

Friday's silence is a central issue in *Foe*. Both Foe and Susan realize that their story will be incomplete if they cannot penetrate Friday's silence. Susan says to Foe, "If the story seems stupid, that is only because it so doggedly holds its silence. The shadow whose lack you feel is there: it is the loss of Friday's tongue" (117).

In *Postcolonial Narrative and the Work of Mourning*, Sam Durrant describes the subaltern characters in Coetzee's fiction in the following way:

> As a way of bearing witness to the negation of subjectivity at the heart of the apartheid, Coetzee incorporates foreign bodies or absent bodies into his narratives, bodies that remain obdurately unfamiliar despite the close attention of the narrators [. . .] He bears witness to the denial of subjectivity that lies at the heart of racial oppression by denying his specters the status of fully realized characters. These specters remain unhomely or uncanny subjects precisely because their narratives are unable to render them familiar by retrieving their respective stories. Such figures cannot be plotted according to the time and space of the subject. (17-18)

In a similar manner, in *Powers of Horror: An Essay on Abjection*, Julia Kristeva describes abjection as a process of the reduction of the self to the body in which the body becomes radically defamiliarized, deprived of the cultural codes by which we recognize it. The abject body is auto-referential; it accrues its own pathos and becomes an image of its own pain. "Significance," Kristeva writes, "is indeed inherent in the human body" (10).

Friday possesses all of these attributes. He is not a fully developed individual but a passive subject, "a shadowy creature" (24) and "a slave and a child" (39). His only activity seems to be obeying the orders of Cruso and Susan. "Had I struck Friday [. . .] would he have borne the blow meekly? [. . .] Had the cutting out of his tongue taught him eternal obedience?" (98), Susan wonders. Friday's severed tongue marks him as the uncivilized, the inhuman, the native, the infant. Following Kristeva's description of the abject figure, his whole self is reduced to and absorbed by his disfigurement – his mutilated tongue – serving as a reminder of all those who have been denied humanity, a reminder of the history of barbarity that underwrites the history of civilization.

Although Friday is not a fully developed character, there are two incidents in *Foe* which allow the reader to gain a glimpse of his interior life. Susan sees Friday floating near the shore on a log. She initially assumes he is fishing but then sees him scattering pedals and buds on to the surface of the water and concludes that Friday is "making an offering to the god of the waves or performing some other superstitious observance" (31). But later she speculates that the log Friday was steering might be a slave-ship which was ship-wrecked and he was scattering the pedals "in memory of some person who perished in the wreck, perhaps a father or a mother or a sister or a brother, or perhaps a whole family, or perhaps a dear friend" (87). Susan's interpretation of Friday's obscure activity invites the reader to assume that, by scattering the pedals, Friday may be marking the place where his fellow slaves lie submerged. In other words, it is an act of mourning in which Friday remembers and laments the loss of his friends.

The next incident concerns Friday's drawings. When examining his drawings on the slate, Susan finds that what seemed to be a design of leaves and flowers is in fact "eyes, open eyes, each set upon a human foot: row upon row of eyes upon feet: walking eyes" (147). The image of the numerous walking eyes seems to suggest the displacement of the enslaved and the colonized as well as the sense of bearing witness to them. Like the scar on Friday's neck "left by a rope or chain" (155), the eyes on feet, that is, the deformed figures without bodies, evoke a whole history of colonial slavery and subjugation.

In his *Mémoires for Paul de Man,* Derrida distinguishes between two kinds of mourning: He associates "successful mourning" with the historicist desire to recover the past. Successful mourning enables the past to be assimilated and digested by translating loss into words and silence into speech. Unsuccessful or "failed" mourning, on the other hand, confronts an indigestible past which refuses to be related. While successful mourning enables us to internalize "the image, idol, or the ideal of the other who is dead," failed mourning, by refusing to recover a history of oppression, "leaves the other his alterity, respecting thus his infinite remove" (6). *Foe* can be described as a novel of "failed" or inconsolable mourning precisely because by testifying to its own inability to verbalize the history of apartheid, it refuses to recognize an end to the time of mourning. As the history of Friday's mutilation cannot be translated into words, the reader is not allowed to assimilate it into his consciousness and then forget it as it happens in the case of "successful mourning." Hence, *Foe* makes a commitment never to forget by inviting the reader to participate in a ceaseless process of remembrance.

In the final section of the novel, there are two descents narrated without quotation marks which suggests that Susan has relinquished her hold on the narrative. On the first descent, an unidentified narrator enters an unnamed house, forces open Friday's clenched teeth, and hears "the faintest faraway roar [. . .] the roar of the waves in a seashell [. . .] the sounds of the island" (154). The second descent is a repetition of the first but with the difference that the unnamed narrator becomes involved in an act of reading. After identifying the house as that of "Daniel Defoe, Author" (155) and thereby entering the house of fiction, he picks up Susan's abandoned manuscript and begins to read it: "Dear Mr Foe, At last I could row no further"(155). As he is reading, he enters the hole in Friday's story (156) where he comes upon a shipwreck which is "the home of Friday" (157), "a place where bodies are their own signs" (157). When he finds Friday, his mouth opens and "from inside him comes a slow stream, without breath, without interruption" (157).

As Sam Durrant points out in *Postcolonial Narrative and the Work of Mourning* (36), the ending echoes both Dante's descent to the underworld in *Inferno* and Spivak's description of the subaltern female in "Can the Subaltern Speak?" In this text, Spivak presents the subaltern female as a character that cannot be represented except by means of an image, more precisely an image of death "that marks the place of her disappearance" (306). At the end of the article, Spivak leaves us with the image of a corpse as a bodily testament to the "no place from which the subaltern can speak" (307). In the same way, the narrator describes the extra-textual location of the last section of *Foe* as "a place where bodies have their own signs" (157). This is the realm of death where Friday's corpse, becoming an "auto-referential" image of its own pain echoing Kristeva's description of the abject body, reduces the narrative to silence, to the postcolonial writer's speechlessness before history as exemplified in *Foe*.

The two descents in the last section enact Dante's descent to Hell. The connection between Dante and Coetzee is suggested earlier in the novel when Foe says to Susan,

> I read in an old Italian author of a man who visited, or dreamed he visited Hell. There he met the souls of the dead. One of the souls was weeping. 'Do not suppose mortal,' said this soul, addressing him, 'that because I am not substantial these tears you behold are not the tears of a true grief'. (138)

This is a reference to *The Divine Comedy*. While Dante is visiting the Inferno, he encounters weeping shades. He is moved by their tears and begins to cry but is powerless to alleviate their suffering as his tears cannot effect reconciliation between God and the condemned. In the same way, Coetzee's novels bear witness to the tyranny of apartheid while remaining powerless to effect reconciliation.

Although Coetzee is acutely aware that, like Dante, he is no more than a tourist in an underworld of suffering, he cannot give up his dream of a place where it would be possible for the writer to descend into "Friday's home" and participate in his suffering by shedding tears of "true grief" for him. This is indicated in the last sentence of the novel which hints at a possible transference of the "slow stream" coming out of Friday's mouth into the tears of the narrator: "Soft and cold, dark and unending, it [the stream coming out of Friday's mouth] beats against my eyelids, against the skin of my face" (157).

Works Cited

Coetzee, J. M. *The Age of Iron*. Harmondsworth: Penguin, 1990.

---. "Jerusalem Speech." *Doubling the Point: Essays and Interviews.* Ed. David Atwell. Cambridge: Harvard UP, 1992. 93-98.

---. *Foe.* London and New York: Penguin, 1986.

---. "The Novel Today." *Upstream* 6.1 (1988): 2-5.

Derrida, Jacques. *Mémoires: For Paul de Man.* Trans. Eduardo Cadava, Jonathan Culler, Peggy Kamuf and Cecile Lindsay. Ed. Cadava and Avita Ronell. Wellek Library Lectures at the University of California, Irvine. New York: Columbia UP, 1986.

Durrant, Sam. *Postcolonial Narrative and the Work of Mourning.* New York: State U of New York P, 2004.

Gallagher, Susan Van Zanten. "History and the Novel in Post-Apartheid South Africa." *Studies in the Novel* (Fall 1997): 376-395.

Gilbert Sandra M. and Susan Gubar. *The Madwoman in the Attic: The Woman Writer and the Nineteenth-Century Literary Imagination.* New Haven: Yale UP, 1979.

Kristeva, Julia. *Powers of Horror: An Essay on Abjection.* Trans. Leon S. Roudiez. New York: Colombia UP, 1991.

Morphet, Tony. "Two Interviews with J. M. Coetzee, 1983 and 1987." *TriQuarterly* 62 (1987): 454-464.

Nkosi, Lewis. "Robinson Crusoe: Call Me Master." *Home and Exile and Other Selections.* New York: Longman, 1983. 151-160.

Spivak, Gayatri Chakravorty. "Can the Subaltern Speak?" *Marxism and Interpretation of Culture.* Ed. Cary Nelson and Lawrence Grossberg. London: Macmillan, 1998. 271-308.

---. "Theory in the Margin: Coetzee's *Foe* Reading Defoe's Crusoe/Roxana." *Consequences of Theory*. Ed. Jonathan Arac and Barbara Johnson. Baltimore: Johns Hopkins UP, 1991. 154-179.

Tiffin, Helen. "Post-Colonial Literatures and Counter-Discourse." *Kunapipi* 9 (1987): 17-34.

Transformation of a Magistrate into a Barbarian: Victimization in *Waiting for the Barbarians* by J. M. Coetzee

Ayşegül Turan
Boğaziçi University

Abstract: The intricate relationship between the colonizer and the colonized is generally reduced to the relationship between the oppressor and the oppressed; however, the emergence of post-colonialism reveals the ambiguous position of the (ex-)colonizer with respect to the colonized. J. M. Coetzee's novel *Waiting for the Barbarians* depicts the in-between situation of a Magistrate, who remains nameless except for the title given him by the Empire, yet hates its men for their torturing of barbarians. The novel is not set in any specific time and place, and gains its sociopolitical criticism from this excess of an ahistorical standing. This paper aims to examine how a member of a colonial power can become a victim of its own practices. The Magistrate experiences the loss of authorial power and social status through physical and psychological torture of his own kinsmen. The vagueness of the line between civilization and barbarity forms one of the focal points of the text along with a representation of the dual nature of reality. The general mood of the novel is shaped around the Magistrate's inner conflicts and dilemmas concerning his position as an agent of the Empire and his existence as a human being.

Because the barbarians are to arrive today;
And they get bored with eloquence and orations.

Why all of a sudden this unrest
And confusion (how solemn the faces have become).
Why are the streets and squares clearing quickly,
And all return to their homes, so deep in thought?

Because the night is here but the barbarians have not come.
And some people arrived from the borders,
And said that there are no longer any barbarians.

And now what shall become of us without any barbarians?
Those people were some kind of solution.

Taking its name from the above-quoted poem by the well-known Greek poet Constantine Cavafy, *Waiting for the Barbarians* by J. M. Coetzee presents us with an allegorical world from the postcolonial period. The novel portrays the decline of a Magistrate who tries to protect the natives/the barbarians of the district but is unable to achieve this. Through his experience of torture by his own kinsman, he also loses his faith in the Empire and his dignity as its servant. Coetzee moves toward a subtler and much more humane understanding of the common colonizer and colonized relationship in the novel. The notions of the oppressor and the oppressed undergo a remarkably profound change as the story unfolds. The fact that time and space in the narrative remain unspecified yields two different interpretations of the text. Judie Newman argues that due to its lack of specific location in time and place it is open to any kind of ahistorical and apolitical readings (127). The counter-argument to this view is that this overly ahistorical standing also extends its sociopolitical criticism beyond any one place and time. The novel is not solely the story of South Africa, Coetzee's country, but of any oppressive society.

The main character, the Magistrate, is an anonymous agent of an undefined empire. He is referred to only as "the Magistrate" and is never given any other name, which makes it clear that he exists only through his title. This emphasis on his official authority and erasure of his identity along with his human traits become significant when he no longer holds his position but becomes a prisoner of the Third Bureau. At the beginning of the novel, he describes himself quite honestly:

> I am a country magistrate, a responsible official in the service of the Empire, serving out my days on this lazy frontier, waiting to retire. I collect the tithes and taxes, administer the communal lands, see that the garrison is provided for, supervise the junior officers we have here, keep an eye on trade, preside over the law court twice a week. For the rest I watch the sun rise and set, eat and sleep and am content. When I pass away I hope to merit three lines of small print in the

> Imperial gazette. I have not asked for more than a quiet life in quiet times. (8)

Newman remarks that the Magistrate is a representative liberal and concerned only with maintaining the status quo, keeping his own hands clean by due observance (130). His life has been as peaceful and calm as he desires until the men of the Empire appear on the scene. The arrival of Colonel Joll disturbs the peaceful picture, and his life takes an unexpected turn with his experience of "the barbarians" and "the workings of the Empire."

The tension in the Magistrate's relationship with Colonel Joll is constantly felt. They first meet as equals, since both are servants of the Empire and on the same side. Yet, neither of them is content with the existing circumstances. Colonel Joll notices the Magistrate's dislike of him. The Magistrate attempts to put a distance between himself and Colonel Joll, yet he finds this impossible to achieve: "[. . .] who am I to assert my distance from him? I drink with him, I eat with him, I show him the sights, I afford him every assistance as his letter of commission requests" (6). The more he spends time with him, the more he becomes disdainful of him. What draws the line between them as agents of the Empire is their attitude towards "the barbarians." The Colonel is in the business of creating the enemy, of "delineating that opposition which must exist," in order that the Empire might define itself by its others (Ashcroft 104). There must be an enemy that will enable the Empire to protect its subjects and reveal its power. According to Colonel Joll, within the Empire, it is the barbarians who threaten the wholeness and security of the Empire. Thus, they must be persecuted for what they have done or, in this case, for what they will do. The Magistrate feels uncomfortable with this manhunt. His attempts to distance himself from Colonel Joll are striking, especially after the Colonel's torture of the barbarians. Yet, from the beginning, the Magistrate knows that this is not so easy, and that he is bound to the Colonel.

The Magistrate feels uneasy about the torture of barbarians by the Colonel, however he does not have the authority to interfere, or at least he does not have the courage to do so. "Of the screaming which people afterwards claim to have heard from the granary, I hear nothing. At every moment that evening as I go about my business I am aware of what might be happening" (Coetzee 5). He seems to neglect what is happening around him, while he is already involved in it. Rather than speaking with a voice of an authoritative narrator, or a strong protagonist, Coetzee narrates the novel in the persona of a weak and wondering man (Gallagher 121). The Magistrate, for most of the time, is unable to recollect the events in a proper way, and he is aware of this weakness. His lack of authority over the events also overlaps with this inability of expression. This aspect of the narration contributes to the realistic depiction of torture. Coetzee does not mention the torture openly but in an oblique manner that corresponds to the Magistrate's lack of linguistic potency. Those who have become subject to torture are incapable of talking about their experience since they are terrorized and paralyzed by what they have been through.

The barbarian girl who has been tortured by Colonel Joll is the first native with whom the Magistrate has such an intimate contact. Up to that point, barbarians for him are those people who visit the town at certain times to buy necessary goods. He never regards them as a potential danger as the Empire does.

> I observe that once in every generation, without fail, there is an episode of hysteria about the barbarians. There is no woman living along the frontier who has not dreamed of a dark barbarian hand coming from under the bed to grip her ankle, no man who has not frightened himself add: with visions of the barbarians carousing in his home, breaking the plates, setting fire to the curtains, raping his daughters. (9)

She is one of the many who has become a victim of the Empire's enemy creating process. Though she has such a significant place in his life, she only exists with her communal identity, a barbarian, and her sex, a woman. Apart from this, she is never given a name, either in her own language or in English. The Magistrate encounters her while he is still carrying the burden of a shared guilt with the Colonel. In order to relieve himself from self-accusation, he develops an unusual relationship with her. In his desire to erase the dirty story of the Empire, he attempts to refresh her mind and body through ritual cleansing (Newman 130). Yet, what he does not notice at first is that he, somehow, behaves similar to her torturers by trying to reveal her deepest and most hidden feelings. His primary aim is to distinguish himself from her torturers but his inability to understand her makes him closer to them than to a kinsman of hers. Susan V. Gallagher argues that the Magistrate participates in the acts of the torturers not only by his first acceptance of the actions of Colonel Joll, but later in his objectification of the woman as the site of torture (128). When the Magistrate realizes this, he is terrified with what he himself is doing: "What depravity is it that is creeping upon me? I search for secrets and answers, no matter how bizarre, like an old woman reading tea-leaves. There is nothing to link me with her torturers, people who sit waiting like beetles in dark cellars. [. . .] I must assert my distance from Colonel Joll! I will not suffer for his crimes!" (47-48).

A comparative look at the Magistrate's relationship with Colonel Joll and the barbarian girl displays that he is suffering from the same problem in these two entirely different conditions. Using Homi Bhabba's notion of "the process of identification," it can be argued that the Magistrate cannot fully establish his own identity in his encounters with both Colonel Joll and the barbarian girl (88). Peter Childs and Patrick Williams assert that according to Bhabha, "colonial identity is a problem arising between colonizer and colonized" (Childs and Williams 123). Through the other, the postcolonial subject can locate and construct its identity (125). At this point, the problematic of "seeing" and "being seen" comes to the foreground in its relation to identifying one's own being. In Bhabha's notion, "the first condition to exist in relation to an otherness is the look" (*The Location of Culture* 44). Namely, an individual must come face to face, literally, to assure his/her difference and to find a confirmation of his/her own identity. However, in the Magistrate's case there is a lack of a proper gaze in his interaction with both Colonel Joll and the barbarian girl. In his relations with the Colonel, the sunglasses are always present, putting an unnatural distance between the two men of the Empire and preventing the Magistrate from defining himself on solid grounds against Colonel Joll. He is not his ally, but nevertheless there is the unbreakable bond of sharing the same heritage that comes from the Empire. In the other case, the barbarian girl's vision is blurred due to the torture she experiences. In her world, nothing is clear or certain. The Magistrate is unable to get the response to his gaze and he suffers from an inability to present himself entirely again. He is neither her father nor her lover; there is no exact situation in which he can position himself against her. The observer, the Magistrate, cannot become the observed one, and "the identity creation process which should take place reciprocally" remains incomplete, leaving him unstable in his identity and unsure of himself (Bhabha 89).

The Magistrate's expedition is the central narrative moment that seals his opposition to the Colonel (Attwell 82). After that point, there is no possibility of being a part of the Empire. This choice also marks the desire to put as much distance as possible between himself and the self of imperialism, namely Colonel Joll. He is aware of the fact that he transgresses the boundary that draws the line between "the barbarians" and the so-called civilized people of the Empire. "We have crossed the limits of the Empire" (77). On his return to the town, he finds himself as the other. His fraternization with the natives causes him to be alienated from his own people. He is no longer the respected, faithful servant of the Empire but "the enemy," as the warrant officer remarks (85). Through his venture to the land of the natives, the implicit resistance of the Magistrate to Colonel Joll evolves into an open manifestation of his dislike of the Empire and its workings.

> I am aware of the source of my elation: my alliance with the guardians of Empire is over, I have set myself in opposition, the bond is broken, I am a free man. Who would not smile? But what a dangerous joy! It should not be so easy to attain salvation. (85)

Ashcroft describes this freedom as an ambiguous one since he undergoes both physical and mental torture from this point onwards (105). What he lives through is not the exact equivalent of the torture experienced by the barbarians. Instead of a demand for confession, the use of torture aims to move him away from his humanity to bestiality. He is not subject to beating, starvation or any other kind of humiliation in his cell, yet his petty sufferings make his situation much more degrading. The essential human needs of maintaining his physical and psychological integrity gain importance: "To lie in a woman's arms in a proper bed, to have good food to eat, to walk in the sun – how much more important these seem than the right to decide without advice from the police who should be my friends and who my enemies!" (105). Even though his torture and imprisonment have physically reduced him to the level of an animal, these experiences also elevate his "moral awareness" and his perspective on the barbarians (Gallagher 130)

The return to the town and the imprisonment hasten his questioning of the notion of "the enemy." The Magistrate is no longer so sure of whether the enemy exists at any time, or it is only a creation of the Empire. Attwell indicates that what is important in the novel is how the Empire imagines the barbarians and the arbitrariness and indeterminacy of the Empire against "the enemy" (71). The identity of the enemy is never apparent; seemingly it is the barbarians but an official of the Empire can turn into an enemy as well, as in the case of the Magistrate. The discourse of otherness is used to formulate the enemy. Coetzee depicts the othering process through his perspective when the Magistrate, too, becomes the other. But the notion of otherness in the novel is not reduced to some kind of a binary opposition between the natives and the townspeople; rather, it is represented as oppressive and false (Gallagher 118). Throughout the course of the narrative, the otherness of the other is called into question, and the differences between the barbarians and the townspeople are deconstructed in different ways.

When the Magistrate no longer belongs to the Empire, he naturally does not turn into a barbarian, either. At this point, the post-colonial individual finds a definition for his in-between position. The Magistrate is "a subject of colonial discourse," and later, he becomes subjected to it like the barbarians (Ashcroft 106). He used to be an imperial official, and now he is an imperial outcast. Colonel Joll, who deprives him of power and dignity, forces him to question his position and standing. Having experienced the torture of the Empire, he is now able to make a comment on himself much more objectively:

> For I was not, as I liked to think, the indulgent pleasure-loving opposite of the cold rigid Colonel. I was the lie that Empire tells when times are easy, he the truth that Empire tells when harsh winds blow. Two sides of Imperial rule, no more, no less. (148-149)

Ashcroft states that "his face turned in two directions; he is both judge and judged, law and transgressor, protector and enemy" (104). This ambivalent position of the Magistrate becomes visible as he goes beyond the boundaries of Empire, steps on the barbarian land, and returns to the land of the Empire.

Throughout the novel, the Magistrate attempts to find an answer to the question of "Who is the enemy?" The apparent answer for the Colonel and the Empire is that the enemy is "the barbarians"; whereas the Magistrate feels uneasy about this answer. The question undermines itself through the narrative. The first enemy to be depicted, the barbarians, turns into a victim of the Empire. The second enemy is the Magistrate, who resists the workings of the Empire and feels close to the barbarians. Upon his return to the town, the Magistrate asserts that there is no enemy, "unless we are the enemy" (77). After he witnesses the brutal torture scene of the newcomers, there is only one enemy who has started all this: Colonel Joll. Another striking question which arises frequently, but implicitly, is "Who is the real barbarian?" Coetzee plays with the civilization and barbarity opposition so masterfully that the arbitrariness of these notions unfolds itself in the stream of events. This also draws attention to the reality behind the appearance. The civilized, educated citizens of Empire do not hesitate to impose violence upon the nameless members of Empire, the barbarians. The line between barbarous and civilized manners is entirely blurred in the novel. Thus, Coetzee reveals the impossibility of establishing clear-cut definitions or categorizations.

Waiting for the Barbarians puts forward the dilemma of the Magistrate by asking the question "Is it possible for the colonizer to become a victim of colonial power?" The question finds an incomplete answer, like the in-between position of the Magistrate. He is not one of the Empire's civilized men any longer, yet he is not a barbarian either. Indeed, these words do not carry any significance in this context. After witnessing the brutality of Empire and the barbarians as its victim, he decides to side with the latter and thus turns himself into "a victim," too. He is not the Magistrate with a capital "m" but just an ordinary citizen, or even inferior to that, in the eyes of men of the Empire. Although this victimization includes physical pain, what hurts him most is the psychological torture of being a part of this empire of injustice and violence. Now he knows that his dream of a peaceful and quiet life will not come true, and he is ready to accept whatever future will befall him as long as "in this farthest outpost of the Empire there exists one man who in his heart is not a barbarian" (114).

Works Cited

Ashcroft, Bill. "Irony, Allegory and Empire: *Waiting for the Barbarians* and *In the Heart of the Country*." *Critical Essays on J. M. Coetzee*. Ed. Sue Kossew. New York: G. K. Hall; London: Prentice Hall International, 1998. 100-117.

Attwell, David. *J.M. Coetzee: South Africa and the Politics of Writing*. Berkeley: U of California P; Cape Town: David Philip, 1993.

Bhabha, Homi K. *The Location of Culture*. London: Routledge, 1994.

Cavafy, Constantine. *Collected Poems*. Trans. Edmund Keeley and Philip Sherrard. Ed. George Savidis. Princeton, N. J. : Princeton UP, 1975.

Childs, Peter and R. J. Patrick Williams. *An Introduction to PostColonial Theory*. London: Prentice Hall, 1997.

Coetzee. J. M. *Waiting for the Barbarians*. London, Random House: 2000.

Gallagher, Susan V. *A Story of South Africa: J. M. Coetzee's Fiction in Context*. Cambridge, Mass.: Harvard UP, 1991.

Newman, Judie. "Intertextuality, Power and Danger: *Waiting for The Barbarians* as a Dirty Story." *Critical Essays on J. M. Coetzee*. Ed. Sue Kossew. New York: G. K. Hall; London: Prentice Hall International, 1998. 126-138.

Bettelheim, Bruno. *The Uses of Enchantment: The Meaning and Importance of Fairy Tales*. London: Thames and Hudson, 1976.

Cixous, Hélène. "Sorties." *Modern Criticism and Theory*. Ed. David Lodge. New York: Longman, 1988.

Grimm, Jacob and Wilhelm. *Grimm's Fairy Tales*. Berkshire: Penguin, 1996.

Grimm, Jacob and Wilhelm. *Selected Tales.* Trans. David Luke. New York: Penguin, 1982.

Hall, Caroline King Barnard. *Anne Sexton.* Twayne's United States Authors Series 548. Boston: Twayne, 1989.

Juhasz, Susanne. "Anne Sexton." *Modern American Women Writers.* Ed. Elaine Showalter et al. New York: Collier, 1993. 309-320.

Sexton, Anne. *Transformations.* New York: Mariner, 2001.

The Ruptured Body and Story of the Female Servant: Angela Carter's "The Fall River Axe Murders"

Esra Melikoğlu
Istanbul University

Abstract: Servants in literature – as well as history – live together with the family of their employers, under the same roof, yet inhabit the dark and narrow spaces in the house: the back corridors, the attic and cellar. On the one hand, they are often a member of the family, yet must suffer to be treated as foster-children in the house as well as culture at large. In Angela Carter's short-story, "The Fall River Axe Murders" (1985), the female servant's – or the invisible hand's – displacement in a class-conscious society is indicated by her reduction to serving hands coarsened by work and bearing the stigmata of the untouchable. These hands cause horror and disgust in the gentility, bent on a life of leisure and beauty. Yet Carter also presents the servant's busy hands as objects of desire in a culture of unproductive idleness and ultimately as the all-powerful hands of fate that merge with those of the equally displaced younger daughter of the house, in an act of revenge upon the oppressive master and mistress.

Bruce Robbins, pondering the hands – a euphemism for domestic servants – in literature, states, "something is missing. Where are the vanished bodies to which these hands belong? [. . .] Amputated, the hands [. . .] are the mark of an absence, an area of non-representation" (ix). And Edward W. Said points out that the servant's "work is taken for granted but scarcely ever more than named, rarely studied," and associates the servant with the colonised abroad, for both are "people on whom the economy and polity sustained by empire depend, but whose reality has not historically or culturally required attention" (75). Indeed, no "ism" has evolved around the figure of the servant, despite the persistence with which, in much fiction, his/her story of marginalisation has been placed in interaction with the stories of the equally marginalised female and colonised subject.

However, literature, and, in particular, eighteenth- and nineteenth-century literature teems with servants. This circumstance evidently reflects the historical fact that either a maid-of-all-works or a whole army of servants – housekeeper, lady's maid, nanny, housemaid, cook, kitchenmaid, scullery-maid, steward, butler, under-butler, groom, valet and others – would keep life going, feed and clothe their employers and nurse their offspring, for aristocratic as well as aspiring middle-class families proved anxious to demonstrate their ability to afford a life of unproductive leisure by keeping servants. Frank Dawes quotes the Official Census which says that, in 1891, in England and Wales, 1,386,167 women and 58,527 men entered into domestic employment, the total population amounting to twenty-nine million (9). In fact, Victorian England owed its prosperity to the servant labouring at home and the native abroad. In literature, some servants remain unobtrusively on the periphery of the events and the narrative, eavesdropping and peering through keyholes to feed on the lives of their betters, as they themselves are denied a life of their own. Others, however, are cast as narrative voice, wielding the power of the pen, and documenting hi/story from downstairs, as in *Pamela or Virtue Rewarded, Wuthering Heights*, *The Moonstone*, *The Turn of the Screw*. Robbins states that "Servants speak on behalf of the family, its past, its continuity over the generations" – and the continuity of culture, at large, we might add – while, at the same time, telling "the story of their own exclusion" (112).

Significantly, according to *Webster's Dictionary*, the word "family" derives from "familia," which denotes, among other things, "servants of a household," and a "household including [. . .] the servants [. . .] the head of the household and all persons in it related to him by blood or marriage". According to this definition, servants are members of their employer's household, that is, they belong to the families they serve, yet must suffer to be treated as foster-children in the house as well as culture, at large. Performing all kinds of supposedly ignoble work for others – from dusting, cleaning the toilets, washing the dirty linen, to killing the mice and vermin – they cause horror and disgust in the gentlefolk, who desire to live in a beautiful and idle world of their own, and servants are thus exiled. We might note here that the artist was once abhorred for the same reasons. Before the emergence of the romantic concept of the independent creative artist, there prevailed the notion of the craftsman or artisan, who was a manual labourer in dirty overalls – this applied, in particular, to the painter and sculptor – working for a master, that is, a patron or commissioner. Physical labour and dependence on a master were, thus, once again, read as signs of inferiority. Historically, servants were – and still are – also considered to reveal innate depravity; employers traditionally raised complaints about their dishonesty, drunkenness, laziness and sexual looseness. They were thought to be utterly dependant on a wise master, who, like a father, would guide them with benevolence, yet also severity if they should prove naughty. The scriptures were quoted in order to argue that God decreed that servants are born to serve their masters. Dawes refers to religion as a "form of propaganda, or indoctrination to keep the lower orders in their place" (119). Did not the bible present Christ as the loyal servant, who patiently bore his cross? Servants were thus expected to remain invisible in the odd spaces of the house: the dark and ill-ventilated back corridors, the attic and cellar. Upstairs and downstairs was usually separated by a door, on one side of which was a crystal knob and, on the other, a humble gunmetal knob. Employers would also usually expect their servants to wear a black uniform to reinforce the lines of demarcation between master and servant (Horn 28). However, living under the same roof, meant a constant overstepping of the boundaries, an intimacy that encouraged servants and, in particular, the nearly equally disempowered children of the genteel house, to enter into surrogate-parent and child relationships or become surrogate siblings or even lovers.

In Angela Carter's short-story, "The Fall River Axe Murders" (1985), the servant, once again, figures as an exclusion, an absence, being reduced to serving hands roughened and reddened by work that ultimately bear the stigmata of the untouchable. Yet Carter also presents these hands as an object of desire in a culture of unproductive idleness and ultimately as the all-powerful hands of fate.

The short-story is a rewriting of the notorious historical Lizzie Borden case of alleged patricide and matricide in 1892, in puritan Massachusetts and in it Carter presents the Irish servant, Bridget, as a partner-in-crime to Lizzie Borden, the daughter of the house. This case, which ultimately exposed the home as a middle-class hell, is summarised in *Benét's Reader's Encyclopedia* – yet no mention is made of the servant. In fact, the 26-year-old maid, who had joined the Borden household several years ago, in 1889, was also suspected of murder, or at least, of entering into complicity with Lizzie, the oppressed female and – irrespective of her being thirty-two – child. One theory has it that Bridget was ordered by Mrs. Borden to wash the windows on the hottest day of that summer and just went crazy (Radin, cited in Aiuto). Another theory states that it was she who did away with the murder weapon, the hatchet, and Lizzie's bloodstained dress (Pearson, cited in Aiuto). What Carter does with these theories is to expand them in order to fill in what is missing: she moves from *what* happened to *why*. The house she presents us is a troubled one, her fiction being an example of "domestic horror," as Gina Wisker notes, related to Gothic literature with its claustrophobic domestic interiors of dark secrets, crimes, "patriarchal tyrannies and revenge" (120). Indeed, the narrator refers to the Borden house as "Bluebeard's castle" (118), and so we are prepared for skeletons in the closet.

As a servant, a female, an Irish immigrant and a catholic, Bridget proves to be four times removed from the centre of power. In fact, old Borden, the master of the house "owns" her by "contract" (104). All the inmates of the Borden house merit a physical body; among them, it proves only the servant who is reduced to a "rough-and-ready hand in the kitchen," (112) as indicative of her displacement. Yet, on the other hand, this hand also exercises great power. Robbins persuasively argues that a servant's coarse hand also showed "the signs of work accomplished, productive value signified and stored up in the hand's strength, size, redness, dirt" (20). Lizzie and her sister are said to be "staring vacantly into space," as they have all the time on their hands and are tortured by such involuntary idleness and parasitism in a patriarchal culture. Bridget's hands that produce plenty – boiled fish, cornmeal mush, Indian pudding, johnnycakes, cookies" (112) – are the only moving and productive things in a world of torturing silence and stasis that eventually unhinges Lizzie's and her sister's minds. Lizzie's only relief from "Stillness, mortal stillness" (106) lies in consumption. The check-book of her father provides her with luxurious clothes, yet with no occasion to wear them; it buys her a ticket to Europe and allows her to write checks for the poor. Her idle and obese step-mother Abbey, on the other hand, "continuously stuffs herself" (112) with the food the servant produces to fill the emptiness in her life. Yet her obese body defines such consumption as sickening. Bridget, the only active agent among these women, is, however, enslaved to a mechanical pattern of labour, set off by the "metallic clang" of her alarm clock that sounds its alarm at six o'clock every morning, shortly after, one by one, all the factory hooters begin to blare. The domestic servant is thus identified with the factory worker, who is imprisoned in a mechanical routine at the assembly line – and has, in fact, become a part of the machinery and material for capitalist exploitation. Still worse, Bridget's labour actually perpetuates the system and machinery that exploits her. The strong, angry, bitter and sarcastic narrative voice in the story, however, does not dwell on this interesting phenomenon – the victim's collaboration with her victimiser – but insists on identifying the servant as victim and the patriarch as victimiser. The "metallic clang" of her alarm clock also links Bridget with old Borden's safe, "that featureless block of black iron" (108). It is, "a slaughtering block or an altar" (108), on which the patriarch, "truffling for money like a pig" (104), in homage to the puritan notion of the elect as distinguished by material riches, has sacrificed the servant.

Bridget's austere and small room upstairs proves emblematic of her dispossession as a servant, reducing her to a blank space or void in a patriarchal world. Her bed is made of cold iron, her sheet very thin and no fire will keep it warm, even in the coldest winter. Here "A banged tin trunk at the foot of the bed holds all Bridget's worldly possessions" (106). The trunk thus constitutes another symbol of dispossession, the fact that it happens to be placed at the foot of the bed also indicating the servant's place at the bottom of a hierarchical culture. That her bed be made of iron, her trunk of tin once again point to her reduction to a soulless machine repeating a mechanical pattern of labour.

The servant emerges, in the face of such oppression, as a split character. On the one hand, Bridget has been religiously instructed to endure great affliction in imitation of Jesus Christ. Her education by nuns, her rosary and print of Virgin Mary, all point to the function of religion as an instrument of oppression. She has also been taught by the nuns to sleep on her back, so that the undertaker will have little trouble in shifting her body into the coffin, should she die in her sleep. She is thus once again displaced, as she has already resigned herself – body and soul – to the hereafter, rather than living in the here and now. It proves significant in this context that old Borden was, in the past, a caretaker, who, so the rumour went, cut off the feet of the corpse, should the coffin prove too small. Bridget is consequently also linked with these mutilated corpses. The reader is told that "she is a good girl on the whole," but "her temper proves sometimes uncertain and then she will talk back to the missus" (106). Despite her occasional rebellion, however, Bridget never dares to talk back to the patriarch himself, and, through her obedient drudgery, keeps the patriarchal machinery going – until the alarm clock inside her goes off and turns her, like Lizzie, into an "angel of death" (121).

Indeed, prior to Bridget's entering into service, a thief, an intruder from the outside world, is supposed to have broken into the Borden house, in the absence of Mr. and Mrs. Borden. This circumstance surely calls for suspicion: the servant might very well have refused to remain offstage any longer and emerged from the periphery to demand entry into the house and world of her social betters – if need be, through force. Robbins draws attention to the servant's claim to kinship as a popular motif in English literature (120). Again, it is "While she snatches a few moments rest upstairs, [that] all hell will be let loose, downstairs" (106), that is, that Lizzie will strike against the patriarch and his wife – once again a suspicious circumstance suggestive of Bridget's complicity in the crime. And again a conspicuous inversion strikes the reader's attention: the servant goes upstairs, while the crime against the employer and his wife is committed downstairs. Upstairs and downstairs carry a strong suggestion of the power position, and curiously enough, Bridget now rests, that is, claims genteel leisure for herself, upstairs, this circumstance suggesting that it is now she who occupies a powerful position. Her solidarity and complicity with Lizzie is further suggested by her refusal to cook Lizzie's much beloved pigeons, which old Borden, tired of their cooing, has killed with the hatchet. The narrative voice recounts that "Bridget the servant girl put her foot down, at that: what?! Make a pie out of Miss Lizzie's beloved turtledoves? Jesus Mary and Joseph!!!" (120). On the other hand, her words are merely an extended echo of Mrs. Borden's order that she cook the pigeons for a pie, which implies the power relation between them, her words, moreover, possessing authority only through her appeal to the authority of religion. Again, the absence of quotation marks that should have marked her direct speech undermines its authenticity and appeal.

Despite the fact that, in the story, the crimes are clearly committed by Lizzie, when presented in the very act of committing them, her presence and that of Bridget merge into one. It could just as well have been the servant who strikes back against her victimisers. Bridget, who dished out twice-cooked fish on a hot day has already, in her absence, been held responsible by Miss Russell, a friend of Lizzie, for food poisoning in the family. Robbins refers to Albert Memmi, who, in turn, quotes Octave Mirbeau, who evokes the idea of the cook holding the life of his master in his hands – a pinch of arsenic instead of salt – and draws attention to this "combination of apparent irrationality with absolute power" (141). Robbins goes on to argue that this combination explains "why so much badinage about murder is overhung with the notion of the servant as Fate, at once avenging and arbitrary" (141). The reader should remember that Bridget's temper has already been said to be uncertain. Again, Horn quotes Charles Greville, who states that a crime committed by a servant against his employer, had "'frightened all London out of its wits. Visionary servants and air-drawn razors or carving knives dance before everybody's imagination and half the world go to sleep expecting to have their throats cut before morning'" (145). The dispossessed servant is thus, paradoxically, at the same time, Fate itself, looming vengefully over the house of his/her employer.

Indeed, when Lizzie suggests that someone has put poison in the milk or the ice, Miss Russell replies that Bridget is always already up and about when the milk man or ice man comes, implying that no such act could have been committed unobserved. Her remark, however, also reinforces the notion of the servant's association with the crime and Fate. Are not her culinary skills, her feeding of Mrs Borden's obese body, indeed, indirect murder? The servant as criminal – this suggestion is also strengthened by the very nature of the burglary that takes place some time before the murder. Lizzie, after a somnambulist trance – and she experiences many "odd lapses of behaviour" (115), as a consequence of living in a sickening home and culture – finds herself at the scene of the crime, dressed only in a corset, a powerful emblem of incarceration, and remembering nothing. We are familiar enough with Freud to take Carter's hint – that she is the supposed intruder or dark man. The act of stealing her step-mother's jewellery identifies Lizzie with the servant against whom is traditionally levelled the accusation of stealing things in the house. In her father's forbidden room, she pockets a row of her father's dollar bills and tries to force open his safe, which as noted above, is presented as an altar or slaughtering block. Money has made old Borden the owner of the women in the house, including the paid female servant. Intruding into his dressing room, Lizzie then assaults his funeral coat, thereby combating his power to doom people to a state of obscurity or literal death. We have already noted Bridget's association with the coffin and old Borden's accumulation of money as an undertaker. And Lizzie's attack continues: her smashing of the flour crock and treacle crock and pieces of furniture also indicates the servant's disownment of her role as keeper of an exploitative order. She has straightened out the patriarch's house, cleaned and polished his pots and pans and oiled his machinery, yet now spreads havoc, turning upside down his world and crippling discourse. Shitting and pissing on the Bordens's matrimonial bed, Lizzie performs the natural functions of the body, which are so abhorred in a genteel, over-cultivated, puritan world, bent on crucifying the body. Committing these acts she also represents the servant, who is traditionally associated with primitiveness, sweat, filth and contamination. Again, that this rebellion be signified through the body rather than speech also suggests the speechlessness of the servant, who must curb her tongue in front of her betters. Yet Lizzie also writes obscenities on the parlour window with a soap of cake, which evokes the idea of the servant as spreading contamination rather than cleaning the house. That Lizzie should write the message on the window might also be interpreted as the unobtrusive servant's desperate attempt to render herself visible to a slighting world. Finally, towards the very end of the story,

Bridget's alarm clock is about to sound its alarm, to announce the beginning of the fatal day. The metallic clang of this clock is not only once again an echo of the hooting of the factories, but its mechanism is interwoven with the machinery of Lizzie's body, "the nerves and muscles of this complicated mechanism won't relax, just won't relax, she is all twang, all tension" (121). The clock – or bomb – that will end, indeed, dynamite the intolerable oppressive stasis in the house – and outside it – is thus ticking inside both the servant and the daughter of the employer as well as the industrial workers.

Once again, the servant occupies a seemingly peripheral position in the story, her fury and insurrection being acted out by another estranged element of culture, yet Carter persistently evokes her presence – even if only through identification or implication – indeed, presents her, "the servant," to conclude with Robbins's words, "as Fate, at once avenging and arbitrary" (141).

Works Cited

Aiuto, Russell. "Lizzie Borden: Theories." *Court TV's Crime Library: Criminal Minds and Methods.* 12 July 2005. 18 July 2005 <http://www.crimelibrary.com/notorious_murders/famous/borden/theories_6.html?sect=7>.

Benét, William Rose, ed. *Benét's Reader's Encyclopedia.* 3rd ed.New York: Harper and Row,1987.

Carter, Angela. "The Fall River Axe Murders." *Black Venus.* 1985. London: Picador, 1986. 103-121.

Dawes, Frank. *Not In Front Of The Servants: Domestic Service in England, 1850-1939.* London: Wayland, 1973.

Horn, Pamela. *The Rise and Fall of the Victorian Servant.* New York: St. Martin's, 1975.

Pearson, Edmund. *The Trial Book of Lizzie Borden.* New York: Doubleday, 1937.

Radin, Edward D. *Lizzie Borden, The Untold Story.* New York: Simon and Schuster, 1961.

Robbins, Bruce. *The Servant's Hand: English Fiction From Below.* New York: Columbia UP, 1986.

Said, Edward W. *Culture and Imperialism.* London: Vintage, 1994.

Webster's Third New International Dictionary Of The English Language, Unabridged. Springfield, Massachusetts: G. and C. Merriam, 1966.

Wisker, Gina. "Revenge of the Living Doll: Angela Carter's Horror Writing." *The Infernal Desires of Angela Carter: Fiction, Femininity, Feminism.* Ed. Joseph Bristow and Trev Lynn Broughton. London: Longman, 1997.

Beyond Gender: Enabling Abuses of Power in Angela Carter and Margaret Atwood

Gillian M. E. Alban
Boğaziçi University

Abstract: Angela Carter's interpretation of the Marquis de Sade shows that women may master in the sexual game if they wish to, as seen with his Juliette, and that characters like his Justine actually enable their own victimization. Carter's and Margaret Atwood's fictional examples similarly demonstrate how frequently the victimizers are enabled by the passivity of their victims, who allow their masters to manipulate them through their own abject behaviour.

Under patriarchy the woman lies beneath the man, playing the sexual game according to male rules and expressing herself in his language. However, is woman always a victim without recourse, is man absolutely the master, or are there times when this myth is a convenient excuse for blaming men for female disempowerment? The work of two feminist writers, Angela Carter and Margaret Atwood, picking their way through the minefield of sexual relations, suggests that the situation is more complex than to sweepingly condemn patriarchy, which, by any other name, would still smell as bad. They expose the frequent complicity of women in their own victimization, suggesting that women should throw off their chains themselves, not allowing themselves to be enfeebled by abuses of power.

Angela Carter's non-fiction work of 1979, *The Sadeian Woman: An Exercise in Cultural History*, presents a radical analysis of power relations in sexual terms, through her reading of the Marquis de Sade. She shows Sade's description of two sisters who exist in a dialectic with each other, where "[t]he innocent Justine is punished by a law she believes is just; the crime-soiled Juliette is rewarded because she undermines the notion of justice on which the law is allegedly based" (103). As a result Carter with Sade reaches the surprising conclusion that when women are prepared to be sexually and morally free, they may exercise power, if they are prepared to abandon their moral scruples in learning the knack of this ruthless game. She suggests that beyond gender, power is in the hands of those who are willing to use it. Traditionally this tends to be the higher class who controls resources, and the male gender; however there is no necessity that this should be the case.

Carter starts with the sexual graffiti of probe and fringed hole, which suggests that "man proposes and woman is disposed of" (6), man is the positive exclamation mark, and woman negative, with nothing but zero between her legs. Following this archetypal view, Freud concludes that "anatomy is destiny" (4). However, Carter's analysis of Sade goes beyond this cliché to suggest that one may often choose one's sexual role, deciding to be mistress rather than allowing oneself to be victim. This requires "a world of absolute sexual license for all the genders" (19). In such a Sadeian world, the infliction of pain or the exercise of power is as significant as sexual gratification. Beyond the biological sex of the participants, male comes to "mean tyrannous and female means martyrised" (24). She cites Sade's liberating manifesto of pornography for women: "Charming sex, you will be free: just as men do, you shall enjoy all the pleasures that Nature makes your duty, do not withhold yourself from one. Must the more divine half of mankind be kept in chains by the others [sic]? Ah, break those bonds: nature wills it" (*Philosophy in the Bedroom*, qtd. in *Sadeian* 37). This is possible in his reductive view of sex as mechanical sensation, a serial excitement of the nerves, "mouth against cunt, cock in anus, tongue on testicles, finger on clitoris" (145); a merry-go-round of kinetic sexuality with no relation to the reciprocity of love, but one allowing the participants a variety of roles, not limited to the position normally ascribed by their physical sex. Here the phallus is reduced to a mechanical device, war instrument, or snake, discharging venom (72), and with the dildo at their disposal, women may master in the sexual act just as well as men do. This view of sex as a variable activity certainly makes it contemporary, beyond a limited heterosexuality.

Carter demonstrates this idea with her readings of Sade's Justine and Juliette, women who take opposing roles within the sexual game, as martyr or master. The masochist Justine cannot learn survival, and persists in locating her virtue in her genitalia (47). This traditional morality of hers taught by patriarchy enables men to subdue women and their offspring through control of their sexual behaviour, requiring female chastity in order to know the paternity of the resulting offspring; of course the only certain parents of children are their mothers. In the position of many stories' heroines, Justine maintains her chastity through repeated savage rapes only by her persistent reluctance and frigidity, thus she comes to define her existence through suffering (75). The perennial victim, she not only invites and causes her own suffering, but she also implicates anyone involved with her. Because she has internalised the master's laws and morality, she is incapable of resisting even to help a fellow victim caught with her in suffering. So while running away with a letter appealing for help and caught by Gernande, she allows him to read this letter and offers herself to him for punishment even before he accuses her, thus reaffirming him in his master status. She thereby causes the death of the mother who had trusted her to save her life (53). Utterly trapped in her role of victim, her obedience invites the violence which she consequently always receives. Evil triumphs over her, and the only limitation to its success is its inability to seduce her into any enjoyment of the acts which she is endlessly forced to undergo.

Carter suggests that "Justine's negative capability for virtue becomes an involuntary affirmation of the humanism that the world in which she lives denies, even if not an affirmation of her own positive humanity, for that exists only by accident" (56). She connects such passive behaviour with screen icons like Marilyn Monroe or Mae West: "Saint Justine becomes the patroness of the screen heroine" (60), where "[f]emale virtue was equated with frigidity and a woman's morality with her sexual practice" (62). Such a woman victim to the Monroe syndrome will sell the image of her flesh rather than its reality, in a market where she does not set the price on her own allure. She passively retains a theoretical virginity, however frequently eyes rape her (67). Caught in this role as zombie or imaginary prostitute, she is not the one to solicit or desire, but rather the prey whom men would rather have slept with than would prefer to sleep with. Citing Monroe's agent's words in 1946: "'I have a call for a light blonde, honey or platinum,' [she suggests that] in this world, women may be ordered like steaks, well-done, medium rare, bloody" (65). This passivity often leads such perfectly passive Monroes to their own death (76-77). In her novel *The Passion of New Eve* Carter creates a film beauty, Tristessa, as exemplar of this Monroe syndrome. The secret of this gorgeous woman, the ultimate beauty, is that she is a man in drag, and has "made himself the shrine of his own desires" (128-129). In this example Carter illustrates the emptiness of female beautification, which creates a mirror image of beauty simply for the eyes of another.

Carter demonstrates her theory of victimization of the masochistic Justine in this novel, *The Passion of New Eve*. The chauvinistic Evelyn has been captured and punished by the Mothers, who under the scalpel recreate him as a perfect woman, Eve. First they get Evelyn to ejaculate, and then they plan to impregnate Eve with his/her own sperm, creating a new race and rejuvenating the world (77). Eve escapes before this impregnation occurs, but she is almost immediately captured by Zero, who incorporates this gorgeous, *Playboy* centre fold woman, into his private harem. Evelyn does not consent to this transaction, and temporarily remains a helpless victim; this is the inescapable victimization which I will discuss later in this paper. What Carter illustrates here, before Eve again escapes, is the complicity of the women of his harem in his brutalization of them. He rapes Eve in front of the seven other wives, and when he makes this newest member his chief wife, the others go for her with a broken plate, "teeth and claws" (89), jealous of her usurpation of their place in his bed. Him they have allowed to appropriate the product of their labour, when they return to him freely with their hard earned money "peddling their asses in Los Angeles" (98). They also allow him to silence them, not allowing them speech, so they communicate in a series of bestial grunts, only whispering when out of his earshot. When Eve tries to explain the situation in the outside world to them, they tell her she "would understand everything in Zero's good time and, besides, [she] shouldn't be talking, anyway, since it was against Zero's law" (99). He treats them as lower than his pigs, amongst whose excrement they live and whom they midwife through their births, and lower than his dog, Cain, who joins him in bed for breakfast after the wife of the previous night is kicked out to serve with the others. The women have swallowed his theory that his sacred fluid is "the balm of Gilead or one true restorative" (92) which he offers them freely, although as Eve observes, these fertile women, some of them mothers of children, are now all sterile with Zero. His entire obsession is with the beautiful Tristessa, or Dyke, whom he believes to have sterilised him since he experienced a sharp pain in the balls while watching her tabloid image, and he is determined to regain his own procreativity by ravishing and destroying her, in revenge for her placing him under this supposed curse. This harem lives subject to his every whim with full complicity in their thralldom to this empty superman follower of Nietzsche and Wagner.

After showing us the self-made victim, Carter goes on to show us the opposite case, Justin's sister Juliette, who learns her modus operandi in the brothel, aligning herself with the powerful, and giving as good as she gets in any situation. Aggrandizing her power and wealth through her mastery of others by causing them suffering, she is driven by two motives; the financial profit which empowers her, and her own libidinal gratification (*Sadeian* 79). To escape persecution she sleeps with the law makers, who extend their Mafia-like protection to her lawlessness (80). Having come through the brothel which leaves saleable women at the mercy of their customers' caprices, her logic is to turn to theft, after Proudhon, for if property is theft, the morality of the outlaw teaches one to redistribute what has been wrongly taken from one (83). In this world Juliette becomes the Nietzschean superwoman herself, transcending the putative impotence of her gender, for Sade shows feminine impotence as a "quality of the poor, regardless of sex" (86). In a world of finite power, any privilege implies tyranny, and the freedom of one takes away that of another (89). We see Juliette in an encounter with her supposedly dead father who weeps to find her; she breaks all taboos when she "seduces him, is impregnated by him, murders him and subsequently aborts his child; so she rids herself of the spectre of his paternal authority over her by a systematic series of ritual transgressions" (92). This monstrous woman glories in her crimes, following the dictum of looking after Number One (101); her life style "living proof that biology is not destiny, since biology may be so easily emended" (104). Carter categorizes Juliette as the show girl who controls her own currency, "the *Cosmopolitan* girl – hard, bright, dazzling, meretricious. She plays to win, this one; she knows the score. Her femininity is part of the armoury of self-interest" (102).

This thesis of mastery regardless of gender, with voluntary victimization to such mastery, can be illustrated in Margaret Atwood's *The Robber Bride,* where we see that beyond gender, an unscrupulous female enemy is as fatal as any male one to her female victims, and in this case there is no wrath like that of a woman's. In this fictional world, the significant characters are all female, and all the victims authorize the robber bride to exert power over them. Like Justine, they allow her entry into their lives and permit her to terrorize them. They all actually love men, however the men they desire are all shown as subordinate to the struggles between the women. The tricks and deceptions of the ruthless Zenia against her three female victims superficially suggest that it could be hard to defend oneself against such a concerted and ruthless attack. However, a closer reading reveals that each woman undermines her own defences against the enemy, feeding masochistically into her savagery. As Atwood says: "people like Zenia can never step through your doorway, can never enter and entangle themselves in your life, unless you invite them. There has to be a recognition, an offer of hospitality, a word of greeting" (134-135), as Lucie Armitt analyses in her study of the vampire in Atwood and others.

Tony is a studious intellectual, and Zenia slips across her defences by being the first to take her seriously. Tony is betrayed into her private palindromic speech in confessing her interest in "raw" or "war" (152) when Zenia asks her a serious question. This brings the alluring Zenia straight under lonely Tony's defences, over her Rubicon. Once on her side, Zenia entraps her by asking her for help with a term paper, and then later suggesting she must confess their plagiarism to the professor, from whom Tony is hoping for a job, at the same time asking for a substantial cheque to help her and West, the only man Tony has ever been close to. Tony helplessly hands over money many times, and Zenia takes up with and drops West at will, reappearing occasionally to repeat her blackmail, while Tony is disempowered emotionally, convinced of West's vulnerability to Zenia's overtures. Thus Tony lives in the uncertainty of losing

West whenever Zenia desires him. She actually reluctantly admires Zenia for her skill in breaking up Tony's marriage, by exposing her own supposed vulnerability to West, who pities this savage wolf (216).

Tony gets wise to Zenia, but Charis is less acute, although her boyfriend Billy, a draft dodger, actually warns her of Zenia's rapacity and duplicity. Zenia's tactic this time is to be fatally sick with cancer, and as she looks ghastly, and arrives saying West has kicked her out, empathetic Charis is happy to look after her, even confiding to Zenia that Billy is a draft dodger. The unhealthy looking Zenia easily makes Charis feel guilty about her health and ability to conceive, and Charis' only defence is her doppelgänger self Karen, who, repeatedly abused by her uncle in childhood, has learnt the self-defensive trick of leaving her body. This other self is the one with which she once made love passionately to Billy, totally out of her own frigid character, and she remains permanently uncertain whether the child then conceived is hers, or whether she was possessed by Zenia during this act. Billy soon leaves after an affair with Zenia, probably having been arrested as a draft dodger. The girls Charis, Tony and Roz establish an anti-Zenia sorority. Tony suggests that Billy is simply shooting practice for Zenia, who "likes breaking and entering, she likes taking things that aren't hers. Billy for her, like West before, was just target practice. She probably has a row of men's dicks nailed to her wall, like stuffed animal heads" (335). After two victories, any further achievement of Zenia seems incredible to the reader.

However, forewarned is not forearmed for Roz, a sharp executive woman who is still naive enough to get entangled with Zenia after her friends' suffering at her hands. Zenia turns up as a researching waitress, with a beautifully reconstructed body, ready for the next kill. Her tactic is her bait of information on Roz's enigmatic migrant father who mysteriously became rich after the war. The intelligent Roz falls for this because of her ethnic insecurity concerning her family roots. So it is Roz who invites Zenia in, to home, firm, husband and all, and soon Zenia ditches him, running off with $50,000. Mitch returns to Roz as he does after affairs, the shadow of his former self, his soul sucked out by Zenia's merciless talons, but this time Roz refuses his pleas, keeping him away from home and children. The three women heave a sigh of relief at Zenia's fake death, but Mitch, still under her aura, accidentally on purpose dies in a boating incident in his utter zombie-like helplessness, while Zenia of course is still alive.

Thus Atwood in this novel demonstrates that the ability to use power against victims is independent of gender, intelligence, instinct, or street cred. A determined predator will smell out any chink in your defences through which to attack, insidiously invade your life and destroy you, enabled by your own weakness against them, which actually invites their attack. Thus she, together with Carter, argues that the rapacious predator is empowered by her victims, who invite her attack even when they know her dirty tactics, which they are unable to make use of themselves.

Carter admits exceptions to this logic of consent to violence, of either gender, as she says, "But if any of the Sadeian victims seem to incite their masters to violence by tacitly accepting their right to administer it, let us not make too much of this apparent complicity. There is no defence at all against absolute tyranny" (*Sadeian* 139). This is the situation that Atwood shows us in *The Handmaid's Tale*, a dystopia of oppression possible if a regime wished to exclude one sex entirely from the active working of its society. Overnight anyone with F on their ID could find themselves without job, money, or legal status, with one touch of the computer. Female roles in this society are divided between housekeeping, concubines, and subservient wives, where women are even forbidden written language, given pictures to do the shopping, almost as bad as the lack of language in Zero's harem. Other than physical labour, their major role is as the wombs of the next generation. Fertile women who have lost status through remarriage or sexual impropriety are made handmaids and joined with infertile older wives of status, in a recreation of the threesome in bed recounted in *Genesis*, when Rachel begged Jacob to give her a child through her handmaid Bilhah. One must bear a child in this society in order to survive, however the children born of these threesome liaisons are removed from their mother within minutes of the birth, and she is moved on to another grouping after a basic period of lactation. The frightening thing about Atwood's dystopia is that it illustrates the awful possibilities for women in a world where patriarchal religions still discriminate against women, especially morally and sexually. It suggests how powerless one could be to remove such a system were it once established. Carter reasons that mythologizing about woman's procreativity guarantees no status for woman. "Because she is the channel of life, woman as mythic mother lives at one remove from life. A woman who defines herself through her fertility has no other option" (*Sadeian* 107). Against a determined tyranny such as shown in this nightmare dystopia there could be little recourse.

Such extreme dictatorial situations excepted, both Carter and Atwood show how frequently it is the complicity of the victim which enables the master or mistress to exercise their power. Of course one needs rather a strong stomach to be able to go to the lengths of the savagery of Juliette, or even worse Eugénie, who takes upon herself the desecration of her own mother, which makes ghastly reading, beyond what I have described here. But certainly Carter suggests that if one is ruthless and determined enough, one may find the world beneath one's feet, irrespective of gender, and therefore that gender does not have the archetypal power we generally ascribe it. Of course this is no theory for the squeamish, for Sadeian mastery is exercised immorally and ruthlessly. It is tempting to think of women as still the oppressed sex, and there are situations of female victimisation, which are at times impossible to escape. Exercise of brute power by either sex is immoral, but often its victims need to resist oppression, instead of sweepingly accusing patriarchy, when it may still be possible to grasp power back from this master. It is often up to the victim, female or otherwise, to actively grasp power over their own life.

Works Cited

Armitt, Lucie. *Contemporary Women's Fiction and the Fantastic*. Basingstoke: Palgrave, 2000.

Atwood, Margaret. *The Handmaid's Tale*. New York: Fawcett Crest, 1985.

---. *The Robber Bride*. London: Virago, 1993.

Carter, Angela. *The Passion of New Eve*. London: Virago, 1977.

---. *The Sadeian Woman: An Exercise in Cultural History*. London: Virago, 1979.

Sade, Donatien-Alphonse-François, Marquis de. *The Complete Justine, Philosophy in the Bedroom, and other Writings*. Trans. Richard Seaver and Austryn Wainhouse. New York: Grove, 1965.

The Victims of Common Passion: The Aesthete as Victim from Henry James to Alan Hollinghurst's *The Line of Beauty*

Murat Seçkin
Istanbul University

Abstract: This paper traces the aesthete figure in the last century and examines the victim status it has sustained in different cultural and economic conditions. Colm Toibin's book *The Master* and Alan Hollinghurst's *The Line of Beauty* are read against the historical and social contexts for they give clues about the place of the aesthete in modern society. Both novels use Henry James as their starting point to show the anti-aesthetic and homophobic nature of contemporary cultures and delineate the nature of creating victims and victimizers.

Our age is said to be more tolerant towards the victims of old prejudices; yet today we see certain groups and institutions victimizing a group or other individuals because they cannot tolerate an individual intellect making choices or some groups' desire to be different from what the corporate business wishes in the global world order.

The artist figure who carried the moniker "the aesthete" has been an object of dislike or even hatred in particular societies. Especially in the English-speaking world, Puritans and the puritanical hegemony always disliked a person who basically deals with a concept like beauty for they deemed it useless, uneconomical, immoral, and even unlawful. The English-speaking world's love of victimizing the aesthete during the last two centuries is the area I will dwell on in this paper. My title comes from Henry James; he has uttered the words "the victims of common passion should sometimes exchange a look" in a letter to a fellow aesthete, John Addington Symonds, in 1884 (Robb 148). Of course, "the common passion" does not refer to love of beauty or to an aesthetic ideal directly. Neither does it carry homosexual overtones, as we would like to hear in the twenty-first century. Their common passion is for Italy and all it represents; so we can conclude that at least James may imply that his (and Symonds') love of Italy may be construed to mean love of beauty. But we also know that these two men were "gay," if we may use this anachronistic word, and there is most certainly an undertone of a "secret" shared in the furtive glance. It was a secret because it was illegal. We know that it is common to use euphemisms like Hellenism for homosexual leanings because it is not only socially but legally impossible to have any. Social structures of the age punished the homosexual as well as the aesthete.

In the English speaking world, Henry James's popularity was unmatched in 2004: he was the subject matter of two of the novels short-listed for the Man Booker Prize in Britain. Alan Hollinghurst's novel *The Line of Beauty* eventually won it; and Colm Toibin's book *The Master* was selected one of the ten best books of 2004 by the *New York Times.* Both novels seem to indicate that there is continuity in England for creating the same victims now as certain hegemonic groups have done in the past.

We see at the beginning of the nineteenth century, poets at first, and later on other artists and intellectuals, define themselves as individuals who do not conform to the increasingly uniform, conservative, and conventional bourgeois society. After the French Revolution, we see that painters, writers, musicians no longer had a niche in society because no class felt any need for their productions or identified itself with their interests. "[The artist] must contrive to live without wage or settled income and therefore was unpractical and imprudent from necessity. [. . .] The bourgeois was [the] enemy [. . .] because he had an objection to the arts, and to the artist, as performing no useful function he could understand" (Gaunt 13). So the bourgeois establishment victimizes the artist as the alien or "the other." This is a simplistic portrait of the middle classes; yet it represents the crude sentiments of those classes rather well. The artist figures at first, in order to defend themselves, have created an imaginary locus called "Bohemia" for them to inure and to reject the conventional requirements of "staid, prudent, small-minded, tight-fisted, traders" and then seek refuge in the movement called "Art for Art's Sake" (Gaunt 11-18). The word "aesthete" was coined in the eighteenth century by German philosophers and it immediately gained a negative meaning in the nineteenth century: "Gwilt's *Encyclopedia of Architecture* criticizes [it as] 'a silly pedantic term,' and adds that it is 'one of the metaphysical and useless additions to nomenclature in the arts in which the German writers abound'" (Gaunt 19). This attack perfectly demonstrates the xenophobic nature of the middle-class attitude towards the arts, artists, and the Germans. The Philistine demonizes the aesthete and sees that figure to be an evil force that disturbs the peace of society which moves progressively towards a perfect future. And the emerging unionized working classes ironically join forces with their oppressors in their hatred towards the person who is thought to be their enemy, the aesthete.

In France, Théophile Gautier and Charles Baudelaire are considered to be the creators of the Aesthetic Movement. Naturally it travels to England and is domesticated there by artists familiar with the Continent, a place that is dangerous in the British mind by itself. The Pre-Raphaelite Brotherhood, Algernon Charles Swinburne, James Abbott McNeill Whistler and others are prominent figures of this movement in England. They have paved the way to the decadent Nineties that culminated in the greatest concerted attack on the movement.

In our minds, 1895 is a crucial year that has played an important part in our discussion: It was the time of great theatrical success for two of Oscar Wilde's plays (*An Ideal Husband* and *The Importance of Being Earnest*) as well as his trials and imprisonment for sodomy. Oscar Wilde is known by the public as the aesthete *par excellence.* The works of Wilde were perceived to be examples of "Art for Art's Sake," and it "was entirely foreign to Victorian England. That Art might go contrary to moral principles or leave them out of account seemed utterly outrageous – the distinction between sensuous perception and sensual indulgence dangerously slight" (Gaunt 24).

This statement by Gaunt may be criticized for its broad generalizations in bringing up a monolithic concept of uniform Victorian England, but we must realize that the popular press and other ideological apparatuses of the establishment were trying very hard to create a very standardized and uniform England. We observe that at the time the Aesthetic Movement degenerates rapidly into a creation of the popular press, rather than the individual artists who come together for a common purpose. The press uses them as objects of derision because the Philistines want to see them in that light. And the arbiters of middle-class morality and taste delight in feeding them a distorted aesthete figure. Oscar Wilde was caricatured in various media to be the most easily recognized "effeminate" man (Sinfield 59). Since the early 1880s, Wilde (and his fellow aesthetes) have been the object of scorn in *Punch* with the cartoons of George du Maurier (Ellmann 130). Gilbert and Sullivan's opera *Patience* openly criticizes Wilde and the aesthetic movement (Ellmann 129). For the middle class Philistines, the crime is the creation of a sort of art and literature they cannot easily understand and therefore they condemn the aesthetic movement and those men who adopt an aesthetic façade. But during the Oscar Wilde trials a much greater catastrophe transpires and the public realizes that some of these artists and aesthetes were practicing homosexuals.

The word homosexual is a neologism late in the nineteenth century and now (in retrospective) some of the figures we see in the Aesthetic movement are known to be secret homosexuals. They were secret because it was against the law of England to practice same-sex passion. It is the trials of Oscar Wilde that informed the public about the connection between the aesthete and homosexual (Sinfield 18).

In Colm Toibin's book *The Master*, we see Edmund Gosse informing his friend Henry James about the trials of Oscar Wilde and opining (like most of Wilde's friends) that he must leave England for France to avoid criminal punishment. We are told that the police and the prosecution are conducting a very thorough investigation on the illegal (that is to say homosexual) activities of others, and Gosse inquires very delicately whether there is any need for alarm in James's case. Gosse brings up the subject gently, and "poignantly poses – or almost poses the key question on James's sexual nature" (Canning). Gosse starts with the words,

> "It is advised, I think, that anyone who has been, as it were, compromised should arrange to travel as soon as possible. London is a large city and much can go on here quietly and secretly, but now the secrecy has been shattered." Henry

> stood up and went to the bookcase between the windows and studied the books. "I wonder if you, perhaps ..." Gosse began. "No." Henry turned sharply. "You do not wonder. There is nothing to wonder about." "Well that is a relief, if I may say so," Gosse said quietly, standing up. "Is that what you came here to ask?" Henry kept his eyes fixed on Gosse, his gaze direct and hostile enough to prevent any reply. (77)

The pathos of "There is nothing at all" is not only implicit in the fact that James has never dallied with rent boys or got involved with male brothels, but in the fact that he has had no sexual life at all. The "direct and hostile" gaze silences Gosse abruptly but the reader is in a quandary; we do not know what to make of James's refusal to acknowledge his sexuality. Is this a denial of his sexual being at the expense of art or is it a manifestation of James succumbing to the laws of homophobic society and suppressing his sexual side?

The Master paints a Henry James that devotes his life to art, or to write "about the conflict between the material life and the life of pure contemplation, the vicissitudes of human love and a life dedicated to higher happiness" (13). These are the words Toibin gives to James when he writes his failed play *Guy Domville*. James chooses a life dedicated to higher happiness and pure contemplation and these make him one of the most revered stylists of English letters. Yet we see the inherent sadness in his character, which has to suppress his homosexual desires and become the pet aesthete in the court of the British aristocracy.

Henry was in the company of these men because their wives wished him to be. The women liked his manners and his grey eyes and his American origin, but more than anything they enjoyed his way of listening, of drinking in every word, asking only pertinent questions, acknowledging by his gestures and replies the intelligence of his interlocutor (22).

He is an erudite, intelligent man-about-town who is adored by the women. The implicit text here is that these women seek him because he is so very different from the men they know. He is known to be the aesthete, the artist, the American, but these words do not sum him up entirely. He is also a repressed homosexual. As men and women are attracted to him socially, they patronize him because he is the sum total of all things they actually dislike. He is in the twilight zone of ambiguity where he is not the typical American or even the homosexual. Therefore Toibin's book succeeds for it shows Henry James as a victim who manages to be the ultimate aesthete. Adam Mars-Jones in his review of the book says that,

> The pillars of the narrative are failure, avoidance, renunciation and withdrawal. Unpromising quartet, but appropriate to a life without obvious eventfulness, and a work with a strong, negative dynamic, structured round the missed opportunity, the faulty choice, the golden bowl with its latent crack, the 'beast in the jungle' whose annihilating leap is delayed and delayed. (n.p.)

In Toibin's book, we see the art of Henry James expounded by a fictional biography and *The Master* comes close to be considered as a parallel masterpiece when juxtaposed with a James novel. We do not seek a happy ending for Henry James or his "outing." It never happened, yet we see the art created by a gay writer who tells us the pathos of being a victim in a homophobic society. By being a victim James has created his art and this story, in turn, makes Toibin's book.

Henry James seals himself up in his art, but the fall of Oscar Wilde has devastating effects on the Aesthetic Movement and the homosexuals. They went underground for twenty years. E. M. Forster had to suppress his novel *Maurice* and stopped writing novels altogether. After the Great War, the aesthete and homosexual emerged in their usual habitat, the public school and the Universities. During the twenties they seem to be thriving; but as W. H. Auden and Christopher Isherwood saw in the thirties, even their gay friends turned against them when they left England for the USA. After the sexual and social revolutions in the sixties, homosexuality was decriminalized, *Maurice* was finally published (in 1971), and all was thought to be going well.

Alan Hollinghurst's novel is the story of the openly gay and (suggestively named) Nick Guest who is writing his doctoral dissertation on Henry James at London University in the early eighties during the heyday of Margaret Thatcher. He comes down to London and becomes a lodger/resident/guest in the Notting Hill town-house of his Oxford friend Toby Fadden. The father Gerald is a recently elected Tory member of Parliament who adores the Iron Lady and the mother is a very rich Jewish woman.

Nick, "like one of Henry James's provincial innocents, is infatuated by a worldly and grand style" (Conradi n.p.); he is critical of the rich people around him yet he is fascinated by their wealth that has accumulated such beautiful objects like their little Gaugin in the master bedroom. He observes that, "Above the drawing-room fireplace there was a painting by Guardi, a capriccio of Venice in a gilt rococo frame; on the facing wall two large gilt-framed mirrors. Like his hero Henry James, Nick felt that he could 'stand a great deal of gilt'" (6). He is a real aesthete that only Oxford University can produce, even in the nineteen-eighties. He is well versed in painting, classical music, and naturally in literature. The Faddens immediately give him the honorary title of "our little aesthete."

The issue of being an aesthete and a gay man is still interrelated; when with the Faddens he visits Hawksewood, Lord Kessler's stately home, he is given the tour of the house by his bachelor host. Kessler might be gay as well, but it is Nick we see going into raptures about the contents of the house.

Lord Kessler himself took him off into the library, where the books were apparently less important than their bindings, which were as important as could be.

> The heavy gilding of the spines, seen through the fine gilt grilles of the carved and gilded bookcases, created a mood of minatory opulence [. . .] Lord Kessler opened a cage and took down a large volume: *Fables Choisies de La Fontaine*, bound in greeny-brown leather tooled and gilded with a riot of rococo fronds and tendrils. It was an imitation of nature that had triumphed as pure design and pure expense. (52)

It is interesting to note the number of times the words "gilded" and "gilt" are used in such a short passage. It also reads like the manifesto of the Aesthetic Movement with final words by Henry James. If the passage had ended with the words "an imitation of nature that had triumphed as pure design" only, it would have been formalism; but Hollinghurst, as a good student of James adds "and pure expense." The man who ordered the book in the court of Louis XV must have spent a fortune on it as well. In the rarefied atmosphere of Hawkeswood we see beauty in Victorian abundance; Kessler and his family achieved it through banking, and that is never forgotten in the universe of the book. But the name Hawkeswood suggests the place is supposed to be a sanctuary for wild (and predatory birds); however we read the history of "nature" in such a brief passage. The eighteenth-century formalized nature in the baroque and rococo styles (La Fontaine and the visual arts) and the Victorians built more gilded cages around it. The last two decades of the twentieth century made everything more commercialized and vulgar. Nick's love of beauty represents the young aesthete's bewilderment and fascination with the splendor around him but he is not mere purchaser but an appreciator. He is like Henry James who sees the vulgarity of display as well as the beauty of the things.

The aesthete as a gay man travels through life in the book both as a guest at the Faddens's and then as the lover of a very rich classmate of his. His lover, in true middle-eastern fashion, is a closeted gay man whose family hails from Lebanon and owns a food retailer chain. Together they use excessive amounts of cocaine, have promiscuous group sex, and publish an artsy magazine called *Ogee*. These are the things Wilde and Douglas might have done a hundred years ago. Our heroes have a project to make a film of Henry James's *Spoils of Peyton*. But instead of following James's advocacy for celibacy and scorn for material things like furniture and objects, they indulge in sex and buy everything around them. The eighties is a decade when some people felt that they existed to shop, have sex and consume conspicuously. The difference between them and earlier times is that Nick feels he is unthreatened by the police for his sexual practices and feels freer in general to pursue his aesthetic aims. Yet, an unexpected disaster awaits him around the corner.

The 1980s are a decade that can be named the Thatcher Years, and they are described best by greed and disease. The Conservative Party was fraught with financial scandals involving its politicians and businessmen and women. Gerald Fadden, in *The Line of Beauty* is a typical member of this regime and he was guilty of "a spot of creative accounting" (442). When the newspapers find out about his illegal financial dealings, they lay a siege around his house and turn his family's life into hell. They are greedy for copy that would sell their papers, and the dirtier the picture the happier they get. They learn about his mistress through the indiscretion of his severely manic depressive daughter Catherine. Catherine also reveals to the press that their "guest" Nick is gay and his lover Wani is dying of AIDS. These are the essential ingredients of a scandal for a few days in the press and they use them liberally.

On the one hand, Gerald Fadden's financial indiscretions lose him his ministerial portfolio. But his almost respectable "crime" does not really ruin him. He gets another directorship in the City and he is still eagerly expected to attend the wedding of the Duchess of Flintshire's son. Socially and economically he is saved after a minor skirmish. Nick, on the other hand, is kicked out of the house and family for being gay. The words used for him show us that not that much has changed since the vicious Marquess of Queensberry accused Oscar Wilde for being a "somdomite." Gerald's friend Barry Groom, the "multiple adulterer and ex-bankrupt" MP, puts all the blame for the financial scandal on Nick's presence in the house and questions Gerald for Nick's presence: "I mean, what's the little pansy doing here? Why have you got a little ponce hanging round your house the whole fucking time?" (476). What bothers Nick is not the rantings of such a bigot but the passivity of Gerald who is supposed to be his friend. He is victimized by disloyalty, betrayal, and finally eviction. He is the pansy, the faggot, the pouf and he might even have AIDS. For all the joy gays bring to the world, and all the beauty they create, they are still regarded as parasites because they cannot "breed themselves" (477). This Judeo-Christian bigotry that has survived for centuries is still flung at Nick.

I have tried to show in this paper that the aesthete and the gay are the victims of social bigotry. These two groups are often the same and they need not do anything to ponder about why they have been victimized because they are to be blamed for anything, especially for all the beauty they create and worship in the world. Both Toibin and Hollinghurst capture the homophobia that is inherent in the anti-aesthetic or anti-aesthete outlook of the bourgeoisie. They also give us scope for the understanding of the fine distinction between creating beauty and the economics of owning it. We see in their novels that each era finds a bugbear to victimize but the aesthete and the gay men and women seem to be common staples.

Works Cited

Canning, Richard. “What Henry Knew - But Never Did: The Master by Colm Toibin.” *Independent Online Edition* 19 March 2004. 20 July 2005 <http://www.independent.co.uk/>.

Conradi, Peter. “Art, and the Cruelty that Goes with It: *The Line of Beauty* by Alan Hollinghurst.” *Independent Online Edition* 11 April 2004 <http://www.independent.co.uk/>.

Ellmann, Richard. *Oscar Wilde*. London: Hamish Hamilton, 1987.

Gaunt, William. *The Aesthetic Adventure*. Harmondsworth: Penguin, 1957.

Hollinghurst, Alan. *The Line of Beauty*. Picador: London, 2004.

Mars-Jones, Adam. “In His Master’s Voice.” *Observer* 22 February 2004. 20 July 2005 <http://books.guardian.co.uk/reviews/generalfiction/0,,1154220,00.html>.

Robb, Graham. *Strangers: Homosexual Love in the Nineteenth Century*. Picador: London, 2003.

Sinfield, Alan. *The Wilde Century: Effeminacy, Oscar Wilde and the Queer Movement*. Cassel: London, 1994.

Toibin, Colm. *The Master*. Picador: London, 2004.

Metamorphoses of a Woman: Twentieth-Century Interpretations of *Medea*

Sema Bulutsuz
Istanbul University

Abstract: The twentieth century witnessed diverse rewritings of Euripides' *Medea*. A woman of extreme intelligence and passion, she has become the epitome of everything undesirable and unwelcome in a wife and mother up until our age, during which she was transformed into an all-purpose heroine. The post-Second-World-War *Medea* by Anouilh was promoting existentialist philosophy with its uncompromising heroine waging war against the whole world and questioning accepted ideas and attitudes on marriage, love, innocence, conformism, and responsibility. Later adaptations gradually became didactic and pedantic: Brendan Kennely's *Medea* was meant to be a comment on the Irish problem within a feminist-environmentalist framework with Medea and Jason as victim-victimiser and colonised-coloniser. Tony Harrison's erudite *Medea: A Sex-War Opera* was a brilliant and entertaining musical, yet shared the same tragic flaw: didacticism.

Tragedy was developed and used for the political, social and psychological moulding of the Athenian citizens, that is, *men*, of the fifth century. A Greek tragedy at its best is concise and indirect, yet able to touch the vital and eternal issues and problems of the world. It is attractive in the way political issues are intermingled with racial, familial, and gender issues and the way the eternal war between the sexes is subtly transformed into current political agenda with profound insights into the nature of main institutions such as family, democracy, state power, and religion.

One of the most complex characters of Greek tragedy as victim and victimiser, Medea embodies the so-called unpredictable, dangerous female psyche lurking in each woman. Yet no great writer could ignore the charm of her passionate revolt and the despicable injustice inflicted on her. Euripides' original re-writing of the story of the legendary Medea is so rich in its conscious and unconscious reverberations that the metamorphoses its heroine has since undergone manifest great variety from the existentialist or feminist heroine to the exploited female body, Mother Earth, and the Palestinian mother.

Euripides' Medea as the Athenian warrior

Euripides was one of the best writers to combine the traditional subject matter of tragedy, that is, myths of the fourteenth century BC, with the contemporary life of the polis. His *Medea* is striking with the code of honour of the Athenian ruling classes that resulted in the butchering of one's own children. In his rewriting of the story of a legendary woman, Euripides creates an extreme situation to oppose the aggressive militarist policies of the Athenian state, to warn Athenians about the oncoming war with Sparta, and to reiterate the old Athenian virtue of moderation by way of a woman who, as the daughter of a barbarian king, betrays her country and her father's house and kills her brother to help the Greek heroes and escape with Jason to the Greek world. She is a loving wife who kills a king to create a king out of her loser of a husband; a wife who is used, abused and exiled by the same husband; a mother who kills her sons instead of nurturing them; an intelligent woman who is feared and dreaded and ostracised by men; a foreigner, an exile, a homeless person, a wandering Jew.

Reasserting herself in both male and female spheres, in social and domestic affairs, she combines and challenges gender roles as well. She acts like a man and prefers the role of warrior to motherhood; yet she is also capable of sacrificing her life and comfort for her husband. Women were considered to be the natural enemy of civilization and the archenemy of the Athenian phallocracy. They were also associated with barbarians and other city states in war with the Athenian democracy. Hence as a "woman," a "barbarian," and a "witch," Medea was "the other" par excellence in fifth-century-Athens. Euripides' Medea stood for the most dangerous forces in Athens: the warmongers.

Yet today, it is impossible to use Medea as a threat for civilization or as evil incarnate. Writers of the post-colonial, post-feminist era trace hints scattered in Euripides' text to interpret Medea as the exploited body and intelligence of women, or as the land of a colonised, despoiled country. They put her "otherness" into use in diverse contexts. As the exploited barbarian, Medea became a symbol of the freedom fighter in the twentieth century. In Africa, Haiti, and Ireland, *Medea* was interpreted as the exploited who fight back (McDonald, "Medea" 302). Medea became black in performances of Hans Henny Jahnn (1926) and Agnes Straub (1933) as a reaction to racist and Nazi policies. In Heiner Müller's *Medeaspiel* (1974) and *Medeamaterial* (1982), Medea is exploited by Jason just as the coloniser exploits the colonised and man abuses the earth. It is now earth's turn to kill man, who has raped her body for years. Brendan Kennelly's Irish *Medea* (1988) and South African black *Demea* (1990) abandoned by the Dutch trekker Jason were later variations of this theme (McDonald, "Medea" 298).

Irish Medea as a political activist

Steve Wilmer points out that tragic characters such as Medea, Antigone, and Prometheus were all portrayed as victims of an unjust authority on the Irish stage. Spokespersons for civil disobedience, they were active transgressors rather than passive victims (2).

> Greek protagonists who have stood up to the state and taken action against the injustices imposed on them are attractive role-models for a beleaguered and oppressed people who are aware that their civil liberties have been severely curtailed. Ireland is at a point of transition. Writers in the south are wrestling with pluralistic values in opposition to the doctrinaire approach of the clergy. Writers in the north are hoping for a democratic post-colonial state while the province still remains under British military control.
>
> [. . .]
>
> The Greek tragedies have been used by Irish poets not so much to express tragedy as to express hope – a hope that comes out of years of tragedy. At the same time the Greek tragedies contain a warning – that pride, inflexibility, intran-

> sigence and extreme actions will only lead to more suffering. The dominant emotion expressed by many of the Irish poets is that of hope for social change, for a change of attitudes and for real peace in Northern Ireland. (5-6)

Brendan Kennely's *Medea* focuses on the exploitation of women by men and of Ireland by England (McDonald, "Medea" 304). Although Kennely tries to retain Euripides' method in combining contemporary issues with the universal strife between men and women, the resulting text sounds like agitprop material rather than drama. A comparison between the original speech of Medea on the predicament of women, which is enough in itself to speak for the women of today, and that of Kennely's Medea, evinces a major defect in most contemporary writers: what they want to emphasise is already contained and subtly expressed by the original and their childish and abortive reinterpretations can only spoil and diminish the originals:

> Of all creatures that have breath and sensation, we women are the most unfortunate. First at an exorbitant price we must buy a husband and take a master for our bodies. [. . .] The outcome of our life's striving hangs on this, whether we take a bad or a good husband. For divorce is discreditable for women and it is not possible to refuse wedlock. [. . .] If after we have spent great efforts on these tasks our husbands live with us without resenting the marriage yoke, our life is enviable. Otherwise, death is preferable. A man, whenever he is annoyed with the company of those in the house, goes elsewhere and thus rids his soul of its boredom (turning to some male friend or agemet). But we must fix our gaze on one person only. Men say that we live a life free from danger at home while they fight with the spear. How wrong they are! I would rather stand three times with a shield in battle than give birth once. (Euripides 317)

Men, the horny despots of our bodies,
sucking, fucking, licking, chewing, farting into our skin,
sitting on our faces, fingering our arses,
exploring our cunts, widening our thighs,
drawing the milk that gave the bastards life. (Kennely, qtd. in McDonald, "Medea" 307)

Medea's statement that she would rather join the fight against an army three times than give birth once in Euripides becomes a manifesto on environmental pollution in Kennely's play:

It is often said that
we women have a comfortable life
in the safety of our homes, while
men go out to sweat at work,
or risk their lives in the terrible
dangers of war. Nonsense.
I'd rather sweat it out
in some stinking hellhole, or
fight a war in a foreign land
than give birth to a brat
who will add to the pollution
of this befouled earth
where even the seas are thick with poison. (308)

One of the best things about a Euripides play is the way the most significant things are implied, rather than stated. In other words, they are emphasised by implication, as if they are there to elaborate the story. Yet the function of the story, or the plot, is to provide a context to say these seemingly negligible things by indirection. Writers of tragedy had to serve the "city" and promote its values. When their own values clashed with those of the state, they resorted to indirection. Besides, fifth-century writers seem to have a keener insight into human soul. None of them imagined to present a character or a situation that is free of strife and guilt. It is impossible to support Antigone without paying due respect to the motives of Creon, or vice versa. Neither Medea, nor Jason is free of guilt and suffering and hence we are given the chance to understand and pity them both and to learn avoiding extremes and choose the "golden means." Didactic efforts of some writers to use, or abuse, Greek tragedy for the dissemination or reiteration of their not very original ideas fail, simply because they are seduced by the richness of implication in a Greek tragedy to think they can exploit it for a cause.

A very apt example is the hopes of the chorus of Corinthian women in Euripides for a better future. Medea's resistance to complying with the dictates of her husband and Creon creates hopes for a new age. The chorus' wish to hear "new songs" about the "wisdom" of women rather than a repetition of old lies about them is a comment on the predicament of women and on the attitude of writers in Greek society. This does not mean that Euripides, whose works are full of insulting and insinuating phrases about women, demanded a radical change in favour of women in society; but it reveals that he was master enough to hint at the injustices and wrongs in ways more powerful than those of our contemporaries. This song of the chorus does not require any explication, elaboration, or specification. The situation and the wish of women are not alien to twentieth-century writers and readers.

> Backward to their sources flow the streams of holy rivers, and the order of all things is reversed: men's thoughts have become deceitful and their oaths by the gods do not hold fast. The common talk will so alter that women's ways will enjoy good repute. Honor is coming to the female sex: no more will women be maligned by slanderous rumor.
>
> The poetry of ancient bards will cease to hymn our faithlessness. Phoebus lord of song never endowed our minds with the glorious strains of the lyre. Else I could have sounded a hymn in reply to the male sew. Time in its long expanse can say many things of men's lot as well as of women's. (Euripides 333, 335)

Kennely elaborates it with supposedly contemporary demands, but the result is only an impoverished version of the original:

> The time is coming when honour
> will be paid to women, when
> their feelings will not be made
> by men, when slavery will not
> masquerade as love, when
> a man's tone of voice will not
> create a tremor in a woman's
> reply, when a woman will
> not live to please
> an inferior man, when a woman
> will not sit in silence while
> her master broods in sullen
> superiority, when decisions
> are her agreement to his
> suggestions, when her hate
> can show itself, articulate
> and pure. Then, too, the
> shadow of justice may be
> thrown across the earth,
> like a warm coat across
> the shoulders of a shivering beggar. (Kennely, qtd. in McDonald, "Medea" 308-309)

Tony Harrison's *Medea* as the revenge of the Great Mother

Tony Harrison's *Medea: A Sex-War Opera* (1985) was commissioned by the Metropolitan Opera. It was merged with Valeria Solanas' SCUM (Society for Cutting Up Men) Manifesto and first performed in this form at the 1991 Edinburgh Festival. As a graduate of Classics, Harrison deconstructs myths in his plays to comment on contemporary political or social myths and mystifications. His *Medea* focuses on an ideological unveiling of all myths to challenge male-chauvinistic ideology and to establish Medea's connection to the mythical past of the most revered fertility goddesses and the long-lost reign of the Mother Goddess as the creator of all life. In his *Medea* notebooks Harrison quotes Neumann who claims that Medea represents matriarchy transformed and reduced to a personal level and negativised: "The ancient mana figure that most clearly represents this principle of transformation is Medea. Like Circe, she was originally a goddess, but has become a 'witch' in the patriarchally coloured myth" (McDonald, "Internal" 306).

The main target of the play seems to be the probing of the nature of myths and their repercussions. The clash between goddesses of the underworld and the heavenly gods is carried to the human level in the form of a clash between woman as the creator and man as the destroyer of life. Harrison's chorus of women states this purpose at the beginning of the play:

> As the sex-war's still being fought
> which sex does a myth support
> you should be asking.
> What male propaganda lurks
> behind most operatic works
> that Music's masking? (370)

The play is successful in its combination of related myths and characters with the story of Medea through well thought out stage directions, use of voices in musical pieces, and most of all, through intertextual references ranging from Euripides to Seneca, Buchanan, Durdik, Mayr, Cherubini, Calderón, and others. This intertextuality is both an homage to previous writers and an assertion of Harrison's unique contribution to the long tradition of rewritings of *Medea*. Yet this rich and provocative play falls short of the original due to its didactic vein, especially at the end, when it becomes a sermon on the predicament of women and an indictment of male chauvinism. If Harrison had managed to harness this didactic strain, the play could have been an entertaining representation of the way patriarchal myths replaced and eradicated the myth of the mother goddess.

Harrison gives two different and clashing versions of the story of Medea by two choruses of warring sexes.

> DOWNSTAGE MAN.
> [. . .] Men overthrew
> the Goddess, women, you,
> ages ago, beyond recall.
> [. . .]
> the Great Mother, 3 in 1.
> She's finished, burned out, done! (374)
>
> CHORUS (W).
> [. . .]
> Beneath *all* Greek mythology
> are struggles between HE and SHE
> that we're still waging.
> In every quiet suburban wife
> dissatisfied with married life
> is MEDEA, raging! (371)

Medea's story is represented by three women, each corresponding to the three stages in the lives of women: Virgin, Mother, and Crone. These are also the attributes of the Mother Goddess. All female roles are interchangeably played by the same three women, who complement each other.

Men are divided into three major categories according to their attitude towards women: the extreme enmity of Hercules is in sharp contrast to the extreme love and understanding between Butes and his wife, and between the King and Queen of Macris. In between, there are ordinary men who ignorantly enact the myths they are taught. The power of women not only as nurturers, but also as destroyers of life is emphasised. All men die at the hands of women: the women of Lemnos kill their husbands; Hercules is killed by the poisoned clothes sent by his wife; Jason is killed by the Mother Goddess; Hylas is killed by voices drawing him into the pit; Butes is killed by the voices of Sirens.

The play starts with a gang of men chanting a multi-lingual hatred song to condemn the effigy of a huge woman who kills her children. She is led to an electric chair, with Jason as the executioner. The electric chair becomes the throne where Creusa and Hypsipyle, Queen of Lemnos, sit. There are two simultaneous processions on the stage: the execution of Medea and the crowning of Creusa with the golden diadem sent by Medea. The crown is the mirror image of the cap used in both the execution and in preparing the poison to kill Creusa and the dragon protecting the Golden Fleece. The two women are "capped" at the same moment as Jason pulls the handle of the switch. The handle is at the same time the tiller of the Argo (367). While Jason pulls the lever, Medea sinks into a pit on the stage from where the GODDESS emerges and to where HYLAS is dragged by water nymphs. It is also the place where the Golden Fleece is guarded by the dragon and where Jason will be buried at the end. Creusa jumps into the pit as well. The triple GODDESS emerging from the pit is accompanied by music. The stage directions say:

> *The* GODDESS *emerges on a revolving platform, and sings as though the three had one voice as some of their ancient names were Nete, Mese, and Hypate, which signify the low, middle, and high tones of the Greek system of scales. The three should be soprano, mezzo-soprano and contralto, and sometimes take alternate notes in their lowest or highest ranges so that the* GODDESS *seems to embody the total resource of the female voice, and by extension the total range of the female. Diva triformis* (Ovid.7.177). *[. . .] There are many different representations of the* GODDESS *(3 in 1) and in all one figure carries a knife in each hand, one a torch in each hand, and the third something like a sickle or sheep hook. In this case* WOMAN 1 [MEDEA] *carries the two knives,* WOMAN 2 [NURSE etc] *the hook, and* WOMAN 3 [CREUSA] *the torches. When the* GODDESS *is*

> *fully risen and rotating on her platform, singing as one voice, we see the 14 children beneath the* GODDESS *rotating in the opposite direction. This forms what is virtually a tableau of death and regeneration, the children being killed and restored to life.* (372)

The story starts with the Argonauts who sing songs to celebrate the freedom of being in the open sea, away from women, but they lament what they are missing:

> Fresh water!
> Wine!
> Fruit!
> Meat!
> Honey [*Butes.*]
> Women
> Women!
> Women!
> Women!
>
> WOMEN! (378)

Harrison represents Hercules as the misogynist and the infanticide. Opposite to this extreme is Butes the bee man, who used to love his wife dearly. Hercules is taken into the Argo for his strength and brutality and Butes for his ability to find his way in the sea. In Lemnos, Argonauts are welcomed by and paired off with women who all killed their husbands. Hercules does not allow his lover Hylas to pair off, but Hylas is seduced by the voice of a girl and drawn into the pit. Hercules, crying after his beloved, is left in the island when Argonauts set sail to Colchis. Before they depart, Butes and Hercules speak about the government of Lemnos:

BUTES.
Maybe this island's a gynocracy
and the Queen here is a gynocrat.

HERCULES.
Gynocrat! What the hell is that?

BUTES.
A woman who controls the state!
[. . .]
They say in the older times of Greece
in the golden ages which knew peace
the female ruled and not the male . . . (387-388)

Butes is the only man who sympathises with Medea on their way to the Greek world. Harrison's *Medea* notebooks contain information about the symbol of the bee. He quotes Bachofen's *The Great Mother* (265-266):

> This makes a beehive a perfect prototype of the first human society, based on the gynocracy of motherhood, as we find it among the peoples named... The bee was rightly looked upon as a symbol of the feminine potency of nature. It was associated with Demeter, Artemis and Persephone. Here it symbolised the earth, its motherliness, its never resting, artfully formative busy-ness, and reflected the Demetrian earth-soul in its supreme purity. (Qtd. in McDonald, "Internal" 309)

When Jason approaches the den of the dragoness to steal the Golden Fleece, Harrison alludes to Seneca's *Medea* in which the image of the snake had played an important role as a symbol of the female element. Voices are directed to create an image of the snake through music and to draw attention to goddesses of the underworld.

After Medea kills her sons, they are stoned and chased by Corinthian men and cry for help. Harrison wants many scenes to be felt as the dreams and thoughts of Medea. Here, Harrison turns back to the old legend of the Corinthian Medea who is said to have 14 children instead of two and who dedicates a shrine to Hera for the protection of children. DOWNSTAGE MAN and DOWNSTAGE WOMAN exchange ideas about the two different versions of Medea. DOWNSTAGE WOMAN says that the story of Medea with two children who are killed by their mother is a lie of Euripides.

The Goddess kills Hercules and Jason. First comes HERCULES to express his hatred of women:

> HERCULES.
> All the sundry monsters that I slew,
> the bloody-jawed hounds and the beasts with scales,
> the terrible dragons with fire in their tails,
> the vicious creatures with torches for eyes,
> all, ALL, were the MOTHER in disguise.
> All the monsters that I ever slew
> were only the great EARTH MOTHER, you!
> the one in the end I couldn't subdue.
> If I lopped off its head, it grew another.
> I killed all the monsters, but can't kill the MOTHER! (434)
>
> GODDESS 3/1.
> Then I drive him off his head
> and he clubs his two sons dead.
>
> SONS OF HERCULES.
> [. . .]
> 2. FATHER, I don't like that look in your eye.
> 1+2. FATHER, you're killing us ! Why? Why? Why?

DOWNSTAGE WOMAN.
He killed his children! I don't hear you
give even a *sotto voce* boo.
He killed his children. So where
is Hercules's electric chair?
A children slayer? Or is Medea
the one child-murderer you fear.
He killed his children. So where
is Hercules's electric chair?

HERCULES.
Death I've never feared at all.
What I feared most was burial,
back in that dark place I hate
from which all Mankind emanate.

At last in death I shall be free
of enfolding Femininity! (436-438)

Towards the end of the play, the chorus of women enters in daily clothes, as contemporary workingwomen going home. They have no make up. Singing a passage from Euripides, they take Jason to put him into the pit.

Harrison repeats the song of the Corinthian women in Euripides as a belated answer to their call. His play is the new song about the superiority of women over men and it also emphasises the fact that nothing really changed:

Did you know that what you hear
is from Euripides' *Medea*
of 431
that's 431 BC!
The breaking of male monopoly
has just begun! (447)

As if that was not enough, he turns back to actuality through projections of newspaper headlines about women killing their children for various reasons. The last headline is a modern Heracles story: "A FATHER CUTS HIS 4 KIDS' THROATS [*The Sun*, 19 October 1983]." (448)

This abrupt shift to daily life at the end of the play spoils everything. On a mythical level, a playful simplicity of diction is still forgivable for a musical. But the reduction of a myth to the quotidian level with infanticide mothers and fathers creates bathos rather than pathos. The name of a recent film adaptation of Medea by Joachim Lafosse, *Folie privee* (2004; Private Madness), is enough to point out the problem of Harrison's play. The play starts as an elaborate examination of Greek myths in terms of sex war and the music and strage directions are successfully used to represent the complexity of myths, yet at the end, the story is brought to a private level, or, the movement is from divine madness to private madness. In the film version, a jobless and aggressive father first beats and then punishes the mother who is separated from him and her lover, who has a warm relationship with the child, by killing his own son. This film is better, because simply dwelling on the problems of our time, it forces the audience to remember the story of Medea that puts the mother in the position of a child killer. In the history of gender relationships, it was usually the fathers who deserted their wives and children and very few women killed her children in turn. Now that the roles are changed and mothers can take care of themselves and their children, the psychology of dethroned men are under threat and on the verge of madness.

Anouilh's Medea as the existentialist heroine

Written in 1946, Anouilh's Medea has an existentialist heroine who scorns ordinary people for their illusion of happiness. Jason and Medea are free individuals responsible for their own actions, yet only Medea excels with her unappeasable hatred of conformism and tries to assert her existence with the ultimate choice: suicide. Anouilh's play is closer to the spirit of Euripides in the richness of its content and its treatment of universal themes without turning into a manifesto, despite the fact that it promotes existentialist philosophy.

Anouilh's *Medea* is timeless, yet the issues are discussed within the frame of the mid-twentieth century. Anouilh takes up the themes hinted at by Euripides by creating a Medea who questions her marriage, her love, and her social status. The common points with the original are the ambiguity of Medea's character vacillating between male and female, between mother and killer, lover and killer, or princess and beggar.

The most important theme Anouilh added to the play is the re-birth of Medea as a new person at the very beginning. Medea and Nurse are at the outskirts of the city next to a wagon which the whole family sleeps in. Nurse laments their lot: "Chased, beaten, scorned, without a country, without a home" (60). But Medea does not miss the comfort and safety of her father's palace. It was her choice and she was fully aware of the consequences of her deed. Her answer "But not alone" (60) is an acceptance of her lot, as long as she and Jason love and support each other. Deserted by Jason, she is now in pain, which is similar to childbirth:

> Help me, Nurse. Something stirs in mc, as in the old days, and it is something that says no to their joy over there, something that says no to happiness. [. . .] I still have something to bring into the world tonight, something bigger and more alive than myself, and I do not know if I will be strong enough. . . . (61)

When she learns that villagers were celebrating Jason's marriage to Creusa, she says,

> Thank you, Jason! Thank you, Creon! Thank you, night! Now I am freed. This time my child has come by itself. Oh, my newly born hatred . . . ! How soft you are, how good you smell. Oh, little black girl, now you are the only thing I have left in the world to love. (62)

The theme of rebirth is the best part of the play. This Medea acquires self-awareness, a sort of negative epiphany that empowers her. She is not the weak princess like Creusa anymore. The similarity between the two brides of Jason is established by Euripides through the sharing of the same clothes and diadem by the two princesses who promise worldly success to Jason.

Following her awakening, Medea is disgusted by her love for Jason. The following passage is a modern version of the original Medea's lamenting of the lot of women. Euripides was emphasising the situation of women as slaves locked in houses. Anouilh's Medea points out the carnal desire that enslaved her:

> What had he done to me, Nurse, with his large, warm hands? He had only to enter my father's palace and touch me with a single caress. Ten years have gone by and Jason's hand no longer grips mine. I have found myself again. Now again I am Medea! I am no longer that woman bound to the smell of a man, that bitch in heat who waits. Oh, shame! Shame! My cheeks are burning, Nurse. All day long I waited for him, my legs open, maimed. . . . Humbly, that part of myself that he could take and give back, that middle of my womb was his. (62-63)

The dialogue between Jason and Medea adds a sex-war theme to the play. But this is a marital war with political implications, rather than an articulately political one. They both express their dream of a life without each other. Yet for Medea "[. . .] this world includes both Jason and Medea" (71). Yet Jason insists on his decision to forget her and their heroic past together and says, "It is not only you that I hate – it is love" (72).

The play turns to the theme of loss of self in love. This was a matter of debate in ancient philosophy, and Anouilh adapts it to twentieth-century marriages. In Euripides' play, the chorus warns women against excessive love for men:

> Loves that come to us in excess bring no good name or goodness to men. If Aphrodite comes in moderation, no other goddess brings such happiness. Never, o goddess, may

> you smear with desire one of your ineluctable arrows and let it fly against my heart from your golden bow!
> May moderation attend me, fairest gift of gods! May Aphrodite never cast contentious wrath and insatiate quarrelling upon me and madden my heart with love for a stranger's bed! But may she honor marriages that are peaceful and wisely determine whom we are to wed! (Euripides 351)

This is a problem for Jason as well:

> I gave you more than a man's love [. . .] I lost myself in you, like a little boy in the woman who brought him into the world. For a very long time you were my country, my light. You were the air I breathed, the water I had to drink, and my daily bread.
> [. . .] The world became Medea. . . . (77-78)

But the real reason why Jason leaves Medea is his desire to become an ordinary man again. He wants to be

> humble. [. . .] *I* want to stop now and be a man. Maybe behave without illusion, as those we used to despise. Just as my father did and my father's father and all those who accepted before us – and more simply than we. To clear a little piece of ground where man can stand in this confusion and this night. (79-80)

Jason explains the function of his new wife as follows,

> [. . .] I will never love her as I loved you. But she is new, she is simple, she is pure. [. . .] From the clumsy fingers of that little girl I expect humility and oblivion. And if the gods grant it, what you hate most in the world, what is farthest from you: happiness, poor happiness. (81)

Ironically, Medea was as pure as Creusa and wanted happiness as much as Jason at the beginning of their adventure. At the end of the play, before she kills the children she shouts:

> Jason! Here is your family, tenderly united. Look at it. And may you always wonder whether Medea, too, would not have loved happiness and innocence. [. . .] think that long ago there was a little girl, Medea, exacting and pure. [. . .] I, too, would have wanted it to last forever and that it be the way it is in stories! [. . .] But innocent Medea was chosen to be the prey and the place of the struggle. [. . .] I still have the innocence to slaughter in that little girl and in these two warm little pieces of myself. (84-85)

The passage about conjugal life and its problems is also to be found in Euripides. Women of Athens were prisoners at home and marriage was a form of slavery, even death, for them. Euripides points out the oppression that drives women crazy in every family: "O womankind and marriage fraught with pain, how many are the troubles you have already wrought for mortal men!" (413). In Anouilh, it becomes an issue between equals, two free individuals whose marriage is getting stale. Both have the power to commit adultery, and here again Medea acts first. The story about Medea's lover who was later killed by both of them is the only passage that does not fit into the overall story. Anouilh apparently wanted to present his modern Medea as an avant-garde and liberated heroine and to emphasise the modernity of his characters.

After killing her children Medea puts the wagon on fire and enters it. Her decision to die is also a rebirth, a return to her old, innocent self. When Jason arrives she shouts at him:

> Now I have found my scepter again. My brother, my father, and the Fleece of the golden ram are given back to Colchis. I have found my country again and the virginity which you tore from me. I am Medea at last and forever! Look at me before remaining alone in this rational world. I am your little

> brother and your wife! I, the horrible Medea! And now try to forget her! (86)

Anouilh ends his adaptations of tragedies by emphasising the contrast between heroes and heroines and ordinary, cowardly people. Medea's heroic struggle against the mediocrity of Jason, who is determined to forget Medea and his past and start a new life, is striking. Giving orders to guards, Jason says,

> Yes, I will forget you. Yes, I will live. [. . .] I will reconstruct my poor and fragile human edifice under the indifferent eyes of the gods. [. . .] Now we must live, secure order, give Corinth laws, and without illusion rebuild a world befitting us, in which to wait and die. (86)

Nurse is simply happy that she's alive. While Medea and children are still burning in the wagon, she claims she also has a word to say and talks about the pleasures of daily routine. Then she asks the indifferent guard whether there will be a good harvest. "No need to complain," says the guard. "There will still be bread for everyone this year" (87).

Medea as the scapegoat

We sympathise and identify with Medea, rather than with Jason or Creon. Facing an injustice, Medea articulates her desires and shattered expectations. Jason is a demagogue in Euripides distorting the meaning of words such as reason, responsibility, and democracy. Jason and Creon are spokesmen of the politicians who send their children to wars to conquer the world, to destroy cities and the so-called barbarian civilizations and who blame women for infanticide. Anouilh's cold-blooded Jason thinks he can find happiness in a rational and orderly society.

Today, in Medea's screams we hear the pain, anger, and hopelessness of Palestinian mothers whose children are left no other choice than becoming suicide bombers. Medea is the power that bombed the monuments to phallocracy in America. Medea is the power that leaves us as speechless and hopeless as the

Greeks in the fifth century in a mutual eagerness to kill and be killed. Medea is also a powerful demonstration of the space where all power relationships are acted on a small scale and where the ground is prepared for large-scale oppression and exploitation: home.

Medea as the supreme scapegoat shares the lot of all monsters in history. Men or women, every group or individual that fought against racial discrimination, injustice, inequality, or war are condemned as terrorists and violators of human rights, and blamed for not being as democratic or liberal as their oppressors. A woman who is intelligent is a witch, an Amazon who threatens her sons and husband. That is why the twentieth-century audience recognises in that angry witch, in that Scylla who devours men to recreate herself, a monster created and perpetuated by phallocracy.

Medea, my sister! You are Cybele dragged by the hair from your abode underground to the blinding sun to be transformed into Athena, Artemis, and Dionysus. You are Demeter forced into serving a male god of fertility, Triptolemus. You are Demeter to give your daughter as the bride to death. You are Persephone stolen from your mother to be given as bride to death. You are Metis devoured by Zeus. You are Lilith punished by God for disobedience to your husband and turned into a child murderer. Medea, my furious sister, my revengeful mother, my broken daughter, it has been thousands of years and we are still Medeas.

Works Cited

Anouilh, Jean. *Medea*. In *Seven Plays*. Vol. 3. Trans. Luce and Arthur Klein. New York: Mermaid, 1967.

Euripides. *Medea*. In *Medea, Cyclops, Alcestis*. Trans. and ed. David Kovacs. London: Harvard UP, 1994.

Harrison, Tony. *Theatre Works 1973-1985*. Suffolk: Penguin, 1986.

McDonald, Marianne. "Medea as Politician and Diva, Riding the Dragon into the Future." *Medea: Essays on Medea in Myth, Literature, Philosophy, and Art*. Ed. James J. Clauss and Sarah Iles Johnston. Princeton: Princeton UP, 1977.

---. "Internal, External, Eternal Medea." *Tony Harrison.* Bloodaxe Critical Anthologies 1. Ed. Neil Astley. Newcastle-upon-Tyne: Bloodaxe, 1991.

Wilmer, Steve. "Radical Reworkings. Prometheus, Medea and Antigone: Metaphors for Irish Rebellion and Social Change." *Didaskalia* 3.1 (Spring/ Summer 1996). 20 July 2005 <http://didaskalia.open.ac.uk/issues/vol3no1/ wilmer.html>.

II

POWER AND VICTIMIZATION IN OTHER LITERATURES

Reading. Writing. Talking. Silence: Ricardo Piglia, Luisa Valenzuela and the Argentine Dictatorship[1]

Dane Johnson
San Francisco State University

Abstract: In 1976, the Argentine military instituted a period of military dictatorship that they labeled "the Process of National Reorganization." Under the guise of "protecting" the nation from left-wing "terrorists," the military would "disappear" (kidnap, torture, and usually kill) alleged subversives. Part of this process was a take-over of public discourse whereby any questioning of the regime was tantamount to subversion. This essay performs a confrontation between the narrative conventions of the regime and those of Ricardo Piglia and Luisa Valenzuela in *Respiración artificial* (1980, *Artificial Respiration*) and *La cola de lagartija* (1983, *The Lizard's Tail*), respectively. At a time when public discourse was reduced to false narratives of patriotic fear or felicity, these two writers broke down traditional narrative conventions as a way to speak the unspeakable and to resist what seemed almost all-powerful. While the focus is on the rhetoric of power and the powers of rhetoric at a specific historical moment and place in two determinedly idiosyncratic texts, this essay addresses more general questions of "the rhetoric of socio-political power and representation of victimhood in contemporary literature" in a coda that connects these two novels to the Latin American genre of "*testimonio*" and to our moment – when specters of terror have gone global.

Do you know where your mother is right now? How can you be sure? Your son? Your daughter? Your brother? Your lover? Are they alive? Right now? How can you be sure?

Do you know what your neighbor said about you yesterday? Your boss? The store clerk? Do you know who they spoke to? Why? Might they have made something up? How do you know?

---

1 I wish to thank Banu Özel for pushing this project forward and Kitty Millet for helping to bring it to an end.

In Argentina, we know now that these paranoiac questions have a name: "The Process of National Reorganization." And we believe them to have a beginning and an end: 1976-1983. We know now that tens of thousands of innocent Argentines were kidnapped and killed by their own government's paramilitary forces – without any trial, without any funeral, without any news – *desaparecido*, "disappeared," as the phrase went. When Ricardo Piglia and Luisa Valenzuela wrote *Respiración artificial* (1980; *Artificial Respiration*) and *La cola de lagartija* (1983; *The Lizard's Tail*),[2] however, they had only the questions of the paranoid, the culture of fear, the supposition of the unspeakable and the burden of the unspoken.

Piglia's novel *Artificial Respiration* begins with a question from one of the narrators to we silent readers: "*¿Hay una historia?*" (*Respiración artificial* 13). But when read, translated, answered, that question fragments into further questions – questions that break down narrative as they war against each other: Is there a story or is there a history? Is there *one* story, or is there *one* history?

But that question is not really the beginning, for who could ignore a dedication "to Eliás and Rubén who helped me to come to know the truth of history" (v) or the poetic, enigmatic sub-title to the first part of the novel, "If I were the Dark Winter" (5), which may refer to a painting by the seventeenth-century Dutch painter Franz Hals, famous for his portraits, and, in fact, the painter of the best known portrait of Descartes, whose name heads up the second part of the novel. But I don't want to rush past the epigraph from T. S. Eliot, for Piglia's narrator urges us to look back at it, at the moment we are looking at – not a portrait – but a photograph: "We had the experience but missed the meaning, / And approach to the meaning restores the experience" (7). Truth of history, dark winters, famous portraits, missed meaning, meaningful experience – now we're getting somewhere, at least to the beginning, "If there is a story," which, we're told, if there is, "begins three years ago. In April 1976" (11), which, if we're not already too confused, happens to be just after the real military coup that instituted the "Process of National Reorganization" on March 24, 1976. That date marks the beginning of a period in Argentine history referred to

2 All citations to the novels are to the English editions unless otherwise noted.

commonly as "*el proceso,*" which could be translated simply – and eerily in this context – as "the process," but can also mean – just as eerily – "the trial." But I'm getting ahead of myself, though behind in Piglia's novel, which has only just begun but quickly reaches back to many pasts as well as beyond to future readers who can not know the present.

Valenzuela's novel *The Lizard's Tail* – T-A-I-L, but T-A-L-E would not be inappropriate, though that would change the tale from the tail that is the name of a whip to the tale of a man who can change his colors as political fashion and fascism dictates; and, besides, the tale of the tail does not work as a homonym in Spanish, though that need not concern Valenzuela, a writer who believes that all "metaphors sustain multiple readings" (Picon Garfield 26), nor this text, the English version of which appeared a little before the Spanish. But I jump, when I want to begin with a beginning before the beginning, which is a warning – "That can not be written" (Valenzuela, *Cola de lagartija* iii; my translation) – which is really what is written, but which passes over a possible subtitle of the novel, "The Red Ant Sorcerer-Gentleman of Tacurú," which ties in to a polyphonic prophecy on a river of blood and twenty years of peace "and enough! Conjunctions revolt me" (vii), which is actually a quote from "The Prophecy," though I share the sentiment and label it testimony to the torture of writing, though it might just as well be testimony to the pain of writing knowing that real torture is over there.

[Do you know where your partner is? Are you sure? Is there a story? A history? One?]

As noted before but too easily forgotten by many, on March 24, 1976, the Argentine military began a phase of brutal military rule that they designated "the Process of National Reorganization." This Process has also been labeled the "Dirty War," which seems appropriately critical of the military, though the term actually began – and we are dealing again with possible beginnings – as a label applied by the military to the work of armed insurgents. Under the guise of protecting the nation from left-wing terrorists, para-military units would "disappear" – kidnap, torture, and, usually, kill – alleged subversives. Part of this process was a take-over of public discourse whereby any questioning of the regime was tantamount to subversion, brutality could be labeled as "reorganization," and the twinning of "nation" to "order" became an excuse to kill thousands of non-violent dissenters – and many who were merely suspected of dissent.

The *Proceso* begins with "Basic Goals and Objectives," at least that is what was decreed a few days after the coup, and some of these follow, in no particular order except to the extent that everything has a particular order, particularly when ordered by the military: "order, work, hierarchy, responsibility, national identity, and honesty in the context of Christian morality." Junta leader General Videla adds publicly, quickly, hauntingly: "The process has goals but no time frame"; "There will be no shortcuts this time, only solutions" (qtd. in Mignone 251). Videla later elaborates upon and justifies the Process in 1978: "A terrorist is not just someone with a gun or bomb, but also someone who spreads ideas that are contrary to Western and Christian civilization" (qtd. in Caistor xiii). In the name of "Reorganization," they shut down the universities; they took control of radio and television; they censored, they questioned, they tortured – thousands were silently disappeared.

Luisa Valenzuela, who went into voluntary exile in New York in 1979, wrote through the fear, finishing *The Lizard's Tail* in 1981 but only publishing its wild ramblings in Argentina after the fall of the dictatorship in 1983. Ricardo Piglia wrote through the fear, staying in Argentina, publishing his erudite, enigmatic scream of witness in Buenos Aires in 1980. These two Argentine novelists wrote through "the culture of fear" in the double sense of writing because of the fear deployed as a weapon by the dictatorship and writing to make it through – to understand and name and possibly transform – this tortured reality. At a time when public discourse was reduced to simplified narratives of patriotic nostalgia and nationalist jingoism, these two writers broke down narrative conventions to explore how the Argentine people arrived at this moment of being split asunder, to explore how the split might be healed without resorting to the frightening mask of lock- or goose-step homogeneity.

From the unspoken dread woven into the short story "Strange Things Happen Here" to the call to "Other Weapons" in the story of the same name to *The Lizard's Tail* itself, Valenzuela has been concerned with exploring linguistic forms and narrative techniques for representing and contesting the dark, patriarchal, militaristic underbelly of cosmopolitan Argentina. Macabre, furiously fragmented and marked by bursts of edgy black humor, *The Lizard's Tail* purports to be the biography of a sorcerer who not only managed to become the Minister of Social Well-being under the chaotic presidency of Isabel Perón but also founded one of the most notorious right-wing death squads, the "Triple A," or "Anti-Communist Alliance." Isabel Perón had come to rule Argentina in the period immediately before the 1976 military coup after the death of her legendary husband Juan Perón and under the long shadow cast by Perón's iconic first wife, Evita.

Turning back to the novel as such, which is much more ferociously foggy on the history above than my summary suggests, the protagonist – the "sorcerer" – has three balls, many more names, and even more disparate representations. He talks to what must have been Evita's finger, walks with the current Generals, and balks at any thought that he could ever be contained, appreciated, or understood. Wanting to name that from which the 1976 dictatorship grew – how, in other words of Valenzuela, "such a supposedly intelligent and sophisticated people like the Argentines had fallen into the hands of this so-called sorcerer" (Picon Garfield 27) – but worried that such naming might only empower the forces of evil, the named narrator, "Luisa Valenzuela," explicitly abandons the text two-thirds of the way through with the sorcerer's mad ramblings taking over. Nameless voices in the capital are either groups of military men or intellectuals, each group allowing a discourse of dread to overtake their action or inaction, respectively. No one can be innocent in such a state; no one can completely avoid the river of blood in a world where tyrannies "now [. . .] have replacement parts" (279).

Piglia's *Artificial Respiration* writes through the culture of fear without naming – or with too many names, too many allusions (as my students inevitably remind me when I have taught this novel). With no present violence depicted, no historically present names named, it is a world of code, a primer on how to read in and of an era when nothing written or spoken can be taken at face value. The first part of the novel is comprised largely of letters, primarily the correspondence between a young novelist in the capital and an uncle from the provinces whom he has never met. The uncle initiated the correspondence in order to correct a mistaken reading of his own history that his nephew had written into a novel. The on-going exchange becomes even more fraught with tantalizing complexity as we come to realize that we are, in a sense, reading over the shoulder of another reader, probably a government spy, who connects these letters to others' that may or may not have any direct relation to the characters above. This obsessive spy/reader is attempting to unpack the supposedly-coded messages of alleged terrorists underneath the heady ramblings of two distant intellectuals. These two intellectuals come to share in their own obsessive quest to unpack the fragmented messages contained in the long hidden but now reopened archives of a 19th-century traitor – or patriot – who had been erased from public history and who happened to be working on a utopian novel consisting of letters written from the "future" – 1979 – which happens to be part of the present of the story we are reading. Or is he a contemporary left-wing "terrorist" masking himself as a 19th-century patriot? The mind reels.

[Is there a history? A story? One?]

With the writing and reading summed up above still unresolved and probably unresolveable, we pack our bags with the nephew and move on to the second part of the novel, which is almost wholly dialogue: a nearly day-long conversation between the nephew – who has traveled to meet his uncle – and the uncle's best friend, a displaced European intellectual named Tardewski who is modeled on Witold Gombrowicz and/or Walter Benjamin and/or Vladimir Nabakov, or, why not, the almost-well-known Polish philosopher of phenomenology Twardowski ("Phenomenology" 660) – the "and/or-ness" of everything being part of the tease and tension of the novel. This sometimes frustrating opening-out is one more narrative technique of feather-bed resistance to – or is it passive acceptance of? – a government that either cannot read even the writing on the wall or, as with the spy of the first part, reads threat into everything. The uncle's absence – a bracingly gentle allusion to the horror of the disappeared – provides space for a free-wheeling discourse that does nothing less than re-write Argentine literary and cultural history, postulate that Hitler and Kafka met each other at the Arcos Café in Prague in January 1910, and leave us with the notion that somehow that meeting might just relate to the sudden disappearance of the uncle, to, even, the past, present and future of Argentina. Fact, accident, and wild speculation whirl in a heady mix as the conversation moves from the train station to the club to the uncle's vacant residence to, finally, Tardewski's home. And the fact of talk is one of the only possibilities for undercutting the illogical self-sameness of the military's mantra of nation, order, and patriotism. Wild talk, empty intellectual drivel to some, is one of the last spaces for teaching a cowered public how to read – "how to associate" (203), as the text reads, with that type of association about the only one possible without threat of death. The opening of another letter brings the narrative to an end, an end that circles back to the beginning, an end that ties up the narrative in an untidy ball of disparate strands.

Neither novel finds or founds a triumphant narrative, for false triumph and the fiction of wholeness constitute the voice of the military in this "dirty war," this on-going trial. The narratives and narrative may have broken down, but accidents of reading, writing, and talking –narrative in all its ceaseless forms – are part of the possible in keeping a variegated Argentine cultural memory alive through the sanitizing – and deadly – "process."

But my summaries – except for the endless beginnings, and this beginning of the end – have smoothed the process of reading these two wild, thorny, elusive texts. And I have joined into a fictional whole two texts that speak in very different – and internally varied – modes. The process of reading – of Lizard's Tails that are whips, of sex that is violence, of violence that can't be named; of narrator's who can't narrate, can't act, can't escape; of *A*rtifical *R*espiration – "AR" – needed for the *A*rgentine *R*epublic – "AR"; of an Argentine Republic in the Process of National Reorganization that is Kafka's Trial and Hitlerian horror; of Kafka's text becoming Hitler's action – the process of processing my reading has become the process of making you hear my truth, the truth? Truth? But have I forgotten what I read? Have I remembered what is convenient? Whose story have I told? How many stories are there?

[Note to self. Still missing: The proliferation of voices. The embedded reading of the reading we're reading. 1979. 1983. – 9/11? – 1930. 1910. 1850. 1492? Follow the bouncing allusion; make note of change from the comic to the horrific – or is it the inability to tell which is which and when is when? Re-read.]

It has been said that war is the continuation of politics by other means. But at moments when the only allowable politics is a war of systematically killing off or driving into exile all possible opposition while controlling all forms of media, all writing and reading becomes political. At moments when this is not the case – our moment here and there in Argentina – we too often eschew the political in reading narrative, the jolting experience of these texts submerged within tidy categories: the experimental novel, the postmodern text, post-Boom literature, or even Argentine narrative of the Dirty War. But the experience of reading these manic, obsessive, disparate narrative breakdowns mimics the fractured and fracturing experience of being an intellectual undergoing The Trial of Reorganization, the narratives remembering and instructing, opening questions of beginnings, leaving us with no certainty of an end.

¿Hay una historia?
Can that be written?
To read is to learn how to associate.
There is a river of blood. Tyrannies are not what they used to be?

CODA: Re-reading and re-vision

If you have comfortably followed all I have written thus far, I have failed, for a confrontation between the narrative conventions of the Argentine regime and those of Ricardo Piglia and Luisa Valenzuela in *Artificial Respiration* and *The Lizard's Tail* defies resolution, even if we declare the novelists as victors over rather than victims of the government. My hope was to provide some sense of being *in* these novels rather than analyzing them from above, and this hope is tied in part to their position within the range of discourses produced during and after Argentina's "Dirty War." During the military dictatorship, the power and powerful rhetoric of the regime silenced most and confused many, inside and outside of Argentina. Experimental literary fiction was one of the few spaces where one might explore unknown and even unknowable truths of the regime while exposing in some survivable way the regime's claim – and construction – of the truth.

But what of victims? They are noticeably absent – in retrospect – in both novels. They jut into *The Lizard's Tail* in a few painful fragments, but the focus is on the source – or sorcery – behind the perpetrators –and the source – or sorcery – behind the public's – or at least the narrator's – passivity. In *Artificial Respiration*, countless passages can be read as commenting on the current situation, but none do so directly. The uncle may well have been disappeared – killed, to be less poetic and less historically specific – but, as in most questions within Piglia's – and perhaps our – world, answers rely on a tissue of fragile texts, on the will to sustain one reading rather than another because we simply do not know the Truth. In part, this silence comes from the condition of writing during rather than after the dictatorship: during, one couldn't know what one wanted to know; one couldn't say what one knew, at least not out loud and certainly not in print in Argentina. Like my attempt to make you live these novels, if only for a few minutes, Piglia and Valenzuela were taking us *in* to a world that could not be rationally comprehended, trying to make us feel what could not be known, to experience a being in without being victim. The silence in these two novels shares both a respect and distance from victims as such in the midst of a nightmare that was Argentine reality. Turning away from actual victims, one might see Argentina – its civil society – as victim, but these two texts do not stop on that kind of memorializing. The dead must be remembered, but that can only be done in retrospect. In the present of these novels and the present of writing these novels and any present of reading these novels, writer and reader are alive, and we can't too easily divide the living into perpetrators and victims.

In contrast to these two novels that say so much so ceaselessly about so many things, the most powerful direct commentary on the state-sponsored terrorism was primarily an empowering rather than cowering silence: later in the dictatorship, mothers of the "disappeared" would gather in the Plaza de Mayo, marching in front of the Presidential Palace carrying signs with photos of their lost sons and daughters. They would not be moved.

Two observations by the authors are particularly instructive as to their posterior perspective on how to read these novels and how they might connect forward and outward. In "Dangerous Words," Valenzuela writes:

> The word is our tool and our enemy at the same time, it is the sword of Damocles sometimes suspended over our heads when we feel incapable of expressing it, of hitting on the key word, the Open Sesame that will allow us to enter into a new text. [. . .] And let's not speak about the silences, which are impossible to speak about anyway. What goes unsaid, that which is implied and omitted and censured and suggested, acquires the importance of a scream. (9)

Less dramatically, but with no less impact on this or any reading, Piglia comments in a 1989 interview:

> I believe that coding is the work of fiction in any context. I don't believe that the ellipsis of political material performed by fiction depends on authoritarian situations. [. . .] What I do believe is that political contexts define ways of reading. (2)

With silenced memory becoming a scream and the code of fiction changed by the politics of reading, we're in a perhaps timeless realm of linguistic and epistemological paradox where relentless questioning of word and world are the norm rather than an aberration.

This *might* be put into contrast with the contemporary Latin American genre known as *testimonio* (often connected to more global notions of "testimonial literature"), which in the collaborative form that most interests me here, is "defined by a speaking subject who narrates her experience of political violence as part of a project of ameliorating social injustice" (Nance 57). With Nobel Peace Prize Winner Rigoberta Menchú's as the most celebrated single example, the emphasis has been on witness transformed into possible action and permanent memory. From the *testimonios* arises a new truth as counterweight to the regime's false truth, witness to past atrocities mingling with utopian hopes for the future. Instead of reading these novels and *testimonios* as opposite discourses, however, I would suggest seeing them as complementary discourses. The truth of *testimonio* is a continual and permanent reminder to see and remember: the unspeakable really happened. These novels, though, open up unconscious "why's" and continual, frustrating, liberating questions.

As the Piglia quotation above suggests, one of these questions is the contextual frame of time. My initial reading of both texts in the early 1990s was from a space-time of victory: the Argentine dictatorship was over; there was a sense that the worst had passed, even chatter of a happy end to unhappy world history after the fall of the Berlin wall. But soon came the rise of new terrors, the terror of nationalisms and fanaticisms that had been suppressed but never defeated. State-sponsored terrorism focused on the revolution from within continues here and there, but the focus has largely shifted to a more dis-membered and global terror, albeit one still grounded and propagated through the rhetoric of singular truth.

Now, I cannot help but see the victims who were rendered in these novels only in absence. The passivity implied in some readings of "victim" had made me turn away from the term, while the call of this conference and my re-reading of these novels in conjunction with rather than in opposition to *testimonio* aided in my re-vision. Now I better see an on-going dialogue with the experimentally adventurous literature of resistance and survival in the Americas, a tradition that I had never thought of as being about victims, even if my focus has often been on literatures coming out of groups that have been victimized. Travel from the Mayan's coded sense of return in a *Popol Vuh* written under the watchful eye of Spanish priests to Frederick Douglass combining learning to read with learning to subvert and on again to Herman Melville's turn on the gentlemanly readers of his day through a look in the uncanny mirror of "Bartleby, the Scrivener's" humanity. Don't pass over Charles Chesnutt's laughing master getting at last laughed at by the human who plays at slave in "The Passing of Grandison." Reel in the heady spin of W. E. B. Du Bois's "how does it feel to be a problem?" landing on the suicidal grandson of slaveholders, Quentin Compson, as he insists, "I don't hate the South, I don't, I don't" in William Faulkner's *Absalom, Absalom!* Cry as Leslie Marmon Silko's "Lullaby" sings the last Navajo lullaby, while the last Navajo dies. Pass on Toni Morrison's remembrance of a middle passage too easily passed over in *Beloved.* Laugh at yourself while laughing at the horror of laughing at Charles Johnson's improbably humorous faux slave narrative *Oxherding Tale.*

The list could go on and on, and they all include the pained and painful representation of victims, a literary litany of abuse and devastation. However, these are also texts of resistance and survival: through memory, through humor, through language, and, in the texts that most interest me – or the parts of text that I tend to notice – through choices in form at all levels that force us to reflect on the relations between language and truth.

It would be nice to end on a positive note – fiction is freedom, say. But *Artificial Respiration* and *The Lizard's Tail* mock such big Truths. After all, isn't that just the kind of mantra that regimes of terror traffic in? Fiction may be freedom, but that includes the freedom for both good and evil. The big essential truth of *testimonio* asks us to never forget. But we will forget a lot; we always do. Memory is always directed, but not always directed in the ways we want, in the ways we know. Terror, to re-phrase Valenzuela, has replacement parts, and victims will always be contemporary.

So I turn to smaller truths, truthful paradoxes, perpetual questions, hoping for resistance, hoping for hope. But a focus on victims can lead to despair, and despair may be an appropriate response to victims in the wake of any Dirty War; it certainly can undercut the utopian truths that too often turn to dystopian realities. I'll end then, on the poet of infinitesimal hope, Samuel Beckett, voiced through his character Molloy: "I must go on; I can't go on; I must go on; I must say words as long as there are words, I must say them until they find me, until they say me – heavy burden, heavy sin" (qtd. in Foucault 215). We must go on reading, writing, and talking through the culture of fear.

Works Cited

Caistor, Nick. Foreword. *Nunca más* [*Never Again*]*: A Report by Argentina's National Commission on Disappeared People*. London: Faber and Faber, 1986. xi-xvi.

Foucault, Michel. "The Discourse on Language." *The Archeology of Knowledge*. New York: Pantheon, 1972. 215-237.

Mignone, Emilio F. "Beyond Fear: Forms of Justice and Compensation." *Fear at the Edge: State Terror and Resistance in Latin America*. Ed. Juan E. Corradi, Patricia Weiss Fagen, and Manuel Antonio Garretón. Berkeley: U of California P, 1992. 250-263.

Nance, Kimberly A. "Let Us Say That There Is a Human Being before Me Who Is Suffering: Empathy, Exotopy, and Ethics in the Reception of Latin American Collaborative Testimonio." *Bakhtin: Ethics and Mechanics*. Ed. Valerie Z. Nollan. Evanston: Northwestern UP, 2004. 57-73.

Picon Garfield, Evelyn. "Interview with Luisa Valenzuela." *Review of Contemporary Fiction* 6.3 (Fall 1986): 25-30.

Piglia, Ricardo. *Artificial Respiration*. Trans. Daniel Balderston. Durham, NC: Duke UP, 1994.

---. *Respiración artificial*. Buenos Aires: Seix Barral, 1994.

"Phenomenology." *The Oxford Companion to Philosophy*. Ed. Ted Honderich. Oxford: Oxford UP, 1995. 658-660.

Valenzuela, Luisa. "Dangerous Words." *Review of Contemporary Fiction* 6.3 (Fall 1986): 9-10.

---. *La cola de lagartija*. Buenos Aires: Bruguera, 1983.

---. *The Lizard's Tail.* Trans. Gregory Rabassa. New York: Farrar, Straus, Giroux, 1983.

---. Valenzuela, Luisa. "Other Weapons." Other Weapons. Trans. Deborah Bonner. Hanover, NH: Ediciones del Norte, 1985. 105-135.

---. Valenzuela, Luisa. "Strange Things Happen Here." *Strange Things Happen Here.* Trans. Helen Lane. New York: Harcourt Brace Jovanovich, 1979. 3-12.

Fascination with Fascism: The Rhetoric of Oppression in Thomas Mann's *Mario and the Magician*

Burcu Kayışçı
Boğaziçi University

Abstract: This paper focuses on how Thomas Mann in his novella *Mario and the Magician* treats the rise of fascism in Italy and Germany through the image of the magician Cipolla. Cipolla is an expert in manipulating people so as to make them act the way he wishes. His hypnotizing power is such that they turn into his slaves. Mann is here questioning the existence of free will: People see the show of their own accord; Cipolla does not force them. But paradoxically they go to see Cipolla only to witness how he destroys the idea of free will. What Thomas Mann seems to say helps to elucidate how Hitler and Mussolini managed to convince masses of people to march with them, and Cipolla is the embodiment of how political rhetoric can change the world order for better or worse.

Thomas Mann's *Mario and the Magician* was written in the period between the two world wars - an era marked by the devastating effects of World War I and the rise of fascism. The war cramped and thwarted all sorts of relationships and the fascist ideas of racial purity, mass fervour, and authoritarian rule resulted in the denigration of the individual and concomitant exaltation of the group. Many writers such as Thomas Mann, Virginia Woolf, and Albert Camus dealt with the clash between between fascism and the individual in their work. While different writers approached the problem of fascism from different angles, their concerns converged: fascism, they concluded, undermines the integrity of the individual.

Mario and the Magician clearly shows that Mann was aware of this threatening situation and his story can be read as a warning for his own country. By 1929 Mussolini had already been in power in Italy, where the novella is set. By referring to the situation there, Mann makes an attempt to warn the German citizens against the dangerous fascination with fascism. Ten days after Hitler accepted President Hindenburg's offer of the chancellorship in 1933, Mann left for Holland on a lecture tour, and he did not set foot on his native soil again until July, 1949. This paper aims to present his story as a paradigm of the rise of fascist rules and to illustrate how the rhetoric of oppression works on people. For this, a two-dimensional analysis of the text will be made. While the first dimension covers the general events in the story that the narrator tells to convey the rise of tension through his family's unfortunate holiday, the second dimension consists of how the show of Cipolla the magician represents oppressive rule and rhetoric. The free will of the people seems to be subjugated to his immense power, and that is the gist of the relationship between oppression and victimhood.

The narrator and his family go to Torre di Venere in Italy to spend a nice and tranquil holiday but things turn out to be different from what they have expected. From the very beginning, one can feel the air of anxiety and hostility that surrounds the family during their stay. Nationalism is on the rise among Italian people, and they implicitly or explicitly want to make the newcomers feel as outcasts. First, the family is not allowed to eat on the veranda for it is reserved "*ai nostri clienti*" (137), "for our customers." Even though they too are clients of the hotel, it is obvious that the waiter is talking about more genuine clients. After a second incident, they have to leave the hotel. The Principessa, one of the guests of the hotel, feels extremely uneasy about the whooping-cough from which the children of the family have recently recovered. Only the youngest kid is troubled by traces of it at times but the aristocrat is alarmed for her own children. No matter how hard they try to show that there is no risk of the illness' being contagious, the narrator and his family are not wanted at the hotel anymore. Even the report of the hotel physician is not enough to convince the Principessa, and they finally move to another hotel. They keep trying to enjoy their holiday but problems won't let go of them. The narrator is very well aware of the fact that something is wrong and disconcerting about the general attitude of people. Talking about his children, he says:

> Ours soon played with natives and foreigners alike. Yet, they were plainly both puzzled and disappointed at times. There were wounded sensibilities, displays of assertiveness – or

> rather hardly assertiveness, for it was too self-conscious and too didactic to deserve the name. There were quarrels over flags, disputes about authority and precedence. Grownups joined in, not so much to pacify as to render judgment and enunciate principles. Phrases were dropped about the greatness and dignity of Italy, solemn phrases that spoilt the fun. We saw our little ones retreat, puzzled and hurt, and were put to it to explain the situation. These people, we told them, were just passing through a certain stage, something rather like an illness, perhaps; not very pleasant, but probably unavoidable. (142-143)

The word "illness" aptly defines the prevailing situation. The hostile and chauvinistic remarks are indicative of this acute illness of the Italian people, including the children, which reaches the ultimate point when the family is labeled as "an offence to the public morals" (143) only because their eight-year-old daughter takes off her swimming suit to rinse it in the sea. People take it as a grave misconduct and there is an outburst of anger. One can easily realize how perplexed the narrator is when giving an account of one gentleman's opinion on the issue:

> The offence against decency of which we had been guilty was, he said, the more to be condemned because it was also a gross ingratitude and an insulting breach of his country's hospitality. We had criminally injured not only the letter and spirit of the public bathing regulations, but also the honor of Italy. (144)

This exceedingly elevated rhetoric and patriotic vocabulary harbor a very dangerous and abnormal tendency if we read between the lines. The little girl's staying naked for a few minutes has nothing to do with the honor of Italy but people are too absorbed in their nationalistic ideals to realize it. It is not a matter of the violation of public bathing regulations either; rather it is implied that one will be excluded and punished if one does not conform to the norms.

The rest of the story proceeds with the narrator's description of Cipolla's show which leads us to the second dimension mentioned above. Having shown his reader the collective loss of consciousness and having established people's fascination with extreme nationalism, Mann goes down to the roots of the problem and poses the essential questions: Why are people so attracted to the idea of fascism? What lies behind the rise of such totalitarian regimes? To find the answers, he uses the extended metaphor of a magical show presented by Cipolla the conjuror as the narrator calls him. Children are excited about the show more than anyone else and on no grounds will they miss it. This excitement has a symbolic meaning as well since the youth are more ready to accept new ideas than the rest of the society for they are less concerned about rationalizing matters. For instance, they are already sleeping when Cipolla appears on stage much later than expected but it takes very little time for them to readapt to the magical environment, and they are lost in amazement soon. The figure on the stage is ugly and weird: "a sharp, ravaged face, piercing eyes, compressed lips, small black waxed moustache, and a so-called imperial in the curve between mouth and chin" (149). His hair is ugly, too, the top of his head being almost bald, and he has a hunchback. He carries a riding-whip in his pelerine. From the very first moment that he has made his entrance, he becomes the center of attention. The audience watches him with ambivalent feelings as Cipolla is both fascinating and awe-inspiring in his colorful fancy clothes. Then he starts his eloquent speech, which attracts even more attention than his looks and his whip. He is outspokenly nationalistic and fascistic, making such remarks as "In Italy everybody can write – in all her greatness there is no room for ignorance and unenlightenment" (156). His actual show begins with arithmetical tests and Cipolla talks "all the while, relieving the dryness of his offering by a constant flow of words" (155). The trick is that he has already written the answers down for the calculations made with random numbers which the volunteers write on the board. He then has the numbers guessed which are written on the paper beforehand and the guess is nearly always right. There is one instance in which one of the guessers admits that he has had in mind to give a certain number but when Cipolla's whip goes whistling through the air, a different one slips out which turns out to be the right one. This incidence is very much in line with what Hannah Arendt says about totalitarian rulers: "Mass leaders in power have one concern which overrules all utilitarian considerations: to make their predictions come true" (349). Likewise, Cipolla consolidates his power and his influence on people by being in control of the whole process and not allowing anything unexpected to happen. He tries a similar trick by cards and of course he manages to find out the chosen ones. But this time he meets a challenge by one of the men in the front row. The man tells him that he wants to assert his own will in his choice and consciously to resist any influence of whatever sort. Cipolla's answer is remarkable; the rhetoric of oppression is at work again. He says:

> You will make my task somewhat more difficult thereby. As for the result, your resistance will not alter it in the least. Freedom exists, and also the will exists; but freedom of the will does not exist, for a will that aims at its own freedom aims at the unknown. You are free to draw or not to draw. But if you draw, you will draw the right cards – the more certainly, the more willfully obstinate your behavior. (162)

His words are an explicit attack on will power and a repudiation of the freedom of choice. They amount to saying "You are bound to do what I tell you to do." The elevated language Cipolla speaks cannot hide the fact that he is trying to impose his will on people rather than let them follow their own choices. This is typical of totalitarian regimes where there is only collective willpower which always follows the leader's will. The subordinates act with the utmost obedience as if hypnotized by the mass ruler. In view of this it is no coincidence that the second part of the magician's show is concerned with hypnosis in which he reaches the height of his power.

"The force possessed by totalitarian propaganda lies in its ability to shut the masses off from the real world" says Arendt (353), and this is exactly what Cipolla does in creating an alternative reality which can be manipulated and dominated more easily. He turns the body of a young man into a board and makes an elderly lady believe that she is on a voyage to India by hypnotizing them, and the lady even gives an account of her adventures. Then a tall, soldierly man is unable to lift his arm after Cipolla tells him that he cannot and cleaves the air with his whip. One of the most striking moments of the show is when Cipolla makes a couple of men dance on stage. Observing the magician and the way his power work on people, the narrator says:

> He had the wit to make his attack at the weakest point and to choose as his first victim that feeble, ecstatic youth whom he had previously made into a board. The master had but to look at him, when this young man would fling himself back as though struck by lightning, place his hands rigidly at his sides, and fall into a state of military somnambulism, in which it was plain to any eye that he was open to the most absurd suggestion that might be made to him. He seemed quite content in his abject state, quite pleased to be relieved of the burden of voluntary choice. (172)

It seems the answer to the questions posed by Mann is contained in these lines. The key factor is "to be relieved of the burden of voluntary choice." Once the leader paves the way, it is easy to follow the path without questioning anything or trying to get rid of his hypnotic influence. One is also exempt from taking responsibilities in this way and as mentioned before the youth are generally keener to take this path. It is a widely known fact that both Mussolini and Hitler had youth corps functioning as active propagandists of their ideology when the two were in power. As it is not a coincidence for Mann to use the image of hypnosis in the story, it is not a coincidence either for Cipolla to choose his volunteers from among young people. According to Feuerlicht,

> Cipolla is an incarnation of the evil power which ugly fascism held over the masses – especially the young, many of whom were glad to escape from their personal freedom, their individual responsibility, and their sense of reality, in order

> to follow the commands of the leader and to act as the others did. (128)

This submission to the commands of the leader necessitates the eradication of individual identity. It creates what is rather a pseudo-identity for the followers which allows very little or no space for personal freedom, just as the leader creates a manipulative pseudo-reality. That is why the young men are dancing on stage thinking that they really want to dance but in fact it is what Cipolla wills them to do. Despite feeling quite uncomfortable about the way the show proceeds, even the narrator cannot leave. The children seem to be a good excuse since they are not aware of what is going on but the narrator and his wife are uneasy about staying as if they have foreseen what will happen next. The narrator asks himself: "Were we under the sway of a fascination which emanated from this man [. . .]; a fascination which he gave out independently of the programme and even between the tricks and which paralyzed our resolve?" (167). The decision mechanism seems to stop operating in their case, too, as though they are conditioned to stay until the end of the show. At this point, it is useful to look at Arendt's commentary on the issue of individuality and freedom. She says:

> [. . .] To destroy individuality is to destroy spontaneity, man's power to begin something new out of his own resources, something that cannot be explained on the basis of reactions to environment and events. Nothing then remains but ghastly marionettes with human faces, which all behave like the dog in Pavlov's experiments, which all react with perfect reliability even when going to their own death, and which do nothing but react. (455)

When we think within Arendt's framework, we can consider Cipolla as a destroyer of individuality. However, the situation is more complicated and paradoxical than it seems. These are people who volunteer to be subdued by the magician. Even if they totally lose control when exposed to his power, they still have the chance to avoid it from the very beginning. Or they can get rid of it at the very moment they start perceiving and questioning. This is exactly what Mario does to overcome the paradox, his solution being a tragic one, though. He appears only at the end of the story, although Mann uses his name in the title. Now there are only Mario and the magician on stage, as the title suggests. Cipolla convinces him to volunteer even if he is hesitant to do so. Then the session of soul-possessing starts once more with Cipolla's attempts to learn more about Mario so as to take everything under his control. He begins with flattering the young man, talking about the beauty of his scarf and his possible popularity among girls with such good looks. Mario is slow to open up and prefers to give short answers to the magician's questions. Then comes the deadly question. "Do you believe in me?" asks Cipolla and is answered by an indefinite gesture. But this does not make any difference at this point for he has already found out the weakness of his victim and is ready to take hold of him. Mario is troubled by his unrequited love for Silvestra and Cipolla is using all his expertise to provoke the poor man. He says: "Is she to give any young gamecock the preference, so that he can laugh while you cry? To prefer him to a chap like you, so full of feeling and so sympathetic? Not very likely, is it? It is impossible – we know better, Cipolla and she" (179).

As he keeps on talking, Mario begins to be hypnotized by his words. Now the hunchback magician appears to the youth as Silvestra, his beloved. "Kiss me!" Cipolla says to the utterly defenseless man who is mesmerized by what he sees; "Trust me, I love thee" (180). How can a person resist such words which, he thinks, come from the person he loves and which he wants to believe with all his heart? Mario's resistance is totally shattered, and he kisses the man whom he thinks is Silvestra. This is the ultimate affirmation of Cipolla's evil power. Now there remains nothing of free will or individual choice but only an absolute subordination to what Cipolla wills. However, the show is not finished yet. The moment Mario comes to his senses and realizes what he has done, he, rather than the mighty Cipolla, ends the show by shooting the magician. For the narrator it is "an end of horror, a fatal end. And yet a liberation" (181).

Thomas Mann portrays Cipolla and Mario from the perspective of an antagonistic relationship. While Cipolla is the voice of the oppressor casting a magic spell on the masses to follow him, Mario embodies the ideals of free will and liberation. He liberates both himself and the rest of the audience from the tyranny of the magician. Ironically, the magician turns out to be the victim at the end for the very same reasons that make him the oppressor. He presents himself as somebody he is not and this is the source of both his power and his downfall. His influence is not genuine for he appears to be different from what he really is. Mario manages to see this, despite a temporary mental block. His killing Cipolla is a symbolic action which signifies the reassertion of free will by getting rid of the hypnotic effect and the removal of the blocks in people's minds so as to make them think in a healthy way again.

Leading his life as a German expatriate deprived of his nationality, Thomas Mann sadly saw that the disease of fascism prevented people from thinking independently. Even if the outbreak of World War II showed that the warning implicit in *Mario and the Magician* was to no avail, Mann's insightful story provides the reader with plenty of food for thought on the dynamics of oppression and victimhood.

Works Cited

Mann, Thomas. *Mario and the Magician.* In *Death in Venice and Seven Other Stories.* Trans. H. T. Lowe-Porter. New York: Vintage, 1989.

Arendt, Hannah. *The Origins of Totalitarianism.* Harvest Book 244. New York: Harcourt, 1976.

Feuerlicht, Ignace. *Thomas Mann.* Twayne's World Authors Series 47. New York: Twayne, 1968.

The Turkish-Greek Population Exchange in the Contemporary Turkish Novel

Lâmia Gülçur
Boğaziçi University

Abstract: In this paper, novels and biographical writing that have appeared in Turkish concerning the population exchange of 1923 are analyzed with reference to the historical background and the reasons for the exchange.

The compulsory population exchange between Turkey and Greece was enacted in 1923 within the framework of the Lausanne treaty. The existence of Greek-speaking people in Anatolia or modern-day Turkey and Turks in modern-day Greece has its roots in past history. The Greek presence in Asia Minor goes back to 1000 B.C., and spans the Ancient Greek, Roman, and Byzantine and Ottoman periods. On the other hand, the first Turks to inhabit what is Greece today were mercenaries settled in these lands by the Byzantines. There is mention of wealthy Turkish merchants in Thessaloniki in the 9th century (İpek 11).

As the Ottoman Empire expanded, it systematically settled Turks in the newly acquired areas. Later, as the Empire declined and retreated, the Turks, as well as those who were not ethnically Turkish but had converted to Islam, were to retreat with it. Those that were Muslims of different ethnic groups were many. Mazowar claims that the Ottoman administration had difficulty at times trying to stop people from converting en masse (127). The retreat was not solely connected with the decline of the Ottomans but also with Christian Europe's integral wish to rid Europe of Turks and Muslims. One authority, Sir John Mariot, claimed that "the primary and most essential factor in the problem [the Eastern problem, the Balkans] is the presence embedded in the living flesh of Europe of an alien substance. This substance is the Ottoman Turk" (qtd. in Mazowar 13). More than five million Turks or Muslims (these were people of Slav, Magyar, Macedonian, etc origin) were driven from the Balkans and the

Black Sea region to what was later to become the Republic of Turkey within the hundred years following the first half of the 19th century (İpek 15).

After the Balkan War, in September 1913, a convention was signed between Bulgaria and Turkey allowing the voluntary exchange of minorities most of whom had already fled to their "respective" countries. The success of this convention led to yet another such treaty being signed in Lausanne in 1923, this time between Greece and Turkey. The agreement came after what Stathakou calls "the inglorious outcome of the expansionist campaign of the Greeks in Asia Minor, which was based on and encouraged by European imperialism" (1066). The compulsory exchange agreement stipulated the exchange of the Greek/*Rum* population of Turkey, except for those living in Istanbul, and Imbroz for the Muslims who resided in Greece, irrespective of their ethnic origin. The only Turks/Muslims who were allowed to remain were those from Thrace (İpek 4). Though not all, a vast majority of these repatriated people had never seen the "homelands" they were sent to. Bernard Lewis claims that the exchange was a matter of sending Christian Turks to Greece and Muslim Greeks to Turkey (12). However, everyone concerned was "returned" to his respective country, enabling an increased ethnic homogeneity in both the nation states. This was the official coloring of what was being done. This is what a linear history of numbers, policies, and politics tells us.

What really happened to these people is the realm of narrative, since narrative is what Bakhtin calls "an authentic site, perhaps the privileged site of social knowledge, precisely because of its polyphonic character as opposed to the monologisms [. . .] of historical writing that remains unaware of (its) passive character" (*The Dialogic Imagination*, qtd. in Aronowitz 163). The exchange was traumatic in that it destroyed the immigrants' point of reference, since it is the community that links its members to something whose existence seems to extend back into time immemorial and forward into the indefinite future. When there is a rupture in this linear cognitive continuity at personal as well as at communal level, a traumatic situation arises. Major life-altering circumstances may be an occasion for "narrative reconstruction," an attempt to bring back autobiographical coherence so that life may be seen as having a purpose and value again (Hinchman 121). Through narrative, these individuals try to find a beginning and end, a meaning and a reason for their lives and experiences.

Narratives of the exchange appeared in Greece almost immediately after the exchange had been completed. This is probably due to the fact that the Greeks had not experienced this kind of uprooting before. What they called the Catastrophe of Asia Minor, the defeat and retreat of the invading Greek army, as well as the displacement of people who had lived in Anatolia for thousands of years, found voice in the novels that appeared within the first fifteen years after the deportation of the *Rum*. One of these novels, *The Land of Blood* by Dido Sotiriou was translated into Turkish in the 1980s (*Benden Selam Söyle Anadolu'ya* [*Give my regards to Anatolia*]) and gained popularity among Turkish readers.

The Turks remained silent for a long time. Various theories were put forward concerning this silence. Some claimed that the Turks who had been uprooted were mostly of peasant stock and therefore did not care to express themselves in writing, while others claimed that the silence was due to the pride in once having been an empire and not wishing to express pain in loss. The truth was probably the fact that the Turks had faced worse tragedies: massacres during the Balkan War, and enmity of neighbors as the Empire retreated till it dwindled to what would become the borders of the Turkish Republic. In short, they had suffered worse fates and learned to bear their misery in silence.

Narratives concerning the exchange began to appear in the late 90s. One of the most prominent of these narratives is Kemal Yalçın's *Emanet Çeyiz: Mübadele İnsanları* (*The Trousseau: People of the Exchange*). The book is the story of Yalçın's search for his *Rum* neighbor's daughter in order to return the trousseau she had left behind when leaving Anatolia. Yalçın's family had kept the trousseau for more than seventy years to be returned when the family came back to their house in Turkey. As Yalçın scours both Greece and Anatolia to find the family, he interviews those that had been forced to leave their homeland.

An old Turkish immigrant tells Yalçın:

> Everyday, I think about the place where I was born and grew up. [. . .] I would like to see my country. I would like to see

> my master Kiratimnu, I would like to see Nahuv Chichipa and say goodbye to them. I am old now; if you go, take them my message; I am Murtaza Acar from Kastro, Mehmet Sipaki's son. I have worked for you; I have eaten your bread. [. . .] the order for the population exchange came [. . .] we left everything, our country, our village, our possessions [. . .] we almost cried. Parting is very difficult.[1] (184)

The story is very much the same for the *Rum* that had to leave. Father Yorgo explains:

> But our country was different. Ayvancik, Sinop was beautiful… We were happy in our country. It wasn't our fault… It seems in Izmir they gave soldiers to the Greeks, but we didn't. It was the English who persuaded the Greeks to attack Turkey and then withdrew. And we suffered… What did you gain from this? Nothing. Everything was wasted... A lot of blood was shed... They shouldn't have had this exchange… we waited for years to return… the people in Sinop cried for us not to leave...War is bad. You Turk, I Greek leave all this behind you. No one wins when there is war. (131)

Each immigrant longs for the landscape of the place that he has left behind and the fruits and vegetables, their neighbors. Muhittin Yavuz from Vrashno explains they had orchards with every kind of fruit: "Our plums were different; they had a different taste. I am ninety-three and I have traveled much. I have not seen or tasted plums like Vrashno plums anywhere" (200). "There were green mountains there. I haven't seen mountains like those here. I cannot forget them," says a woman originally from Thessaloniki (218). "Our village had eighteen windmills. We had a lot of land. We planted maize. [. . .] You could plant a person and he would become a man. Our world was that fertile," claims

1 All translations are the author's.

another (218). "Crete was the heaven in the Mediterranean! It was such a beautiful place. I cannot tell you. [. . .] Everything was beautiful there! Our homeland was a place to cherish. Its people were real men," says an old man from Crete (270).

The feelings are the same for people who were forced to go to Greece. "It's the season. If we had some Aydın figs, we could eat a bowl now" says Angela Katerini, who had to leave Anatolia and go to Greece, "Ah, those Aydın figs" (144), while Tanasis Bakırcıoğlu talks abut the smell of newly baked bread, the cheese, the butter, and the cream, the hundreds of kilos of grapes they harvested. "They don't have these things in Greece! I have to explain these things to them," he claims (113).

In short, the land of desire and plenty of good relations with neighbors is the land that has been left behind. The stories of these immigrants are also full of the good relations between neighboring villages of Christian and Turk. Each one has a memory of the harmonious life they had together until the politics of war and nationhood entered the picture. Each immigrant has a memory of a person from the other group helping them in time of need: a Turkish soldier who enabled his neighbor to escape; a priest who protected his Turkish neighbors from the Greek militia; a kind mill-owner who shared his food with his Greek neighbor in time of need; a Turk who kept his Greek neighbor's daughter's trousseau for seventy years to return to her when she came back to her village. They all remember deteriorating conditions during the time of war. Another theme they have in common is their belief that they would ultimately return to their true country. Many report that they did not marry outside their tight communities so that things would be easier when the time came for them to return.

Berber relates the story of one of these families that had to leave Greece. Again the reader is faced with the anguish of parting and the strangeness of the country that the family has to settle in since it is their homeland. Feride, the subject of the life-story, reports: "At school they asked my brother why we had left our country to the enemy and come to theirs" (Berber 48).

These are the life-stories of those who were forced to leave. The images that emerge are similar: the land of desire and plenty, of friendship and comfort is the land that is left behind. The new country is strange and hostile to the newcomers.

İskender Özsoy's work *İki Vatan Yorgunları* (*The Disillusioned of Two Nations*) is a collection of interviews which also underline the fact that those people who were repatriated suffered since they were, as Lewis says, actually total strangers to the country that was supposed to be their homeland. Raziye Oğuş, one of his interviewees says: "The gendarmes took us from the boat to our new house. They rang the bell. The owners were inside. [. . .] The owner of the house didn't want to give up her house. Then they went crying to Greece. We too had cried when we had to leave Janina" (114).

Among the fiction that has appeared an important novel concerning the political background and the incidents of the years previous to the exchange is Kemal Anadol's *Büyük Ayrılık* (*The Great Separation*). The book is part research and part fiction dealing with the decline of the Ottoman Empire during the first part of the 20th century and its repercussions on the lives of the people of the Aegean: the Armenians, the Greeks, the Turks who lived and traded in harmony between Foça, Ayvalık, and Midilli. This well-documented work gives the lives and political beliefs of the people concerned. It also dwells on the harmony between the groups and exposes the fear and enmity that was engendered between these people as a result of politics.

Another noteworthy book is Ayla Kutlu's *Sen de Gitme Triyandafilis* (*Don't Go Triyandafilis*), a story about a rich Greek family of Izmir and their mentally retarded, beautiful daughter Triandafilia who is left to the servants when the family have to flee. The story is about the love of the nurturing family for the girl and the social makeup before the exchange.

Other novels seem to have been written by the children and grandchildren of Cretans who were forced to leave. The reason for this might be that the Cretans were fiercely bound to their land. Very few Cretan Turks knew Turkish and some changed their religion to say behind. Research, in fact, points to the fact that the Cretan Muslims and Christians were from the same stock, since only soldiers were sent to Crete. They married and stayed. Women and men converted from Christianity to Islam and vice versa in time. So that if a Muslim wanted to marry a Christian, she would change her religion, and if a Christian wanted to marry a Muslim the reverse would happen.

Giritli Mustafa (*Cretan Mustafa*) is part fiction part history, claims the author, Ertuğrul Erol Ergir. His aim, he says, in writing the book is to record the cries of the people of the population exchange so that the Mediterranean will become a lake of peace and prosperity. The story of Mustafa, the son of a Cretan Muslim, tells of the close relationship between the Greeks and the Turks living in Crete and the tension that arises between them due to international politics. The story ends with the family's moving to Turkey and leaving their past and their country behind.

Ahmet Yorulmaz seems to be the most prolific of these writers of Cretan origin. I will refer to two of his novels: *Savaşın Çocukları* (*The Children of War*) and *Girit'ten Cunda'ya ya da Aşkın Anatomisi* (*From Crete to Cunda or the Anatomy of Love*). Both novels start off in Crete and end in Ayvalık. *The Children of War* deals with the beginnings of the enmity between the people of Crete. It too, like the narratives of Yalçın, deals with the harmony between the communities until international politics takes hold and friction mounts. The hero Aynakis Hasan is ultimately forced to leave his country for Ayvalık. But the tale is woven with good relations between the small communities. The reason for the enmity emerges as the politics of Venizelos and the lethargy of the Ottoman Empire, the sick man of Europe.

The Anatomy of Love is also about initial good relations and the understanding the two communities have for each other. It is about the illicit relationship of a wealthy Greek Cretan, Marigo, and Hasanaki, a handsome Turk. When Hasanaki has to leave Crete for Turkey he leaves behind a pregnant Marigo, who tries to bring up her son Haralambos to be tolerant of Turks. The story ends with Haralambos coming to Ayvalık and meeting his father after his mother's death. Haralambos changes his name to Hasan and remains in Turkey to marry a Turk. Both stories dwell on the underlying politics of change. On the fact that there was no difference between Muslim and Christian Cretans, Greece started sending large numbers of immigrants to Crete in order to be able to claim the island, which had been conquered from the Venetians in the 17th century and which had a population of almost equal numbers until the end of the 19th century.

Another novel by a Turk of Cretan origin is *Kritimu: Girit'im Benim* (*Kritimu: My Crete*) by Saba Altınsay. It too deals with very much the same theme. The protagonist İbrahim and his family have close relationships with their Christian neighbors. They share the joys and sorrows of family life with their neighbor Hrisula, a relationship that remains unchanged although tension grows between the two groups and life becomes dangerous for both Muslim and Christian. One of the prominent Muslim citizens of Hanya, Aziz Bey, asks: "Let us say that the Cretan Christians are rebelling to attain their independence. Let us say that they are protecting their lands. But may I ask whose land this is? Is it not ours also? Christians and Muslims, we all came here from other places and settled in Crete. How do they know who is more Cretan?" (Altınsay 196). This vital question seems to be one that remains in the minds of Cretan Turks after several generations.

Works Cited

Altınsay, Saba. *Kritimu: Girit'im Benim.* Istanbul: Can, 2004.

Anadol, Kemal. *Büyük Ayrılık.* Istanbul: Doğan, 2003.

Aronowitz, S. *Dead Artists and Live Theories*. New York: Routledge, 1994.

Bakhtin, Mikhail M. *The Dialogic Imagination: Four Essays*. Trans. Caryl Emerson and Michael Holquist. Ed. Michael Holquist. Austin: U of Texsas P, 1981

Balkan, Arif. *Cumhuriyet Türkiye'sinin İnşası: Anılar.* Istanbul: Papirüs, 1998.

Berber, Engin. *Rumeli'den İzmir'e Yitik Yaşamlar İzinde*. İzmir: Stil, 2002.

Ergir, Ertuğrul Erol. *Giritli Mustafa.* İzmir: Türkelmat, 2003.

Hinchman, Lewis P., and Sandra K. Hinchman, ed. *Memory, Identity, Community*. New York: State U of New York P, 2001.

İpek, Nedim. *Mübadele ve Samsun*. Ankara: Türk Tarih Kurumu, 2000.

Kutlu, Ayla. *Sen de Gitme Triyandafilis.* Istanbul: Bilgi, 2000.

Lewis, Bernard. *The Multiple Identities of the Middle East.* New York: Schocken, 1998.

Mazowar, Mark. *The Balkans*. London: Phoenix, 2001.

Özsoy, İskender. *İki Vatan Yorgunları*. Istanbul: Bağlam, 2003.
Sotiriu, Dido. *Benden Selam Söyle Anadolu'ya*. Trans. Atilla Tokatlı. Istanbul: Can, 2001. Trans. of *The Land of Blood.*
Stathakou, Katilena P. "The Compulsory Exchange of Populations between Greece and Turkey after 1923: The Case of the Muslims of Crete." *Cross-roads of History: Experience, Memory, Orality*. Vol. 3. Proceedings, 15-19 June 2000, Boğaziçi University. Istanbul: Boğaziçi University, 2000. 1066-1070.
Yalçın, Kemal. *Emanet Çeyiz: Mübadele İnsanları*. İstanbul: Doğan Kitapçılık, 1999.
Yorulmaz, Ahmet. *Savaşın Çocukları*. Istanbul: Remzi, 2001.
---. *Girit'ten Cunda'ya ya da Aşkın Anatomisi*. Istanbul: Remzi, 2003.

Willfully or by Force? Resistance and Surrender in Orhan Pamuk's *The White Castle* and Kobo Abe's *The Woman in the Dunes*

Özlem Öğüt
Boğaziçi University

Abstract: This article focuses on the ways in which *The Woman in the Dunes* and *The White Castle*, two novels by two internationally acclaimed contemporary novelists, Kobo Abe and Orhan Pamuk, respectively, call into question universalizing and essentializing notions of identity through their portrayal of the traumatic encounter of their protagonists with their 'other,' which marks the beginning of an intense power struggle and an emotion-laden love-and-hate relationship between them. Both the entomologist/schoolteacher from a big city in twentieth-century Japan and the Venetian scholar taken prisoner by Turkish soldiers while sailing from Venice to Naples in the seventeenth century are deeply frustrated and cannot think of anything but escape when they are forced to live as the captive of a person who they initially consider as fundamentally different from themselves: the woman who lives in a sand pit in a village in the middle of nowhere and endlessly struggles against the accumulating sand, and the Ottoman Hoja (master/teacher) who is obsessed with science, cosmology and the secrets of his being. Both protagonists end up staying on their own freewill as their new lives expose the limitations of their own systems of knowledge and social existence, and open vistas into a more inclusive and multi-dimensional understanding of life, in which the categories subject/object, internal/external, self/other become fluid.

In her *Chaos Bound: Orderly Disorder in Contemporary Literature and Science*, N. Katherine Hayles refers to two general branches within chaos theory. The first posits "the spontaneous emergence of self-organization," and that "entropy-rich systems facilitate rather than impede self-organization," according to which chaos is seen "as order's precursor and partner, rather than its opposite" (9). The second branch distinguishes chaos from true randomness, which shows no discernible pattern, pointing to the deeply encoded structures existing within chaotic systems (9).

Hayles underlines that a major fault line developed in the episteme due to the "destabilization of a dichotomy as central to Western thought as order/disorder," which is also underlined by other theoretical enterprises such as post-structuralism, especially deconstruction, which "exposes the interrelation between traditional ideas of order and oppressive ideologies" as well as the death of the subject (16-17). In this context, Hayles naturally refers to Michel Foucault's works, which focus on the pivotal role of power in the creation of systems of knowledge as well as the limitations they impose on the human mind, including monolithic conceptions of subjectivity, which, in accordance with the dominant epistemes, is generally based upon the dichotomy between the 'self' and the 'other.'

What constitutes the parallelism between Orhan Pamuk's *The White Castle* and Kobo Abe's *The Woman in the Dunes* is primarily the ways in which they undermine not only the conceptions of nature and culture, which are based upon the dichotomy of order/disorder, but also essentializing views of subjectivity. In other words, they de-naturalize or de-universalize categorically and hicrarchically ordered notions of time, space, body and identity, by displaying their contextuality and fluidity, and manifesting the tendency of natural phenomena towards entropy, which may defy the solidity of all established systems.

Both novels revolve around the tension-laden love-and-hate relationship between two main characters that constantly alternate in their roles as oppressor and oppressed, victimizer and victim, master and slave. In each novel, one of these characters experiences a traumatic encounter with his 'other' into whose snare he falls without much hope for escape although escape is all that is on his mind. The interaction between these characters and their 'others' during their 'captivity' makes them more and more conscious of the limitedness of their preformed and deeply ingrained conceptions of life with all its social, moral, emotional ramifications, and prepares them for an alternative mode of existence, perhaps even resistance. They both end up staying of their own will.

The White Castle is set in seventeenth-century Istanbul. The two protagonists are the Ottoman Hoja, meaning "master" or "teacher," in this case both, who is obsessed with unraveling the secrets of the universe as well as his being, and the narrator, an Venetian scholar taken prisoner by Turkish sailors while sailing from Venice to Naples, who, as a Westerner is supposed to guide and assist Hoja in his scientific endeavors. Thanks to a few books of anatomy, he manages to take with him he can pass as a doctor and is given the privilege to work with Hoja. He admits that he had luck in the whole matter: "After I'd treated a few Turks using my common sense rather than knowledge of anatomy, and their wounds had healed by themselves, everyone believed I was a doctor" (16). Throughout the novel, the Venetian and Hoja experience the joy of success and often jealousy that comes with it or the disappointment of failure when they work on or put to practice their scientific projects such as the production of fireworks, weapons to be used in wars by the Ottoman army, the prediction of the course of the plague, even their dream interpretations for the Sultan. In all of these endeavors, chance, in addition to common sense and scientific knowledge, emerges as a determining factor in their success or failure. Sometimes an experiment, which consistently yields mediocre results, creates a miracle during its public demonstration whereas another one, which they regard as promising may thwart their expectations when it is put into practice.

In *The Woman in the Dunes*, set in late twentieth-century Japan, a big-city schoolteacher, an amateur entomologist at the same time, takes his equipment and embarks on a short-term vacation or rather an expedition in the dunes by the ocean with the purpose of discovering a new species of insects. As he is walking in and around a little village which consists of several houses carved into pits in the sand, several feet below the ground level and accessed through a rope ladder, he is told by some old men sitting in front of the cooperative building that he missed the last bus and will have to spend the night in the village. They take him to the house, or rather the hole, of a widow in her thirties. He is appalled by the woman's life style, which requires an ongoing struggle against sand and sand slide. The endless cycle of work, which consists of shoveling the constantly accumulating excess of sand and collecting it in buckets which are then picked up by men assigned for this job is shocking for him. Despite all these efforts, sand keeps invading her space. It comes flying in with the wind, falls from the walls and ceilings. It clings to one's body. The limited amount of water brought by the "basket-men" is almost useless in the face of the all-pervasive power of sand. To his dismay, he finds out that he cannot even take a bath that night because the woman's water supply is replenished only on certain days. Even if he could, soon he would soak in sweat due to immense humidity and the sand would stick to his face and body. Still, he feels a certain kind of excitement, thinking he is going through an extraordinary experience, an adventure, and looks forward to the following day, when he can leave the hole and continue his expedition. However, his real struggle against nature, specifically sand, the woman and the village community starts with his discovery the following morning that the rope ladder has been removed. From then on, he is forced to help the woman with her routine work because the basket-men refuse to let him use the rope ladder, but at the same time this is his willful struggle for life because if he does not help the woman the pit-house may collapse on them. In this respect, the man's struggle is similar to the Venetian narrator's in *The White Castle* since he is forced to help Hoja – after all, he is in the position of a slave – but at the same time he hopes to become a freedman as a reward for his achievements. However, neither Hoja nor the pasha (the general) of the army will make him a freedman unless he converts to Islam, which he refuses to do despite all threats. Furthermore, Hoja and the pasha use the Venetian to impress and gain the favor of the young Sultan in the hope to eliminate their rivals in an ongoing power struggle. The pasha, who is afraid of being poisoned, appeals to the Venetian about the slightest health problems he experiences. Hoja's competition for the position of imperial astrologer gains impetus through joint projects engaging his imagination and the Venetian's. Moreover, a former slave who had converted to Islam many years before reveals that "they" always keep a slave who is useful to them such as himself, never granting permission to return to his country even if they grant his freedom.

A parallel can be drawn between the two protagonists' selfless struggle for liberation and the fact that they are not referred to by their names in the novels.

With the exception of the entomologist, whose name appears for the first time almost halfway into the book, not to be mentioned again except in a couple of cases, none of the four main characters are referred to by their name. In *The White Castle*, it is 'I' and 'Hoja,' or towards the end of the novel, when the two become indistinguishable, it is the pronouns 'I' and 'he' that designate the two or rather both, whereas in *The Woman in the Dunes*, the woman and the man are referred to as 'the woman' and 'the man' except for a few instances, and that is when the man's name appears in the newspaper announcements which report him as missing. All of the above designations suggest both their urge to exist as individuals and their being subsumed in a category. Both novels bring to the readers' attention multiple social strata and power structures that prevent the emergence of individuality in the environments in which the protagonists live. What may initially appear as the account of the relationship between two individuals in each novel is in fact full of implications concerning the power structures surrounding them, and as these two individuals gain insight into each other, they realize the influence of those power structures on their lives and their self-conceptions, which appear rather limited once they are exposed to other such systems, which are also epistemes, but different from their own. As Michael Payne points out in his *Reading Knowledge*, in which he discusses Foucault's work, what constitutes the charm of such another system of thought is that it exposes the limitations of our own means of ordering things (48). Abe and Pamuk display the process of their protagonists' realization that it is precisely the restrictions of their own system of knowledge which causes their limited view of their 'other's' life and his/her understanding of the universe.

In *The Woman in the Dunes*, the man's aim is to establish his name in scientific circles by discovering a new species, in other words, to stand out as an individual but at the same time he wants to belong to a certain category of scientists, the ones whose names are associated with the species they found. Unwittingly, he associates himself with another being, an imaginary insect, when he says that the efforts of a discoverer are "crowned with success if his name is perpetuated in the memory of his fellow men by being associated with an insect" (10). He is particularly interested in finding one that displays a great degree of adaptability by surviving in this world of sand, which is in such close vicinity to the sea. Ironically, as the events unfold, it is not only the woman with her animal-like existence but also himself who can be associated with the species he is looking for, an analogy, which he has a hard time to accept. Hence the long period of frustration and rejection as well as his many unsuccessful attempts to escape. Despite all his careful calculations regarding his weight, the slope of the sand hill around the pit, the humidity level, the angle of his body vis-à-vis the slope, the speed of the flow of the sand, in order to achieve maximum efficiency in his climb up, the sand defies his scientific knowledge and turns all into entropy. Sand slides and absorbs his body as if to remove the boundary between them, to force him to adapt. As he admits, "there was no escaping the law of sand" (17).

One of the most striking images of the kind of adaptability, which fascinates the man, is to be found in the part of the novel in which he observes the woman's naked body, with only her face covered by a towel, while she is sleeping. The curves of her body are covered by sand and look like sand dunes, the visible form of the inextricable link between her and her environment. Sand also connects him with her because it is like a blanket that covers all bodies whose movements can hardly be conceived of as distinct from the motion of the sand. It all folds and unfolds endlessly in a way that is reminiscent of Deleuze and Guattari's conception of "plateaus," a term that they borrow from Gregory Bateson who defines it as "a continuous, self-vibrating region of intensities whose development avoids any orientation toward a culmination point or external end" (Bateson, qtd. in Deleuze and Guattari 21-22). Deleuze and Guattari describe "plateaus" as "between" things, and point out that

> *Between* things does not designate a localizable relation going from one thing to the other and back again, but a perpendicular direction, a transversal moment that sweeps one *and* the other away, a stream without beginning or end that undermines its banks and picks up speed in the middle. (25)

Indeed the village of sand is a territory that cannot be assimilated into either order or disorder, form or non-form; it is in an undifferentiated state which N. Katherine Hayles associates with chaos (19). According to the man it is madness although he soon realizes that life in this village is yet another system, which is not any more binding than the one that marks his life in the city. Sand recalls the existence of other loci of power, which are equally pervasive but may be less visible or tangible. In his preface to his *Madness and Civilization* Foucault contends,

> We have yet to write the history of that other form of madness, by which men, in an act of sovereign reason, confine their neighbors, and communicate and recognize each other through the merciless language of non-madness [. . .] We must try to return, in history, to that zero point in the course of madness at which madness is an undifferentiated experience, a not yet divided experience of division itself. (ix)

In *The Woman in the Dunes*, sand compels the man to what Foucault calls "thinking beyond his reason" and "marking the caesura that establishes the distance between reason and non-reason" (ix). Indeed, the formation of sand and its flow defy reason despite its clear scientific definition as "an aggregate of rock fragments. Sometimes including loadstone, tinstone, and more rarely gold dust" (Abe 13). For the man, the explanation that sand came from fragmented rock and was intermediate between clay and pebbles is not a satisfactory one because "If a true intermediate substance were involved, the erosive action of wind and water would necessarily produce any number of intermingling immediate forms in the range between rock and clay" but "there are in fact only three forms that can be clearly distinguished from one another: stones, sand, and clay" (13). He is even more puzzled by the fact that "there is almost no difference in the size of the grains whether they come from the Goby Desert or from the beach at Etnoshima" (13). As such, sand unsettles the dualism of order/disorder. Moreover, the man's contrast between "the ceaseless movement of sand" and "the dreary way human beings clung together" (15) testifies to his awareness of the stagnation of his social existence, which finds expression in the following passage, in which Abe craftily mixes humor with pathos. The man refers to the socially sanctioned form of love:

> Sexual intercourse is like a commutation ticket: it has to be punched every time you use it. Of course, you must check to see that the ticket is genuine. But this checking is terribly onerous; it corresponds precisely to the complications of order. All kinds of certificates – contracts, licenses, I.D. cards, permits, certificates of title, authorizations, registrations, carrying permits, certificates of memberships, letters of recommendation, notes, leases, temporary permits, agreements, income declarations, receipts, even certificates of ancestry . . . every conceivable type of paper must be mobilized into action. (137)

For the first time in his life the man experiences with this woman, whom he often finds repulsive and pitiable, what he calls "sexual desire in general or sex in particular" (136), which refers to a state before the evolution of "particular sexual tastes" (136). He compares this to hunger, which does not discriminate between particular kinds of food: "Food exists only in an abstract sense for anybody dying of hunger; there isn't any such thing as the taste of Kobe beef or Hiroshima oysters. But once one's belly is full, then one begins to discern differences in taste and textures" (136). This notion of desire is rather similar to the one posited by Deleuze and Guattari in their seminal book *Anti-Oedipus*. As Ronald Bogue writes, for Deleuze and Guattari desire is essentially unconscious and indifferent to personal identities and body images; it is pre-personal and pre-individual (Bogue 89).

The transcendence of the boundary of individual consciousness and the dissolution of the dichotomies of subject/object or self/other finds a rather poignant expression in *The White Castle,* in the Venetian narrator's cognizance of the striking similarity between Hoja and himself when he first meets him: "The resemblance between myself and the man who entered the room was incredible!

It was me there" (22). On another occasion later, the pasha says that whenever he tried to recall the Venetian 's face, Hoja's had come to his mind, which engenders a conversation about twins and look-alikes "who were frightened at the sight of one another but were unable, as if bewitched, ever again to part" (37). This is indeed what happens as the novel progresses.

Hoja's house becomes the arena of a relentless power struggle between these two characters who supposedly belong to two different worlds. They alternate in assuming superiority, and torture one another with words, silence or indifference, a state that can never last too long since both realize how much they need and depend on each other in order to fulfil their aims. Initially, all that Hoja wants is to emulate the scientific minds and inventions of people from the West, to whom he refers as "they" and sometimes as "fools," a term, which he uses also with reference to Muslims who resist being enlightened by his knowledge. On the other hand, the Venetian's only aim is to obtain his freedom and return to his country, which he thinks he can do by fulfilling the requests of Hoja and other notable Muslims. He vehemently refuses to convert to Islam, all the while thinking that "they" are "fools."

Years go by, in the course of which the two disclose their innermost selves to each other in their dream narrations, stories from their lives, and confessions of their fantasies, secrets, sins and lies. The narrator's prophetic dream about "an endless, sleepless night" following the death of his closest friend with whom he had got into the habit of "thinking the same thing at the same time," and how he feared that he might be "presumed dead and be buried alive with him" (62) foreshadows the climax of the novel when the narrator and Hoja look at each other's half-naked bodies in the mirror.

The two of us were one person! This now seemed to me an obvious truth. It was as if I were bound fast, my hands tied, unable to budge. I made a movement to save myself, as if to verify I was myself. I quickly ran my hands through my hair. But he imitated my gesture and did it perfectly, without disturbing the symmetry of the mirror image at all. He also imitated my look, the attitude of my head, he mimicked my terror I could not endure to see in the mirror but from which, transfixed by fear, I could not tear my eyes away [. . .] He shouted that we would die together [. . .] Then he said he had taken possession of my spirit; just as a moment before he'd mirrored my movements, whatever I was thinking now, he knew it, and whatever I knew, he was thinking it! (82-83)

The erasure of the boundary between their bodies is unnerving for the narrator because it unsettles his sense of selfhood. As Deidre Lynch contends, "The human face was supposed to function as a rigid designator: as a distinct sign belonging to the same distinct person in all possible worlds [. . .] A face indexed character: a social norm, a determinate place on the ethical map where every person had a proper place and where distinction was contained within limits" (Lynch 116-117). Another reason why he becomes distressed is the possibility that the swelling on Hoja's belly might not be an insect bite but a symptom of the plague that infected the city. He is terrified by the thought that Hoja might be passing the illness on to him when he gets closer to him or touches him, especially when he says, "I know your fear. I have become you" (83). The narrator writes, "He's doing this because he enjoys going outside of himself, observing himself from a distance [. . .] like someone struggling to awake from a dream" (85-86), which is reminiscent of his prophetic dream, with the only but significant difference that Hoja replaces him as the one who is having the dream.

The relationship between body and mind which becomes manifest in this part of the novel reflects Maurice Merleau-Ponty's conception of self as oriented being and the world as universal flesh, which involves an intertwining of the body with other bodies as well as a relation between mind and body based on reciprocity and reversibility: "a being of depths, of several leaves or several faces, a being in latency, a presentation of a certain absence" (136). It is not hard to discern the parallelism between Merleau-Ponty's ideas of "universal flesh" or "oriented being" and the concept of "plateaus" discussed earlier. Both dispense with the categories of inside and outside, subject and object, a view that is also highlighted by the recurrent motif of the Möbius circle in *The Woman in the Dunes*, which is defined as "a length of paper, twisted once, the two ends of which are pasted together, thus forming a surface that has neither front nor back" (99). The experience of looking at the mirror, which constitutes one of the prominent motifs of Pamuk's novel, is analogical to the Möbius circle. Hoja thinks that "just as man could view his appearance in the mirror, he could examine his essence within his own thoughts" (65), thus becoming both the subject and the object of his perceptions and thoughts. Thus, two people looking at the mirror can also gain insight into themselves and one another simultaneously and detect a deeper-lying connection or flow between each other which may call their individual identity into question, as in the case of Hoja and the Venetian. For Hoja, self-distancing and merging his identity with another may herald the long-sought death of his ego, which is also implied by recurrent references to his fearlessness in the face of the epidemic. He welcomes another, a multi-faceted view of existence, which also becomes evident in his comment on a Spanish miniature painting: "Reality may have been flat like that in the old days [. . .] But now everything is three-dimensional, reality has shadows, don't you see; even the most ordinary ant patiently carries his shadow around on his back like a twin" (49). Hoja's ecstasy upon seeing his body and mind as confluent with the Venetian's can be compared to George Bataille's interpretation of laughter:

> The truth of life cannot be separated from its opposite and if we flee the smell of death, "the disorder of the senses" brings us back to the happiness that is connected with it. The truth is that between death and the endless renewal of life, one cannot make a distinction: we cling to death like a tree to the earth by a hidden network of roots.
> [. . .] If we didn't naively draw from the wellspring of suffering, which gives us the insane secret, we could not have the transport of the laughter. (Bataille 116)

Hoja laughs because he can see the world as the narrator sees it, can understand what the latter thinks and feels. He speaks enthusiastically about how he is going to take the narrator's place, exchanging clothes with him, cutting his beard, and how the Venetian will let his beard grow and make Hoja a freedman so that he can return to Italy in the narrator's place, all of which are extremely disconcerting for the narrator:

> I was terrified to realize he remembered everything I had told him about my childhood and youth, down to the smallest detail, and from these details had constructed an odd and fantastical land to his own taste. My life was beyond my control, it was being dragged elsewhere in his hands, and I felt there was nothing for me to do but passively watch what happened to me from the outside, as if I were dreaming. (84)

In fact, Hoja himself has revealed to the narrator as much of his life, desires and sins as the narrator exposed his heart and mind to Hoja. The two, sitting at the opposite ends of the table have recorded the narratives of each other and (re)constructed a life story, a life story that belongs to both. Not only the bodies and minds but also the writings, the narrative voices, of the narrator and Hoja intersect in the novel. Hoja and the Venetian indeed switch roles and places at the end of the novel. At this point, however, they become one in their roles as narrator. Like a Möbius circle, the narrative coils in and out, and the narrators appear as mirror images of each other, distinct and identical at the same time.

The Venetian, in his capacity as the narrator, which turns out to have been an illusion on the part of the reader since the narrator is Hoja at the same time, had stated early in the novel that he was trying to invent a past for himself while writing this book, *The White Castle*: "I already sensed then that I would later adopt his manner and his life-story as my own. There was something in his language and his turn of mind that I loved and wanted to master. A person should love the life he has chosen enough to call it his own in the end; and I do" (63). His attempt to appropriate and master ironically suggests willful surrender. The efforts of both Hoja and the Venetian narrator to achieve supremacy over one another, whether it be in Istanbul or Italy, whether they physically inhabit or fantasize about these different places, result in their realization of the infinite shades and layers of their identities.

The ending of *The Woman in the Dunes* is of a similar character. The man surrenders his being to the woman: "He abandoned himself to her hands as if he were a smooth, flat stone in a river bed. It seemed that what remained of him had turned into a liquid and melted into her body" (232). The passage signifies his realization of the inextricable bond between himself and the rest of the universe, endlessly folding and unfolding as the Möbius circle, as sand. He had stated earlier in the novel, "I rather think that the world is like sand. The fundamental nature of sand is very difficult to grasp when you think of it in its stationary state. Sand not only flows, but this very flow *is* the sand [. . .] You yourself become sand. You see with the eyes of sand. Once you're dead you don't have to worry about dying any more" (99). At the end of the novel he cannot suppress "a natural laughter" – suggestive of Bataille's take on laughter, exemplified earlier – when he finds water beneath the buckets and discovers that the sand was "an immense pump" (234). "The change in the sand corresponded to a change in himself. Perhaps along with the water in the sand, he had found a new self" (236). When the long-awaited ladder is finally at his service, he feels "There was no particular hurry about escaping. On the two-way ticket he held in his hand now, the destination and time of departure were blanks for him to fill in as he wished" (239).

The Woman in the Dunes and *The White Castle* thematize an individual's captivity in a culture which shocks and frustrates him because of its radical difference to his own, but gradually leads to his realization of his entrapment in the very episteme which he had accepted as his own and whose boundaries he had not questioned before. Both protagonists transcend those boundaries, by submitting willingly to a new lifestyle whose shocking and frustrating characteristics turn out to be liberating in the sense that they dismantle all established dichotomies imposed on their minds, including a sense of selfhood based upon a distinction from an 'other.' Neither *The White Castle* nor *The Woman in the Dunes* uses the motif of a journey as one that leads to the protagonist's self-discovery, but as one that proves instrumental in the discovery of the potential what he may be. The subjectivity of the man in Abe's novel cannot be dissociated from the endless flow of sand which simultaneously shapes and is shaped by him and the woman, while in Pamuk's novel both Hoja and the Venetian emerge as the narrator, never allowing the reader the possibility to read it in a unidirectional way. *The White Castle* is endless and circular like the endlessly repeating cycle of life in *The Woman in the Dunes*. The process remains to be enjoyed.

Works Cited

Abe, Kobo. *The Woman in the Dunes*. Trans. E. Dale Saunders. New York: Vintage International, 1991.

Bataille, Georges. *The Impossible.* Trans. Robert Hurley. San Francisco: City Lights Books, 1991.

Bateson, Gregory. *Steps to an Ecology of Mind.* New York: Ballantine Books, 1972.

Bogue, Ronald. *Deleuze and Guattari*. New York: Routledge, 1989.

Deleuze, Gilles and Felix Guattari. *A Thousand Plateaus: Capitalism and Schizophrenia*. Trans. Brian Massumi. Minneapolis: U of Minnesota P, 1987.

Foucault, Michel. *Madness and Civilization: A History of Insanity in the Age of Reason.* Trans. Richard Howard. New York: Vintage Books, 1988.

Hayles, N. Katherine. Chaos Bound: Orderly Disorder in Contemporary Literature and Science. Ithaca: Cornell UP, 1990.

Lynch, Deidre. "Overloaded Portraits: The Excesses of Character and Countenance." *Body and Text in the Eighteenth Century.* Ed. Veronica Kelly and Dorothea E. von Mücke. Stanford: Stanford UP, 1994. 112-143.

Merleau-Ponty, Maurice. *The Visible and the Invisible*. Ed. Claude Lefort. Trans. Alphonso Lingus. Evanston: Northwestern UP, 1968.

Pamuk, Orhan. *The White Castle*. Trans. Victoria Holbrook. New York: Vintage International, 1990.

Payne, Michael. *Reading Knowledge: An Introduction to Barthes, Foucault, and Althusser*. Oxford: Blackwell, 1997.

Victimhood and Deliverance in Naguib Mahfouz's *The Harafish*

Fiona Tomkinson
Yeditepe University

Abstract: This paper discusses the themes of victimhood and deliverance in Naguib Mahfouz's novel *The Harafish.* It presents the novel as being simultaneously an example of the deliverer myth and an analysis of its limitations. It argues that there is a tension in the text between, on the one hand, a celebration of the myth of the deliverer as one who resists class oppression and overcomes internal temptations, and on the other, the recognition that there are other forms of victimhood, including the oppression of women, against which such a deliverer is largely helpless, or in which he may even be complicit. Ultimately, the novel presents the human condition as an existential victimhood from which only a partial escape is possible. This interpretation can, I contend, be supported by the unveiling through translation of the mystical Persian poetry scattered through the text.

Naguib Mahfouz's 1977 novel *Malhamat al-harafish* is at once an extended meditation on what it means to be a victim and an exploration of the extent to which deliverance from victimhood is possible. In this paper I will claim that despite Mahfouz's supposed return to the genre of the Arabian tale in this work and other novels of his fourth period (*Naguib Mahfouz: A Biography*), what we are given in *The Harafish* is both a mythical account of deliverance from victimhood *and* a critical analysis of the deliverer myth, posing the questions of whether deliverance can ever come from a single figure and what are the limits of deliverance *per se*. I shall argue that the novel simultaneously offers the possibility of human escape from victimhood and the sense that this escape can never be complete, and that it is all too easy to exchange one form of victimhood for another.

Victimhood in *The Harafish* assumes various guises, but the narrative voice leaves us in no doubt that its basic form is the daily suffering of the common people, the *harafish*, worn down by poverty and hard labour, deprived of education, at the mercy of outbreaks of plague, oppressed by the rich 'notables,' and by clan chiefs who claim to protect them, but who only do so in the sense of taking protection money. However, within this basic context we are also presented with various other versions of victimhood: self-destruction through drink, drugs, lust and greed; the victimization of women by their menfolk and by society at large; and the universal victimhood of the human condition subject to illness, old age and death. The novel can be read as an account of the way in which these forms of victimhood interact with the main theme of social injustice conceived in terms of class oppression.

The Harafish consists of ten tales narrating the story of the al-Nagi family over several generations: thirteen generations to be precise, though the author leaves us to count them for ourselves. In the world of the novel, the temporal is vague, but the spatial very precisely delineated. Most of the action takes place in one particular alley of Cairo, presented as an almost self-sufficient microcosm. We understand that the clan chiefs are laws onto themselves, that no-one will ever testify against the crimes they commit and that the police rarely venture to interfere in the affairs of the alley. In sharp contrast to other novels by Mahfouz, such as *The Cairo Trilogy,* there is no reference to historical events or social change, no mention whatsoever of any colonial power in Egypt and only the briefest references to central government. The resulting impression is of a claustrophobically confined space, within which relations between the *harafish* and their oppressors take on a timeless quality.

Harafish is a pejorative word in Arabic, suggesting the scum of the earth rather than the salt of the earth, but Mahfouz defiantly takes it up and uses it in a positive sense. Catherine Cobham's 1994 English translation for the American University in Cairo Press retains the Arabic word *harafish* in the title, but other possible translations would be *The Epic of the Rabble* or *The Epic of the Riffraff.*

The use of the word *malhamat*, or 'epic,' might be taken to suggest that the *harafish* take on something of the role of the epic hero, as man of action, warrior or exiled wanderer. Members of the al-Nagi family do in fact assume all of these roles, though sometimes in so doing they cease to be *harafish*. But, on the contrary, the common people as a body are for the most part of the novel presented as passive and static – victims who do not struggle against their fate.

This can be illustrated by a passage at the beginning of the novel describing how the *harafish* react to an outbreak of plague and to the government advice on this subject transmitted by the *sheikh* of the alley:[1]

> They listened intently. Could the government save them from catastrophe?
> "Avoid all public gatherings and crowded places."
> They looked at one another in astonishment. They lived their lives in the street. At nights the harafish congregated under the archway and in derelict buildings. How could they avoid crowds?
> [. . .]
> "And hygiene! Always remember to take precautions!"
> The mocking eyes of the harafish looked at them from behind masks of caked dirt.
> [. . .]
> "Is that all?" someone asked eventually.
> Amm Hamidu replied in a tone which invited no further discussion, "Say your prayers and accept the Lord's judgment."
> The crowd broke up despondently. The harafish went off to their slums exchanging sarcastic jokes. The funeral processions went on without a break. (34-35)

The *harafish* are obviously in need of a mythical deliverer, and they are going to get one when Ashur-al Nagi gains the position of clan chief. Ashur's origins are both mythical and prosaic: like many a mythical deliverer, including Moses, he is a foundling: an abandoned child raised by a pious blind *sheikh*, who grows up to be virtuous hero of giant-like stature. However, as a young

1 The plague is probably a cholera epidemic from the description of the symptoms (vomiting, diarrhoea and sudden death), but it is typical of the novel that we are not given any more scientific information than the harafish themselves possess.

man, he also appears to be of limited intelligence and enterprise, passive and docile, an unlikely candidate for leadership. It is only the onset of the plague which galvanises him to action. The *harafish* need deliverance from death and from oppression, but, ironically, Ashur will attempt to provide deliverance from death, and in failing to do so, give deliverance from oppression. He will not save the people of the alley from the plague, although, prompted by a dream, he feels that he has a divine mission to do so by persuading them to flee into the wilderness. Fatalism, fear of the unknown, the poor's reluctance to leave their livelihoods and the opposition of the authorities all conspire against him. He is not even able to persuade his first wife and her three sons to follow him into the desert, but escapes with his second wife, Fulla, and their son. He returns to find the alley deserted: it slowly sinks in that everyone is dead. Ashur has by now acquired some of the mythic aspects of a Noah or a Lot, but if measured against the Moses myth can only be seen as a failed deliverer. Again somewhat ironically, he only metamorphoses into a popular saviour after rather guiltily succumbing to the temptation of going to live in the deserted but richly-furnished house of one of the alley's rich families.

He uses his newfound wealth to benefit the new *harafish* who settle in the alley, not only distributing alms, but giving the unemployed a means of earning a living, and building an animal's drinking trough, a fountain and a small mosque. Therefore, although he is finally caught and imprisoned for his illegal appropriation of wealth, when released, he is welcomed as a hero by the populace and the clan chief's men go over to his side: he "became clan chief without a fight" (57). This is the point at which many a deliverer myth ends; but the epic of the riff-raff is only just beginning. Ashur himself does not disappoint, but sets himself up as a kind of urban Robin Hood:

> As the harafish expected, he set about his duties in an entirely different manner from his predecessors. He returned to his trade as a carter and lived in the basement room of his earlier days. He obliged all his followers to work for a living, thus eliminating the thugs and bullies. Only the rich had to

> pay protection money, which was used to benefit the poor and disabled. (57)

He is sustained in his task by the sound of chants from the dervish monastery, which is a closed world within the world of the alley. This is despite the fact that the "meanings of their sweetly intoned cadences were hidden from him behind a veil of Persian" (11). The dervishes are markedly outside the normal relations of sociopolitical power. They "do menial tasks like the poor" (11), and hid themselves away when Ashur in his early days came to offer himself as their servant. From time to time, as the story progresses, a line or couplet of Persian will float in the background as a counterpoint to the turmoil and distress of the Nagis and the *harafish*, like a message from those who have freed themselves from the relation of victim and victimiser.

It is a mystical consolation of which the characters will be in need as the story progresses, and the legend fades. After Ashur's mysterious disappearance, his son, Shams al-Din, courageously attempts to carry on his legacy until defeated by old age and death. But the leadership then passes to Ashur's grandson Suleyman, who begins well, but becomes, to a degree, corrupted after a second marriage to a rich woman, and finally loses the position of clan chief after suffering a stroke brought on by family troubles. Subsequent generations of his family are unable to follow in the footsteps of Ashur: sometimes a member of the al-Nagi family regains the position of clan chief, but only to be an unjust leader of a gang of thugs in the old style, as is the case with Wahid in the sixth generation, Galal in the eighth and Samaha in the eleventh, or else to be a humane and idealistic leader who does not have the physical strength to maintain his position, such as Samaha's half-brother, Fath al-Bab.

In addition, the legendary al-Nagi family, whilst remaining painfully conscious of its glorious past, is dogged by misfortune and scandal to the extent that even its innocent members come to be despised by the *harafish*. Members of the family murder one another: there is even one case of fratricide and another of parricide; other members of the family disappear, or are forced into exile; the reputation of its womenfolk is tainted in various ways.

Possibly the most scandalous case of all is that of the clan-chief Galal, who under the delusion that he can gain immortality by following the instructions of a magician, lives for a year in seclusion, neglecting his people, and builds a minaret without a mosque. He enjoys a short period of success and imagined immortality, only to be poisoned by his jealous lover, the former prostitute, Zaynat the Blonde, and to meet an ignominious end with his head plunged in the animal's drinking trough which his ancestor Ashur had provided for the community.

However, all is apparently restored in the thirteenth generation of the al-Nagi family by the appearance of another Ashur who brings back the golden days of the first, but with a crucial difference as to means: he seizes power through urging the *harafish* themselves to take control of their own destiny, to finally play an epic role in their own epic. In a conversation in the marketplace, Ashur uses a vaguely Socratic technique of question and answer to urge them to reach a true consciousness of their situation and to make the progression from waiting for the return of a deliverer to becoming their own deliverers from victimhood:

> "What could restore our alley's fortunes?"
> "The return of Ashur al-Nagi," answered several voices.
> "Can the dead come back to life?" he murmured, smiling.
> "Of course," someone replied with a laugh.
> "When you're alive you're alive, and when you're dead you're dead," he said firmly.
> "We're alive but not living."
> "What haven't you got?"
> "Bread."
> "Power, you mean," said Ashur.
> "Bread's easier to come by."
> "Not at all!"
> [. . .] "Do you want to become clan chief?"
> [. . .]
> "Even if I became an honest, upright chief, what good would it do?"

> [. . .]
> "Even if you were happy when I was there what about after I'd gone?" asked Ashur.
> "It would be back to the bad old days."
> "We don't trust anyone. Not even you!"
> "Wise words," smiled Ashur.
> They burst out laughing.
> "But you have faith in yourselves!" went on Ashur.
> "A lot of good that does us!"
> "Can you keep a secret?" asked Ashur seriously.
> "Just for you!"
> "I had a strange dream. I saw you armed with clubs." (397)

The dream becomes reality with a combination of the epic deliverer engaged in single combat and the awakening to self-consciousness of the proletariat. Ashur takes on the clan chief, Hassuna, in a battle which ends with Ashur lifting his opponent high over his head and hurling him into the alley "where he lay senseless and robbed of his honor" (402). But while the fight is taking place:

> there was a surprise which hit the alley like an earthquake. Nobody was prepared for it. The harafish poured out of the lanes and derelict buildings, shouting, brandishing whatever weapons they had been able to lay their hands on: bricks, bits of wood, chairs, sticks.

It isn't a velvet revolution.

> The harafish surrounded the men of the clan and beat them with sticks and bricks. The lucky ones were those who escaped.
> [. . .]
> The number of combatants made the fight without precedent in the alley. The harafish, the overwhelming majority of the

> populace, had suddenly joined forces and prevailed over the clubs and long sticks. This sent a violent tremor through the private homes and businesses. The thread holding things in place had been broken. Anything was possible. (402)

However, authority is not completely dissolved into anarchy: "Contrary to expectation, chaos did not follow. They closed ranks around their chief, with dedication and obedience" (403).

The novel closes with the recurring theme of the choice between being a victim of one's own desires for a better life or victimising oneself by remaining in poverty. Ashur's mother encourages him to take a rich wife, saying "I don't think there is any justice in being unfair to yourself" (405). But he refuses, although he knows his mother hankers for a better life and despite his own dreams of living in a mansion with a soft-skinned woman: "I am not going to be the one to destroy the most magnificent structure in the alley!" (405). It is also significant that in making this resolve he expressed his desire to be independent of the *harafish*, even as he glories in his political dependence on them:

> He was determined that his refusal should come from within him, and not be the result of pressure from the harafish. He wanted to be better than his ancestor. The first Ashur had relied on his own strength, while he had made the harafish into an irresistible force. His ancestor was carried away by passion; he would stand firm like the ancient wall [. . .] That was his sweetest victory: his victory over himself. (405)

So he marries a woman of the *harafish*, Bahiyya, the hairdresser's daughter, "after seeing her and making inquiries on his own behalf" (405) – an idealistic courtship by the standards of the world portrayed in the novel. He then celebrates by pulling down Galal's mosqueless minaret, symbol of the futile wish for immortality and of the isolated ego detached from the body politic.

If we focus on Ashur's moment of victory, it is very easy to interpret *The Harafish* in terms of the summary which the AUC edition provides: "a mythic tale, a compelling story of human weaknesses – pride, dishonesty, lust, and greed – and the greatness of which we are capable when we overcome them." This religious or liberal humanist myth could be replaced with a Marxist one focusing on the *dénouement* in which the harafish become aware of their own political power. Neither of these 'mythic' interpretations would be entirely wrong, but they focus on class oppression and the succumbing to internal spiritual weakness as the only kinds of victimhood.

There are, however, two disturbing undercurrents in the text which subvert the moral clarity of these views: we can call them *the question of the female* and *the question of death*: questions which are implicitly linked through the unfolding of the plot.

It is very clear from the novel that human beings suffer victimisation not only from class oppression, but as the result of gender and as the result of the general miseries of the human condition, subject to old age and death, miseries which may never be abolished, but which can be ameliorated if too much fatalism does not prevent this. Unfortunately, the characters who are most successful in overcoming class oppression or in controlling their own weaknesses frequently increase the victimisation of women in doing so, either by denying them the opportunity of rising out of poverty for fear of compromising their own integrity, or else gratuitously, as when Shams al-Din intervenes to prevent his mother's remarriage, thereby causing her decline and death. Conversely, the mad Galal's protests against the acceptance of death, arising out of the loss of two female figures in his life, both invite sympathy and pose ethical and political questions which should not be ignored.

Sometimes, of course, women are victimised by the oppressors of the *harafish*, who do not hold love or family life sacred. For example, when Samaha, the great-great grandson of Ashur, refuses to relinquish his fiancée to the clan chief al-Fulali, al-Fulali has her murdered and Samaha falsely accused of the killing. Yet the record of the Nagis and the *harafish* on a woman's right to choose her own marriage partner is no better. Moreover, paradoxically, the arbitrary acts of the clan chiefs can sometimes be a liberation for women, as in the case of Zahira, who gets rid of two unwanted husbands after the clan-chief commands them to divorce her. Zahira, "husband collector" and "social climber" (275), is presented not simply as a greedy *femme fatale*, but as an existentialist in quest of self-realisation: "A movement each day, a jump each week, and a great bound each month. She was discovering herself layer by layer" (236). She is also intoxicated at the prospect of escaping the usual female role of victim. Hearing the astonishing news that "A woman's the new clan chief in Birgawan!" a "secret fire" stirred inside her, making her realise that,

> a woman's weakness is her emotions, and her relationships with men should be rational and calculated. Life is precious, with vast possibilities, limitless horizons. Love is nothing more than a blind beggar, creeping round the alleyways. She sighed and said to herself, "The only thing worse than having bad luck is putting up with it." (236)

She is not mourned by the *harafish* when, after her fourth marriage, her second husband, Muhammad Anwar, takes his revenge by smashing her beautiful head to pulp. But Zahira, like Clytemnestra, might get the feminist sympathy vote.

Zahira's attitude to the uses of her femininity as a means to realising the possibilities of existence is coloured by her sense of transience: she is determined "not to lose a moment of her life" (259). For Galal, conversely, the question of the female leads to the question of death. It is the murder of his mother Zahira before his eyes which initially gives rise to his attitude of non-acceptance of death. He asks the imam at Quran school why people die, and when unsatisfied with the explanation that it is the will of God, he is tied down by the feet and beaten (275). The last straw for his sanity comes when his betrothed, Qamr, catches what seems to be a simple cold and dies on the eve of their wedding. His reaction takes him to the opposite extreme of the fatalism of the *harafish*, to the assumption that human beings are responsible for every misfortune which befalls them. As his sanity gives way, he tells himself:

> I hate Qamr. [. . .] Don't grieve over a creature so quickly destroyed. She broke her promise. Didn't respect love. Or hang on to life. She welcomed death with open arms. We

> live or die by the strength of our will. *There is nothing more revolting than a victim.* People who invite defeat. Cry out that death is the end of life [. . .] This outlook is the product of their weakness and their illusions. We are immortal. We only die as a result of betrayal or weakness. Ashur is alive. He worried about people confronting his immortality, so he disappeared. I am immortal. [. . .] The dervishes only keep their doors closed because they are immortal. Has anyone seen them holding a funeral? They're immortal. They sing about eternity, but nobody understands them. (288, my italics)

After Galal takes power as clan chief, his preoccupation with death makes the idea of social justice meaningless to him:

> His life appeared to him in sharp relief, the features and the colors clearly visible, right down to its ludicrous, definitive ending. His mother's shattered head, his childhood trials and humiliations, Qamr's ironic death, his unlimited power and dominance, and Shams al-Din's tomb awaiting one funeral procession after another. What was the point of being sad or happy? What did strength mean, or death? Why did the impossible exist? (291)

When his father tells him people are asking when justice will be done, he replies, "What does it matter?" since "They're dying like flies all the time, and they don't complain." To his father's retort that "Death has rights over us, but you have it in your power to eradicate poverty and indignity," he merely shouts "Damn these stupid ideas!" (291).

Deluded as Galal's dream of immortality is, he has a point. Preventing people from dying like flies is doubtless a more important political agenda than the redistribution of wealth *per se*. Perhaps one of the most pressing ethico-political questions of our time is how to strike a balance between the desire to push at the limits of the human condition and the desire to focus on doing the good which is well within our power. In concrete terms, to strike a balance between devoting too much money to battling with incurable diseases when people are still dying of preventable ones, and, on the other, holding back medical research until the poor are no longer with us. Mahfouz's narrative voice does not present Galal's views as anything other than a tragic error, a deviation from the path of his illustrious ancestors, but the structure of the novel itself leaves us the possibility of a more subtle and ironic reading.

The main irony is that the attitude which Galal is protesting against is one which Ashur had also confronted at the beginning of his mission. When attempting to persuade his wife to flee the plague, she replies, "It's not for us to resist death, Ashur" (36-37). In a sense, Galal is only exaggerating the existential protests of the ancestors whose legacy he is supposedly betraying: Shams al-Din, son of Ashur, was also remembered as the one who "fought old age" (296).

Reading only slightly against the grain, we come to a position where both acceptance of poverty and the will to escape it can be considered forms of victimhood, as can both the acceptance and resistance of death.

This ambivalence is reinforced by the closing scene of the novel, a scene in which a door both does and does not open. After midnight, the second Ashur leaves the crowds to listen to the songs in the monastery square. At this moment, the barrier between the world of the dervishes and the world of the *harafish* is at last abolished:

> A creaking sound spread through the darkness. He looked at the great door in astonishment. Gently, steadily, it was opening. The shadowy figure of a dervish appeared, a breath of night embodied.
>
> "Get the flutes and drums ready," the figure whispered, leaning towards him. "Tomorrow the Great Sheikh will come out of his seclusion. He will walk down the alley bestowing his light and give each young man a bamboo club and a mulberry fruit. Get the flutes and the drums ready." (406)

This turns out to be a dream or hallucination, but Ashur reacts to it with affirmation not disappointment:

> He returned to the world of the stars and the songs and the night and the ancient wall, grasping at the tail ends of his vision; his fingers sunk into the waves of majestic darkness. He jumped to his feet, drunk on inspiration and power. Don't be sad, his heart told him. One day the door may open to greet those who seize life boldly with the innocence of children and the ambition of angels. (406)

But then another door opens, for the reader, if not for Ashur: the door between incomprehension and comprehension. For the first time in the text, the chants of the dervishes are given not in Persian, but in English in the AUC translation – (presumably in the original this will be the first time they are given in Arabic). The last lines of the novel are an affirmation of ultimate mystical deliverance, of the illumination which follows the dark night of the soul:

> *Last night they relieved me of all my sorrows*
> *In the darkness they gave me the water of life.* (406)

Yet this lifting of the veil of Persian only makes one all the more curious as to what lay behind it in the previous untranslated couplets. At least, I was sufficiently curious to have them translated: unlocking their secret gives us a new slant on the theme of victimhood in the novel.

In the eyes of the pious *harafish* the chants are the otherworldly songs of those liberated from victimhood, sin and desire, songs whose orthodoxy they surely do not doubt. They are, in fact, quotations from the fourteenth-century Persian poet Hafiz, a heterodox mystic who was almost denied a Muslim burial. From what we can reconstruct of his life, Hafiz was also a victim: victim of childhood poverty, apprenticed to a baker after his father's death, victim of unfulfilled passion for Shak-e Nabat, a beautiful woman glimpsed through a window in the rich quarter of the city where he had gone to deliver bread. The first Ashur-al-Nagi with his horror of alcohol might well have been shocked to discover that the author of his beloved chants achieved enlightenment at the age of sixty after drinking a cup of wine ("Hafiz: Biography"). We can only speculate as to whether the other characters would have been ultimately distressed or consoled to discover that the mysterious chants to which they were listening speak of the moon-like face of the beloved, of wine, of the pain of separation, of the fine dividing line between sensible action and insanity, of the hypocrisy of the religious, of eyeballs shedding tears of blood.[2]

---

2 The eleven quotations given in Persian in the text can be translated as follows. Thanks to Dr Osman Gazi Özkuzugüdenli of the Turkology Research Institute, Marmara University, Istanbul, for translating the lines to Turkish so that I could translate them to English. Any errors are my responsibility alone.

1) *Ay furughe mahe hosn as ruye rakhane shoma*
Abruye khubi az chahe zanakhdane shoma. (8)
Oh, my love, the moon of beauty reflects your face;
Beauty is honoured in the dimples of your chin.

2) *Ze geryeh mardome chesh nesheste dar khunast.* (19)
My eyeballs are bloody from weeping.

3) *Joz astane tovam dar jahan panahi nist.*
Sare mara bejoz in dar havale gahi nist. (39)
There is no shelter in the world for me other than your door,
Other than this door there is no place to which I can turn.

4) *Salahe kar koja va mane kharab koja*
Bebin tatavote rah az kujast ta bekuja. (98)
Where is the discipline of the flesh, where am I?
Look at the difference, where the road comes from and goes to.

5) *Ananke khaq ra benazar kimya konand*
Aya bovad keh koshahe chesmi bema konand. (144)
Those who with their glances turn earth to jewels,
I wonder if they will bestow a glance on us as well?

6) *Darin zamane ratiqi keh khali as khelalast.*
Sarahiye meye nab o satineye ghazalast. (152)
At this time the most faithful friend is made
Of a jug of unmixed wine and a book of verse.

What the unveiled lines suggest, however, is that deliverance is not a process which can be completed without a struggle: and that maybe it is never completed once and for all. The novel ends as the dervishes sing of the resolution of sorrow: perhaps tomorrow they will sing again of unsated longing.

To conclude, there is a line of Hafiz's not quoted in the novel, which could nevertheless be taken as its epigraph: it closes a quatrain referring to those who suffer the pains of unrequited love as belonging to a select club, but one whose membership is nevertheless completely open: in a modern translation the line runs: *Join us if you can put up with the crap.* ("Rubaiyat," 42, 4)

A contemporary message from the fourteenth century to the would-be deliverer of victims.

---

7) *Darde mara nist darman al-ghiyath*
Hejre mara nist payan al-ghiyath. (182)
Have mercy! There's no remedy for our pain,
There is no end to our separation.

8) *Naqdha ra bovad aya keh ayyari girand.*
Ta hame sume'e daran peye kari girand. (200)
Will the day come when they weigh everyone in the balance?
If that day comes, they'll catch all the pious red-handed.

9) *Har ankeh janibe khoda negahdorad*
Khodash dar hame hal azbala negahdorad. (223)
Those who obey with the minds of faithful lovers,
God in every case and state preserves from harm.

10) *Bir mehre rokhat ruze mara nur nanamdast*
Vaz omre mara joz shabe dijur namandast. (374)
Your face like sunshine is hidden. The light of my day is over;
Only a pitch-black night remains of my life.

11) *Did keh bar joz jur o setam nadasht*
Beshkast ahd o zoghame ma hich gham nadasht. (393)
Have you seen? My beloved, but placed there to rebel and reproach me.
She broke her oath and cared nothing for our pain.

Works Cited

Hafiz. "Rubaiyat." *Hafizonlove*. Ed. Shahriar Shahriari. 1999-2005. 16 July 2005 <http://www. hafizonlove.com/divan/index.htm>.

"Hafiz: Biography." *Hafizonlove*. Ed. Shahriar Shahriari. 1999-2005. 16 July 2005 <http://www.hafizonlove.com/bio/index.htm>.

Mahfouz, Naguib. *The Harafish*. 1994. Trans. Catherine Cobham. Cairo: The American University in Cairo Press, 2001

Naguib Mahfouz: A Biography. Cornell University Library. Middle East & Islamic Studies Collection. 16 July 2005 <http://www.library.cornell.edu/colldev/mideast/mahfz.htm>.

ibidem-Verlag
Melchiorstr. 15
D-70439 Stuttgart

info@ibidem-verlag.de

www.ibidem-verlag.de
www.edition-noema.de
www.autorenbetreuung.de

act-compliance

471